Design Secrets:
Furniture

50 Real-Life Projects Uncovered

Laurel Saville
Curated by Brooke Stoddard

© 2006 by Rockport Publishers, Inc.
First published in paperback in 2008

First published in the United States of America by
Rockport Publishers, a member of
Quayside Publishing Group
100 Cummings Center
Suite 406-L
Beverly, Massachusetts 01915-6101
Telephone: (978) 282-9590
Fax: (978) 283-2742
www.rockpub.com

Library of Congress Cataloging-in-Publication Data
Saville, Laurel.
    Design secrets : furniture / Laurel Saville ; curated by Brooke Stoddard.
        p.   cm.
    ISBN 1-59253-218-7 (hardback)
    1. Furniture design. I. Stoddard, Brooke C. II. Title.
    NK2260.S28 2006
    749'.320904—dc22

                                              2005030319
                                              CIP

ISBN-13: 978-1-59253-439-5
ISBN-10: 1-59253-439-2

10 9 8 7 6 5 4 3 2 1

Layout and Production: Raymond Art & Design
Cover Design: Madison Design & Advertising, Inc.

Printed in China

To JEL for holding my hand and my heart.

—Laurel

contents

Aspen sofa, page 136

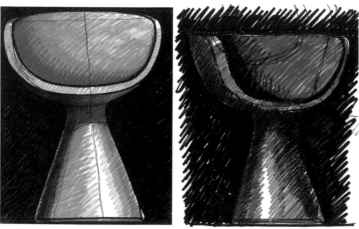

introduction

Designers are generally a dissatisfied lot.

When they use an object, they want to change it, redesign it, make it better, or make it more closely fit their idea of what the thing should be. When the question arises, "Does the world really need another sofa, table, or shelf?", their answer is a resounding "Yes." They are optimistic with just enough ego to say, "Not only do we require new versions of what we already have, but I am the person to make this product more functional, versatile, beautiful, unexpected, or elegant…" And they are also opportunistic, finding myriad ways to more fully utilize, exploit, subvert, or reinvent materials, manufacturing processes, technical innovations, and production techniques.

Furniture designers may love or revile the computer, but If they don't use it themselves, they work closely with someone who does. In this day and age, a designer needs to make friends with technology. They are process-oriented, paying so much attention to each phase of the design continuum that the final product sometimes seems an incidental result. It is not so much that they are risk takers or rebels (although they may be), but they just don't notice the conventions attached to accepted wisdom. Their creativity often springs directly from this inability to see the limitations that others take for granted. But, the very best designers also respect the constraints placed upon them by clients, the needs of the human body, or the physical laws of the universe. These restrictions are a welcome challenge that forces them to think around, through, or above and beyond, to find a more inventive solution.

It is the work of these designers that we profile in the following pages. Their furniture may offer a place to rest, but that is only one dimension of the object. A table may also be a piece of sculpture; a wall divider unfolds like a paper party lantern; laser beams give a chair an otherworldly shape; a shelving unit expresses a frozen moment in time and space; a daybed tells a story from childhood; a night bed recalls a spectacular winter vacation; an outdoor seating system enhances social interactions.

It may be true that in most cases, for so many of us, a chair is just a chair; but not in this book.

Laurel Saville

Advanced Polymer Cantilever Chair, PearsonLloyd

"I don't think you stumble across **innovation**," says Luke Pearson, of **PearsonLloyd**. "You have to find a **strategy** to get there.

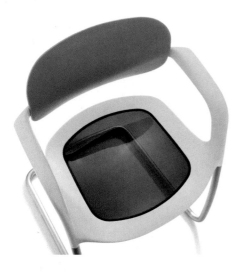

The Advanced Polymer Cantilever Chair by PearsonLloyd for Fritz Hansen utilizes the latest in plastics technology to improve the function and performance of a classic silhouette. *Credit: Fritz Hansen*

"You have to find a way to create from a blank canvas by surrounding yourself with the components of knowledge. We design from the ground up so we can always ask first, 'Why are things like this?' This is the only way to find innovation."

When design partners Luke Pearson and Tom Lloyd decided to apply this strategy for innovation to what Pearson calls the "old and established archetype" of a cantilevered chair, they set out first to understand why so little had changed in the chairs' design over the years. Their answer lay in the materials. "The steel tubes at the heart of these chairs are a very easy material to use. It's cheap and works well," says Pearson, "However, in the last five to seven years, there's been huge development in plastic technology. The reason for working in plastics is that most cantilevered chairs have a welded structure when you get to the seat. Welding more steel under the seat is heavy and takes time, so you're adding weight and assembly time," he notes. "As industrial designers, we started looking at bikes and other high-performance items and saw that plastics were taking the place of metals and alloys." After consulting with some plastics engineers, they began to find materials that might work. "We came up with the structural principles early on, and the beauty of what we got is that it reduced the chair to as few components as possible."

Top: PearsonLloyd feels that hand-carving models is a critical part of the design process that brings humanity and improves aesthetics; but they also value the technology of programs like PRO-E to create the CAD build for their Cantilever Chair. *Credit: PearsonLloyd*

Bottom: A CAD drawing shows the detail that goes into the shaping and the joining of each component part. Almost every part is simply snap-fit together. *Credit: PearsonLloyd*

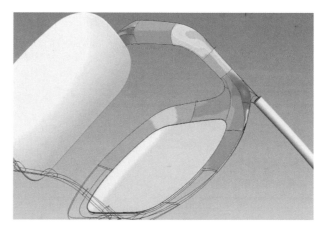

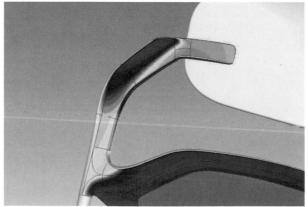

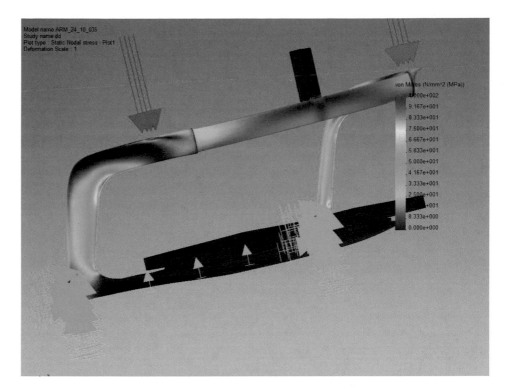

FEA images show stress analysis and potential material deformation. The Cantilever Chair is made with several different high-tech materials including plastics and polycarbonate. *Credit: PearsonLloyd*

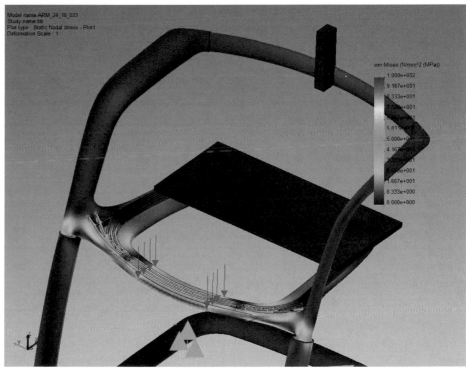

Another screen shot from the FEA points to stresses that may be applied at various points on the chair. The material choices help improve the dynamic qualities and comfort of the chair. *Credit: PearsonLloyd*

Pearson also points out that using plastic lends some fundamental ergonomic benefits to the chair. "When you weld the seat, you kill some of the dynamic qualities of the cantilever. And this is its major advantage over a four-legged chair. When you sit in a regular chair, you get a shock loading into the spine because the back legs don't bend. By using plastic, we could maximize the dynamic quality of the chair. When you sit in our cantilevered chair, the front legs bend to reduce shock loading. We also designed the seat platform in such a way that it flexes progressively," Pearson continues, "so at the front of the chair where it needs maximum stiffness, there's no flex; in the back, there's more. The seat platform responds to your movement, so you don't need a cushion. You have a flexible, supportive structure that responds like a human being stands, by shifting weight from one leg to another."

The plastic also confers another advantage important to Pearson: "It has a long life and it's possible to recycle it. We think you have a responsibility to consider how much material you'll use. We didn't want to use any more material than we needed to. The life energy cost of the chair, the material usage, is equivalent to driving a European car about 120 kilometers," he notes. The plastic itself is used primarily in office furniture, but also for automotive parts and other components where high performance is required. Made with a high glass fiber content, the resulting material is, according to Pearson, stronger than aluminum, with the added benefit of greater flexibility, yet has a high-tensile capacity.

The completed chair is actually constructed of several different materials. While the main skeleton is ISEF plastic, the central section of the seat pan is polycarbonate, the backrest is ABS plastic, and the bottom tubular section is steel. Perhaps most interestingly given this variety of parts, "There are no fixings on the chair," Pearson points out. "Everything is snap-fit except for the back, which is glued to the arms."

PearsonLloyd developed the chair with their own, in-house prototyping capability that balanced technology and old-fashioned handwork. Pearson fears that, "Computers are dumbing down that intuitive difference you get between people. Programs work the same way no matter who is working on it. They're a tool, but not a creative tool. Of course, we do a 3D computer drawing," he says, "but you need to have a one-to-one model. The computers were used to verify the stress analysis and minimize the use of material. The most important thing is that with all the technology and computers, there's nothing like carving a complex form by hand and seeing it emerge in front of you." He explains their process: "What we did in the studio to develop the design language, was we carved it by hand out of blocks of hard foam until it looked right. It's a little bit like looking at a car and one tiny dent will change the entire line. In some cases, we'd sand off a millimeter to change the way the light fell on a curve. This is so vital to making something for the human scale. The emotional involvement is dependent on sight and touch. Which is why I think as a designer we have to be very wary of the design process. We can't think that because it looks a certain way on a computer screen, that's the only way. There's an awful lot of intuitive ability that's relevant to making things by hand. We had a parallel process of engineering running with aesthetics at all times. It was very inefficient and labor intensive. But at the end of the day, what we've got is what we want. It's all about the communication between the hand and the eye, as they are the two portals through with you judge something three dimensional."

Pearson and his team also balanced other demands as they developed their cantilevered chair. "There are two great extremes that drove us," he says. "One is beauty. If a thing is beautiful and compelling, people will look after it, and this is a very good way to create a value system in objects. We need to do this because we're creating so much environmental damage. And it should also be as efficient in manufacturing as possible. We try to balance our design ambitions with those things at both ends of the spectrum," he explains. "There's a great pleasure as a designer to know that you've done both to get something to be beautiful and compelling, and also that, when someone looks into it, they'll understand how much careful thought goes into how and why it's made."

Looking back at their creation now, Pearson says the thing that surprises him most is quite simply that it works. "That's the wonderful thing," he says. "We set off with a dream of producing this beautiful, minimalist, sculpted object, and without sounding arrogant, I have to say that we we're very happy with it. It's wonderful to spend two and a half years on something, and then look at it and see exactly what we wanted." He pauses and adds, "In fact, it turned out better than what we wanted."

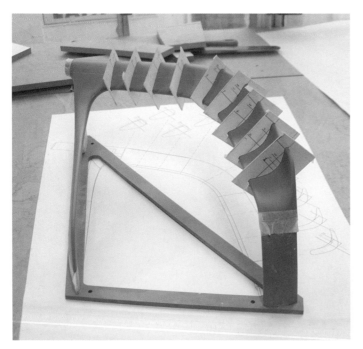

⬆ Once a model is made with CNC (computer numerical controlled) machinery, it is then altered by hand to achieve the final form to ensure the piece is pleasing to the hand and eye in real life, not just on the computer screen.
Credit: PearsonLloyd

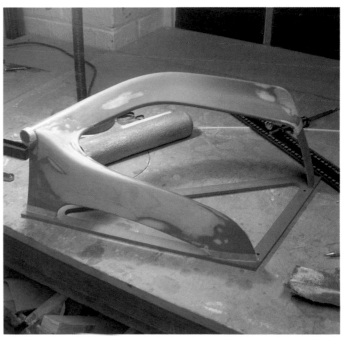

⬆ A model receives fine-tuning adjustments, including shaping and sanding to give each curve just the right tactile quality, and even to improve the way light strikes the object.
Credit: PearsonLloyd

The high-tech materials mix in the Advanced Polymer Cantilever chair allowed PearsonLloyd to push the design of this "old and established archtype" to a more comfortable and elegant form. *Credit: Fritz Hansen*

Boson Chair, Studio Patrick Norguet Normally, designers use **technology** and manufacturing in the **service of design,** starting with an **idea** and then finding a **means** to make the **concept** real. For the **Boson chair**, Patrick Norguet turned this **process** inside out.

The Boson armchair and footstool use manufacturing processes more commonly used in the automotive industry to create a seating cocoon that is both retro and techno in its outlook. *Credit: Artifort*

While working with a company that develops prototype cars for Renault and other French car companies, Norguet became inspired by seeing how they fabricated fiberglass, making structures that were both thin and strong. "I took the material from its manufacturing environment and applied it to the design world," says Norguet.

The borrowing of materials from one arena and using them in another is common for Norguet, who started his career designing window displays and creating special events for Louis Vuitton. He has since moved freely in the worlds of fashion and luxury goods, architecture and interiors, as well as product and furniture design. Recent projects include designing new event space and showrooms for Renault, window displays for Van Cleef & Arpels, retail stores for Marithé and François Girbaud, and cosmetic products for J. P. Gaultier, as well as furniture, carpets, and lamps for a variety of well-known manufacturers. Norguet has also participated in several group design shows. He points out that his "Rive Droit" seating system was inspired by watching a television program on Italian textile design and thinking how much fun it would be to mix fashion and furniture. "I am inspired by many sources and mix them all quite freely," he says.

After seeing some of the possibilities offered by fiberglass, Norguet used computer graphics to conceive the chair. "The idea was to work out an organic form that could be reassuring and cocoon-like, and also to optimize the material so we could make it as thin as possible," he says, describing the process. "I wanted to use a minimum of matter to create a maximum of aesthetic." He then brought the design to the car manufacturer, which made prototypes that went to the furniture manufacturer, Artifort. Artifort was interested in the chair but didn't have the technology to manufacture it, so they went back to the car company and both companies worked on realizing Norguet's vision together. According to Norguet, "That was what this design is all about: to mix the industrial world with the design world."

Norguet points out that there was a bit of ". . . culture shock in this process. We went in to this big industrial company and brought this design for a piece of furniture, which is of course on a much lesser scale. Of course they were interested," he says, "because it seemed like a crazy idea, but a very interesting one. It was really funny to see a machine making a car, and then two hours later, making a mold for a chair."

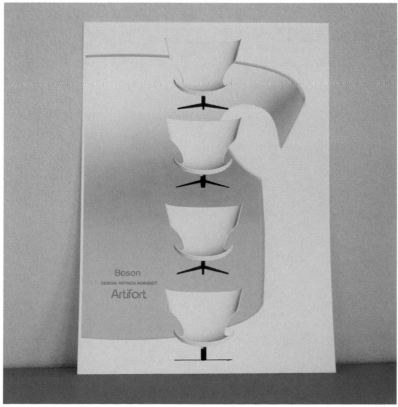

Preliminary sketches show the Boson's unique curvilinear shape, with arm supports cut out of, rather than added onto, the fundamental form. While different foundations were considered, including feet, production economy dictated setting the chair on a circular stand. *Credit: Patrick Norguet Studio*

Computer renderings show the sleek, slender, and supportive back, which embraces the seated person. The faintly automotive feel to the curves and cutouts reflect the manufacturing process as much as the design sensibility. *Credit: Patrick Norguet Studio*

The manufacturing process offered its own challenges, especially because of Norguet's goal to make the most slender profile possible, and still have the chair be strong enough to support someone. "We had to find the best technological solution to fit the best aesthetic solution," he points out.

The exterior of the Boson chair is made of white fiberglass that can be painted any color. Foam is injected onto the fiberglass shell and then upholstered. Originally, the chair was designed to have feet, but to achieve economy of shape and contain costs, the feet were replaced with a stand and circular base. Norguet prefers the footed version and hopes to offer the chair in both options before too long. Either way, the resulting shape hearkens both to the past and the future. "Aesthetically, it reminds us of '60s design," says Norguet. "There's a wink to the '60s because of its organic form, but the material and manufacturing make it futuristic."

Then, just to add some mystery to the already space age, improbable nature of the overall aesthetic, there's the name of the chair. A Boson is a theoretical, fundamental particle associated with a theoretical, quantum field, neither of which has yet been proven to exist, despite decades of research by physicists. Norguet finds this all very intriguing.

Of course, the Boson chair is quite concrete and applicable in a wide variety of real-life settings. Norguet envisions the chair as a comfortable addition to environments as varied as an airport lounge or a family home. "I see an accumulation of Boson chairs," he says. "Not just one, but as a cluster of little islands where people can feel private and relaxed."

While on this project Norguet had complete freedom to design wherever his vision and the manufacturing process took him. He also finds designing to a client brief equally stimulating and challenging. He points out that when a client has their own agenda concerning aesthetics, or there are limitations imposed by technology or marketing, these very constraints can provide their own inspirations. "These cases are interesting," he says, "because when you are limited, it boosts your creativity. Working on a brief means working with other people's ideas and meeting other people and looking into other technologies. It's about exploration of other possibilities and other cultures, and that's inspiring."

Norguet describes his design process as ". . . very intellectual, so things end up being very coherent in the end. The idea is to approach every project in a neutral way and not have a recipe or reflex." And how does he keep himself fresh and neutral? "By forgetting everything that's come before."

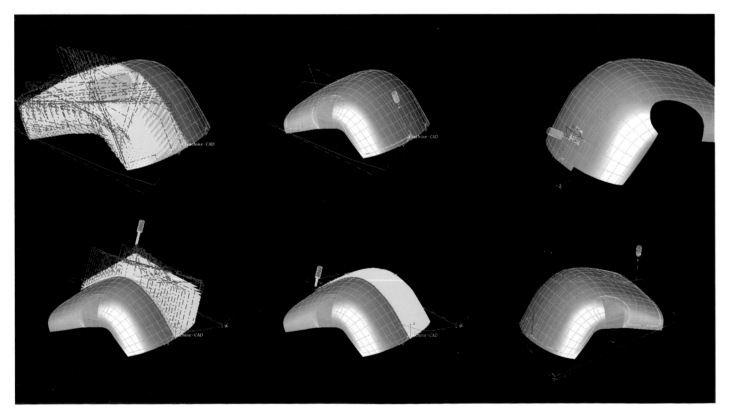

⊳ Using a resin material called LAB (liquid adhesive bond), the manufacturer uses a milling machine to make a form that will be used to shape the fiberglass —a kind of mold for the mold. *Credit: Studio Patrick Norguet*

⊳ The LAB has been milled down to what looks almost like an inside-out version of the Boson chair. *Credit: Studio Patrick Norguet*

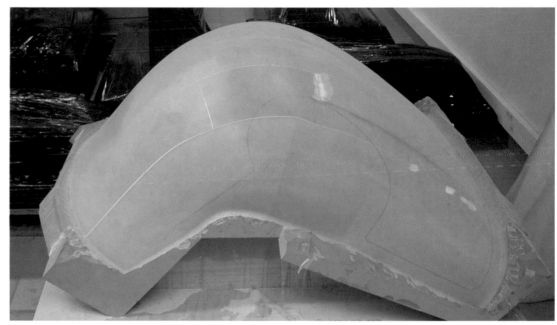

⊳ Using molded fiberglass allowed Norguet to create the most slender of profiles and still have the necessary strength to hold the shape of the Boson chair. *Credit: Studio Patrick Norguet*

⊲ Opposite top: Computer renderings from the milling machine show the ultimate form the block of LAB resin material will take on. *Credit: Studio Patrick Norguet*

⊲ Opposite bottom: Digital files and drawings created at Norguet's studio direct the work of the milling machine. This rendering—showing the exact form of the chair mold— has been generated by the milling machine's operating system. *Credit: X-3D image*

Buttercup Chair, Blu Dot Design and Manufacturing Blu Dot is a trio of **college friends** who came together after independent careers in art, architecture, and marketing to **design** and manufacture "furniture for **everyday** people with everyday needs."

The Buttercup Chair, made of molded plywood, began with the simple premise of creating an extremely comfortable lounge chair. *Credit: Blu Dot*

President John Christakos puts it simply: "The three things we're about are elegant design, simplicity of manufacturing, and affordability. We're trying to take the elitism out of design."

With these fundamental principles in mind, Christakos and his partners Maurice Blanks and Charlie Lazor at Blu Dot set themselves the seemingly straightforward task of making a lounge chair that was comfortable. "Comfort was the main goal; a must, the genesis, and what everything we did hinged upon," says Christakos. Comfort in a chair is usually associated with upholstery. But part of Blu Dot's mission is to use mass manufacturing to make things affordable, and upholstery is "a craft, not an automated process," according to Christakos. They also considered plastic but found the cost of injection molds prohibitive. "So we narrowed in on plywood. It was something we could afford to work in, the molds are relatively inexpensive, and we hoped that the curvilinear shapes that we could get would yield something comfortable. Plus, we'd never worked with it before and wanted to experiment."

The first part of the experiment was to create sketches and cardboard models. "At that stage, we were just looking at forms," Christakos points out. "Most of our previous pieces were rectilinear, and it was nice to get back to something more formal, more sculptural." As they began to focus on a few shapes, they built more refined cardboard models, then went to foam core models, and finally made preliminary molds in their own shop. They shaped pieces of the rigid, pink insulation foam that's readily available at any building supply store, laid a stack of veneers with glue in between them over the molds, then stuck the whole contrivance into a vacuum bag and sucked the air out of it, forcing the veneers down over the mold and clamping them there until the glue dried and the veneers took on the shape of the mold.

In between the cardboard models and pink foam prototype, Blu Dot spent a lot of time tweaking the shape to maximize the chair's comfort. They used a seating buck, described by Christakos as "a crude contraption to play around with angles and curves, height, pitch, angle of the back relative to the seat, the curvature of the back, the height of the arms, the position of the arms, etcetera."

⬙ Top: Blu Dot uses the straightforward tools of cardboard, tape, and a big black marker to turn rough ideas and conceptual thoughts into something that's starting to look like a chair. *Credit: Blu Dot*

⬙ A seating buck helps designers determine the angles and proportions of a chair's back, seat, and arms to ensure the final product will be comfortable for a range of body types, sizes, and shapes. *Credit: Blu Dot*

⬙ Standard building insulation provides an inexpensive, easily accessible, simple-to-shape material that Blu Dot uses to create an initial mold. Shrink-wrapping sheets of veneer to the form provides the first round of prototypes. *Credit: Blu Dot*

But they also utilized the basic sit test, getting a dozen or so people in sizes from petite to well over 6' (1.8 m) tall to take a seat and comment on how it felt. "I discovered that the section between my shoulder and elbow must be short because I always wanted the arms to be higher," Christakos quips.

"Of two shells we worked with, we discovered in prototyping that one was not possible to make," he continues. "Plywood can only bend in on one axis at one time, like a piece of paper. One of the designs had this condition embedded in it, and we didn't discover this until we started prototyping. In order to fix it, we would have killed the form." So they focused on what would become the Buttercup.

The next step was to find out how to make the back and the seat work together. Christakos explains: "We trimmed the pieces we'd made by hand and then began to play with the connection between the two parts—the seat, which includes the arms, and the back. We ended up with a joint between the two pieces that is not decorative, but functional. The shape is such that if the glue failed, the joint would hold it in place. We used the geometry of the joint to take some of the pressure off the glue and create a shape that is almost self-supporting. We ended up with something that looks like one continuous ribbon of bent plywood."

The final development step was to create a base. After exploring several options, "we came to the conclusion that the base needed to sit in the background as much as possible," says Christakos. "We wanted to put this beautiful form on a pedestal. The chair feels like the petals of a flower, so we focused on creating something that's like a stem." The base also swivels, which Christakos points out is an especially nice feature for enhancing conversation.

⊘ Prototyping allowed the designers to understand the possibilities and limitations of plywood. Discovering that it could bend in on only one axis, like a piece of paper, allowed them to home in on the shape that would become the Buttercup. *Credit: Blu Dot*

After prototyping, Blu Dot does its own production modeling and drawings and then sends everything to a factory for real production. The Buttercup is manufactured in Poland, and production models feature a decorative face veneer over a core of birch. The veneer is rift sawn, which Christakos says produces a very straight grain that helps accentuate the form.

Christakos found that even though their goal was comfort, they were still surprised by the results. "We never expected it to be that comfortable. The geometry, the opening, and the dramatic curve in the back, all let you just slip right in, and then the chair just grabs you."

Christakos feels that working as a collaborative practice makes the final design much stronger and more refined. "Nothing comes straight from my sketchbook to the real world," he says. "Individually, we'll each spend time sketching or making models or some other representation of our ideas and then we'll get together, pin things up, share what we like and don't like, and why. Normally, a few clear ideas start to emerge, and we'll take it from there to the next level of detail. It's like sanding, going from 60 grit, to 80 grit, to 120 grit."

And being actively involved along the entire continuum of initial inspiration to actually selling furniture pieces confers other benefits that end up improving the end product as well. "Because we produce most of the things we design, we live with the practical realities of making, distributing, and servicing products," Christakos says. "We're engaged with the more pragmatic concerns like, will we be able to ship it, is it useful, does it solve a problem, will a customer know how to use it, is it produceable in a repetitive way with low defects? These concerns are baked into our process from the beginning. Often, the end form is like the residue of the process, and the product is what's left over after being driven by just plain problem solving. The form becomes inevitable, as opposed to subjective."

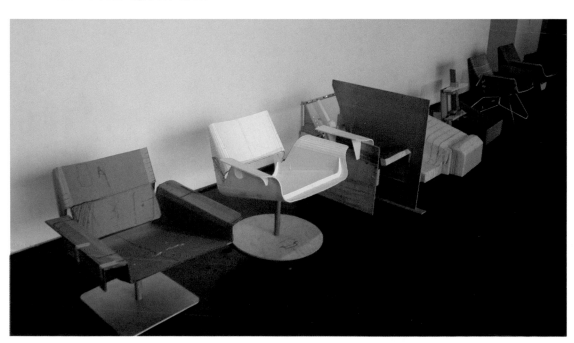

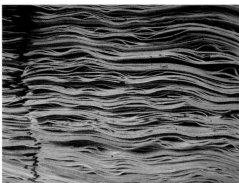

Layers of veneer are glued together and then slid into the mold that will giave them their signature curvature. *Credit: Blu Dot*

The sensuous curves of the Buttercup Chair are designed primarily for comfort. The pedestal was designed to be reminiscent of a flower stem. *Credit: Blu Dot*

Blu Dot chose to work with plywood because it was cost effective and could easily be molded. They wanted to experiment with a material that they hadn't worked with before, and they knew this material would keep the chair affordable. *Credit: Blu Dot*

Cikrak Chair, Adrien Gardère "I wanted to study traditional crafts in **India** and other places in **Asia** in order to project how they could be **reconsidered** and made relevant to **contemporary design**, not for the cheap manufacturing

The Cikrak Chair by Adrien Gardère for Perimeter Editions is the result of years of working to find modern uses for Indonesian indigenous materials and craftsmen. *Credit: Philippe Chancel*

The traditional Indonesian shovel, made from woven bamboo, inspired the Cikrak Chair. Production of the chair is helping to preserve local crafts knowledge, as these shovels are being replaced by cheap plastic versions. *Credit: Adrien Gardère*

and local labor, but on the contrary, for their enriching and inspiring traditional know how, that might be disappearing otherwise."

So, began a great adventure for Adrien Gardère that spanned several years and many trips from France to various parts of Asia. "The idea was to try and understand the phenomenon where the process of production is responding to a lot of demands from the occidental world that conform to our stereotypes as to what is local or Asian or Indian, rather than a truthful and genuine reality," he says. "It is looking for the convergence of design and sustainable design." The process began when he won a fellowship to study and work in India. There, among other projects, he collaborated with the National Institute of Design (NID), set up in the mid 1960s in Ahmedabad, following Charles and Ray Eames's 1958 India Report. "With 5 selected students of NID, I designed a full collection of furniture," Gardère notes. "The idea was not to be a gimmick or a monkey design of what is exotic or local. The idea was to go very deep into the understanding of the crafts, to understand the manners and attitude of the crafts, and to see if there was an approach or technique that could be transposed, or a material that has interest, or a form that has such a strength that it deserves to be reconstituted." This year of study resulted in seven pieces of furniture that were shown around Europe, but never went beyond the prototype phase.

About a year later, Olivier Debray, the director of Surabaya Alliance Française in Indonesia, Olivier Debray, contacted Gardère to see about creating some furniture that reflected the same philosophy and approach of his Indian collection. "It was very important for me to have some local training, to root my experience in Indonesia, and to have a real exchange of know how," Gardère says, "so I could train people at the same time that I would learn from observing." He worked with three local design students who became his trainees.

Gardère hoped that this time his creation would go beyond prototypes. "The idea was to not only identify the local craftsmen and their know how, but also to identify the local producers and the local small factories that we could follow up with and learn along the way about what we didn't even know what we were going to make yet," he laughs. They began by traveling the countryside looking for materials, shapes, and techniques that might be extrapolated to a chair. They settled on an indigenous, traditional Indonesian shovel that is very strong, used for a wide variety of tasks, and is made in several different sizes. "But it was disappearing," Gardère notes. "It took us a lot of time to find craftsmen that were still making them, because they are now using plastic." They also began experiments with splitting and

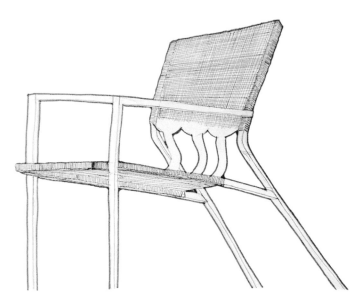

Left: A first sketch shows the distinctive angle of the back legs, as well as the beautiful pattern created by weaving rattan over a metal frame and among three pieces of split and bent bamboo. *Credit: Adrien Gardère*

A "very first try on a metal frame" shows the key elements that need to come together for the final chair: bent metal, split bamboo, and woven rattan. Perhaps unfortunately, colored ribbons will not be included on final production models. *Credit: Adrien Gardère*

The bamboo pieces are bent in a shape that provides comfort as well as support. Early prototypes were made with whatever tools local craftsmen had on hand or could create. *Credit: Adrien Gardère*

bending bamboo. "In this way, the chair is totally drawn and designed naturally," Gardère notes. "It has grown around and from the bamboo techniques and prototypes. It's not that we pasted the bamboo artifacts onto the chair. It's not something we designed and then thought, oh we'll make it in bamboo. It's very much a result of the processes and mechanics of the bamboo that we'd researched, adapted, and extended. The chair kind of fluidly raised out of that process."

The production model is made of stainless steel metal that is bent, rather than soldered, "… to make it a little softer and more welcoming." The unusual angle of the back legs and the curve of the bamboo reflect both aesthetic and functional concerns. "We wanted this continuity between the seat and the back," Gardère explains. "And that this would happen with the bamboo itself. Structurally, we could not have the backrest rely on the arms, so we needed a link between the backrest and the back feet. Also I wanted to almost contrast the softness and sweetness of the molded bamboo element, the part where it is one piece before it explodes in fingers." As well, Gardère notes, "We had to step from seat and backrest with the same element. I wanted continuity of material. We had to bend it respecting the structural capac-

ity of the bamboo. We could not make a straight angle or it would have broken. We needed a curve that the bamboo would support." Finally, the three pieces of split and bent bamboo are woven with native rattan, which is treated with a fungicide and then given a protective coat of varnish.

The chair is made from three pieces of bamboo that are split at each end and then woven into a chair seat and back around a metal frame. This prototype was shown at the Paris Furniture Fair, Salon du Meuble de Paris, ". . . not to be sold, just to show the result of the experience," Gardère says. But, as luck would have it, a new company, Perimeter Editions, was looking for limited edition products by a few select designers, saw the chair, and wanted to produce it. "What I really wanted happened in the sense that the chair found a distributor," Gardère says, "but I wanted to be very faithful to the process. It had to be produced in Indonesia." With a lot more work finding the right craftsmen to make the metal frames, and setting up workshops with the same craftsmen they originally trained to do the weaving, the Cikrak chair became much more than a cross-cultural, somewhat academic experience.

The Cikrak chairs are being made in an existing factory that has set aside a section for these specially trained craftsmen. "The company is small," Gardère notes. "For the moment, we're working on orders of fifteen at a time." But in addition to the satisfactions of seeing his creation somewhat industrially produced, he's also helped a group of people find new uses for important aspects of their indigenous culture. "They are very conscious of the need to feed their creativity," Gardère explains. "They very well know that they are very much limited to a Western order of production, which is stereotyped and impoverishing their know-how. They are very conscious of the benefit they can gain from new applications of their know-how." Summarizing the whole experience, his enthusiasm is palpable. "It's a good adventure and a great satisfaction. This is kind of my secret garden design, and it's also political in a way. It's a way of trying to take into account what I like in the world, and also trying to set up projects that are not just ego-centered, but are part of exchange and cooperation, and in this very limited way, part of sustainable development. It took a whole range of people and cooperation, and I find this very exciting because other projects are not usually as humanly rooted."

⊘ Bamboo provides a critical structural element—as well as natural beauty and comfort—to the Cikrak Chair. Three pieces are split at either end, while the middle section remains whole to provide support between the seat and back. *Credit: Adrien Gardère*

⊘ This flat, test version of rattan woven around bamboo splits reveals the natural beauty of this traditional craft, so evident in the utilitarian shovels that were the genesis of the entire project. *Credit: Adrien Gardère*

Gardère started with a cardboard mock-up of the chair before experimenting with bamboo, which was ultimately used. *Credit: Adrien Gardère*

A detailed shot shows the sensual curve obtained in the bamboo structural supports, along with the delicacy of the woven rattan, which together create a very strong, versatile, and comfortable chair that uses traditional techniques to create a thoroughly modern statement. *Credit: Philippe Chancel*

Corallo Chair, Fernando and Humberto Campana

"This **chair** is an example of how **something** that is very **complicated** for typical **industrialization** can be made," says Humberto Campana of the Corallo chair **designed** by him and his brother **Fernando**.

Each Corallo chair is individually handmade of bent and welded wire, following the form created by the Campana Brothers. *Credit: Edra*

Opposite top: The design for the Corallo chair was decidedly simple—create lines floating in air, as this early sketch shows. *Credit: Fernando and Humberto Campana*

Opposite bottom: In a later drawing, the Corallo chair takes on a more definite, organic shape. The Campana brothers find inspiration in both the urban and rural worlds in which they split their time. *Credit: Fernando and Humberto Campana*

It is also an example of how, in the creative process, nothing really gets lost, and even things that have been set aside for a decade can suddenly spring back to life. When Humberto started making chairs back in the early 90s, he fabricated a seat made of wire and wood rings. "It was very sculptural and one of a kind," he says. "We kind of forgot about that project until the art director of Edra came to the studio one day and saw a photo of this other chair and asked us to make something like this concept with another shape."

Working from the concept of lines floating in air, Humberto began simply by bending pieces of steel wire. "We started with real scale, one-to-one," he recalls. "I bent a lot of materials, created a lot of lines, and then we started welding them one to another to create the structure. We create a volume, even though we don't know what will be the final shape, and then, just like sculpting, like someone who works in marble or wood, we start to take away material to sculpt the chair itself and to make it comfortable." He continues, "There were several phases, little by little, but the sculpture came first and the function came after."

When the handmade prototype was finished, the brothers sent it off to Tuscany where skilled craftsmen followed their basic form to create this highly fashioned armchair. Even though Edra has developed a kind of mold around which the wires are bent and welded to create the overall shape, every Corallo armchair is basically made by hand. "Each one is different from the other," Humberto points out. "This humanizes the design. We don't want to put a standardization on the chair. We want to have a human touch. These are semi-industrialized, but they need the human hand to help them."

Once Edra saw the shape of the seat finalized, they named it Corallo, which means coral in Italian, and painted the piece its signature color. Humberto remembers, "The first one we did was rusted, without any paint or varnishes. But this one is painted so it can be out in the garden and can be comfortable. The paint has a kind of plastic in it, so it's softer in contact with the body." However, he notes, "It's not a chair to sit in for many hours, I will confess. It's something that you could use a pillow with. That would be fine with me. It doesn't matter to me how people are going to use it. The most important thing is for us to make the concept, to bring something new, and then it starts walking on its own, and I'm not responsible for it anymore."

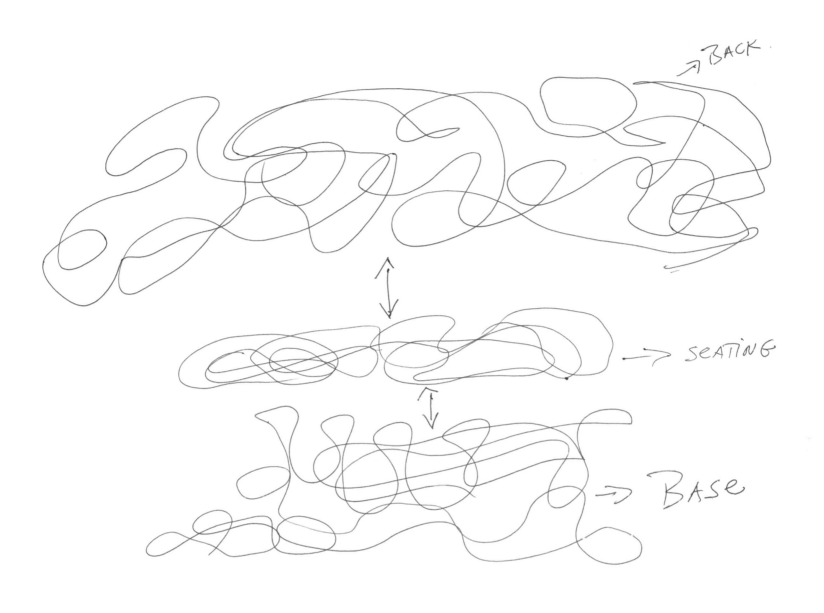

→ BACK

→ SEATING

→ BASE

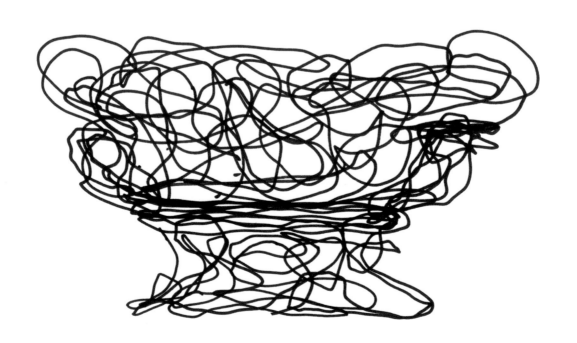

The Campana brothers collaborate on all their designs. Fernando was trained as an architect and Humberto as a lawyer. "But I gave that up," Humberto says, "and then I started making small things and got involved in iron sculpture. I thought I was going to be a sculptor, and then furniture design just arrived in our lives." Fernando is reportedly the rational force of the team. "I'm much more into ideas," Humberto says. "He puts my foot on the ground so I don't dream so much. He gives function and stability to the work." The coming together of these opposite approaches is not without its sparks. "We have a constant dialogue, and sometimes it is very explosive," Humberto says. "We have lots of disagreements. It's funny that we are always trying to convince each other that one is right and the other is wrong. It's like two characters in a David Lynch film."

The brothers collect their ideas from places as different as their own sensibilities. They grew up in the countryside and still spend every weekend in this rural setting, far away from the vibrant and culturally rich, urban atmosphere of San Paolo. "We look for inspiration from the ground to the sky," Humberto says, "from the clouds in the sky to the rocks and in the very colored, textured, compressed world of San Paolo. We need them both and like to make a shock between these two different worlds in which we live."

The brothers work through all these disparate influences in a decidedly civilized way. Humberto describes their process: "Every day, we go and have a coffee, and we make it into a kind of meeting, and we talk about projects and to just be away from the studio and see the life of the streets. I like everyday to have an idea, and Fernando likes to have time away from the idea. He comes from a distance, as he is not involved manually with the piece. Sometimes, he arrives and finishes it. He can see it more clearly, where I am so involved with the piece, I can't see it any more. Every day, we just talk about creation. There is no formula for how we come to agreement. I never thought about it because it just comes." The brothers also have other designers in their studio who bring ". . . fresh eyes and minds to the creative process, and their opinions are very important. Sometimes, they give the final opinion, and they break the deadlock."

Even though his background as a sculptor clearly influences his work, Humberto feels there are important differences between design and art that need to be understood, and then transcended. "Even though my work can be very sculptural, my main concern is that it belongs to people's houses. We are not artists, we are designers," he says. "We like to point out new directions, new questions about how to use furniture. We like to be outsiders, to pervert materials that exist in the market to create another function with that material." He continues, "I don't like barriers—this belongs to art, this to design. Today, we need to embrace everything. Today, everything is coming to design. Modernity is to make a fusion of everything."

Top: Metal rods are bent by hand and placed as whim and aesthetics dictate in early stages of developing the first chair that would later become the Corallo.
Credit: Fernando and Humberto Campana

More pieces of bent metal are added to give the Corallo chair arm supports. The production models are made in a similar way, by bending wires over a rough form and welding them together.
Credit: Fernando and Humberto Campana

Bottom: Once the generous proportions of the seat are created, the form is set atop a temporary support to finalize its proportions.
Credit: Fernando and Humberto Campana

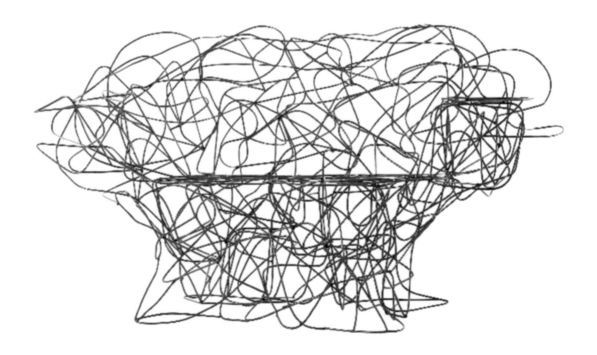

△ Final shaping of the first prototype resulted in a chair that looks both sculptural and natural, as if it grew into its ultimate form. *Credit: Fernando and Humberto Campana*

▽ The Corallo chair, as produced by Edra, is covered with a brilliant coral paint that not only protects it from the elements but also contains rubber to make it more comfortable against the skin. *Credit: Edra*

Ultimately, the pleasures of the Carollo chair are quite simple for Humberto. "It looks like a cloud of lines in the sky," he says. "I like this. It gives me happiness when I see it. It gives me the sensation of lightness." And when others look at it? "When people see it, there is a smile on their face," Humberto reports. "Especially children. They love our furniture. They seem to make an emotional connection to the chair. This is what is missing today in furniture, this emotion, this connection to the spirit. The world is saturated with rationalism. People need to work more with intuition and a sense of humor. In this era, we need this."

Decompression Space Chair, Matali Crasset

"This chair had a very **specific** brief at the **beginning**," says Matali Crasset. "FeliceRossi **gave** the same base to four or five **designers**. They had a chassis, and then they **were** to do four or five models on the same **technique**, like a car."

The Decompression Space Chair creates a relaxing environment by offering pockets cut out of the foam for resting elbows and hands. *Credit: FeliceRossi Srl*

The base provided by the furniture manufacturer was to be made in roto-molded plastic. "They sent the drawing and said we had to finish it," says Crasset, who immediately saw the raw potential in the simple structure. "I decided not to cover the base," she says. "It is an industrial piece and well-finished. It was quite a big structure, and I realized that I wanted to do the opposite of the arm chair, where there are big soft shapes on each side to hold your arms. I wanted to do the opposite and let the arms fall inside because it's a more relaxed position; you put your arms along your body to relax. That's why it's called a decompression space. To have the body be in this position is to make a situation to relax, to forget, and get imagination on that point."

For Crasset, design is less about the object itself and more about the space it will inhabit. "In a way, I always start with the context," she says. "I'm doing a piece for a company, or a specific interior, or a hotel, so you have to deal with atmosphere and how you want people to feel in the space. You always have a context of development with a project." But with this project, the context and the product became one and the same. "The brief was already very different," says Crasset. "When I suggested to leave the chair open and keep the structure visible, I thought they would refuse it because it was not the idea. But the opposite happened. They found it very interesting."

As she began to work out a form for the chair, Crasset spent a lot of time thinking about what it is to rest. "I did some experimentation about the decompression space and how can space can create a kind of restful atmosphere," she says. "I did some trials about resting with space and it was quite interesting to find the same disposal, but for a domestic application and with the armchair," she explains. "I did this idea of inverting the armchair. It is a kind of negative armchair. The arms are inside out." This project also turned Crasset's usual design interests inside out. "It is something which is very different than other things I do," she says. "I hate to dictate to people. I prefer to make a base and let people be free to move. With the shape of the armchair, it's a proposal to rest. It's a fixed proposal. Usually, I'm working on modularity, movement, not having a product that is dictating something. In a way, this is an invitation to keep quiet. It makes sense."

The base of the chair is a shell of plastic, available in five different colors: pink, light blue, white, royal blue, and green. The seat is made of molded foam with small pockets where elbows and hands can find a comfortable nest. Contrasting colors of foam accentuate these areas. "The more difficult part was to have a very good shape," says Crasset. "We had to make a mold for that part

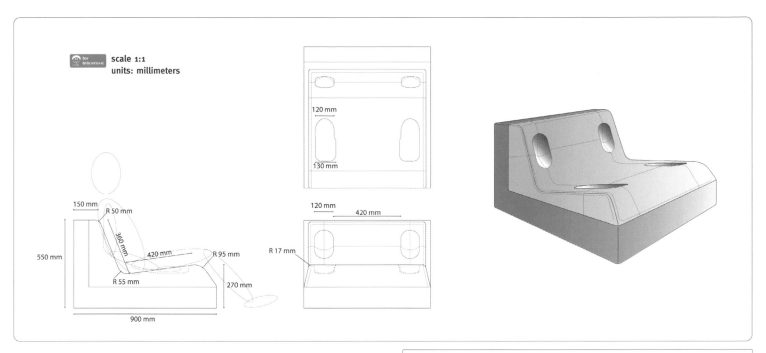

scale 1:1
units: millimeters

120 mm

130 mm

120 mm
420 mm

150 mm
R 50 mm
360 mm
420 mm
R 95 mm
550 mm
R 55 mm
270 mm
900 mm
R 17 mm

⊘ Above: A technical drawing of the Decompression Space Chair shows the comfortable slant of the seat, as well as the dimensions of the cut outs, which are shaped to reflect and invite the hand and elbow that will be resting there. *Credit: Matali Crasset*

⊗ Left: The base of the Decompression Space chair is fabricated of plastic made in this mold. The manufacturer gave several designers a drawing of a "chassis" and asked them to finish it into a piece of furniture. *Credit: FeliceRossi Srl*

⊘ Right: To create the chair base, raw polyethylene is put into the mold, which is then placed in this machine where it is heated and rotated to spread the raw material evenly inside the mold. *Credit: FeliceRossi Srl*

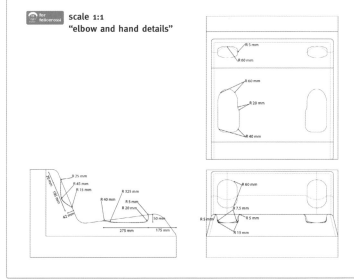

scale 1:1
"elbow and hand details"

R 5 mm
R 60 mm
R 60 mm
R 20 mm
R 40 mm
R 25 mm
R 45 mm
R 15 mm
R 325 mm
R 40 mm
R 5 mm
R 20 mm
42 mm
50 mm
275 mm
175 mm
R 60 mm
R 7.5 mm
R 5 mm
R 5 mm
R 15 mm

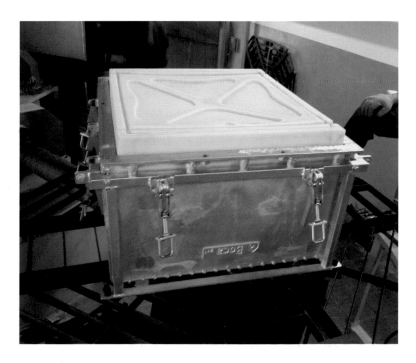

to make sure we get a good cut. The shape inside the cut out part is not just round," she notes. "It's shaped like a hand. It goes from wide to narrow to make people think of having their hand there." According to Crasset, the foam is attached to the plastic with Velcro strips. "So you can take it out," she says. "You can change the fabric or whatever." The small contrasting strip between the seat and the plastic base is "where it is elastic for comfort," she notes.

"Normally," she says, "this would be made of wood or steel. This project is very light. The molding is very light. There is air inside. You have a very thin layer of plastic and then the foam. It's empty inside; it's a closed shape. Only the outline is plastic. It's strong; it's enough." The piece is finished with four small metal feet, also in contrasting colors that further lift and lighten the entire piece off the floor just a bit. Crasset points out that you can put the Decompression Space chairs side by side to create a sofa of any size or seating capacity.

Crasset has also expanded how the chair can be used in other ways. "Here's a little story," she says. "I am doing another project, an exhibition about design and the domestic application for sound. I put a remote control where the hand is. You have a database of sound and text and the idea is to mix them, to select sound and text and try to mix them together. The idea was to no longer get music—that is very easy   but what can we do with it, and how do we give it meaning." At the Abitare il Tempo, an interior design fair in Verona, Italy, Crasset created an entire Decompression room. "We used the same chair," she says, "and it was green and yellow. The idea was to get a rest, but also to get energy. The color was to give to energy."

When she considers this inside-out chair, she finds that the self-contained and suggestive nature of the Decompression Space is its most intriguing aspect. "I like the idea that this furniture has its own way of working," she says. "I don't care about the shape. The more interesting thing is the attitude it can propose to you. I like to have a product that engages the person. You like it or you don't, but if you do, you have a deeper relationship with the piece. You have the same mood as the piece of furniture."

Top: A prototype of the molded piece is cut apart to check the thickness of the plastic. Crasset so liked the finished look of the plastic base that she decided to leave it exposed and simply add a foam seat.
Credit: FeliceRossi Srl

For the MIXtree exhibition, Crasset implanted a remote control into the hand pocket of the Decompression Space. Users manipulate fragments of sound and spoken text to create an interactive music experience.
Credit: Patrick Gries

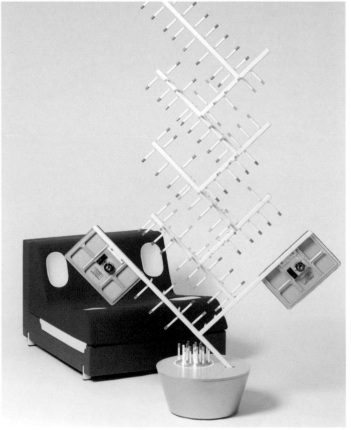

The Decompression Space Chair offers shoppers a place to rest in the midst of the Lieu Commun store in Paris. *Credit: Patrick Gries*

At the Abitare il Tempo interior design trade fair in Verona, Italy, Crasset created the Flux 04, an entire decompression room, where the chair shape was to provide rest, even as its color was designed to create energy. *Credit: Matali Crasset*

Dora Chair, Studio Palomba Serafini "In this special moment we are looking out for something more, something, how can we say, like a sort of metrosexual design," says Roberto Palomba.

The Dora Chair from the husband and wife team Palomba Serafini for Zanotta uses advanced molding techniques to create a textilelike pattern directly on the plastic surface. *Credit: M. Zambelli*

"I like masculine and rigorous, and I like geometry and also something that is minimal, but why do I have to be boring?" he asks. "Me too, I also dress with blue jeans, but why can't I use a flower T-shirt? I am a man, a straight guy, but also I can wear something that can be decorated, that can be more joyful." The Dora chair reflects not only these masculine and feminine influences—Palomba shares the studio with his wife, along with ten other designers and staff—but also multi generational and multicultural design inspirations. According to Palomba, "The main idea is that you can do something rigorous or rational, but it can contain something absolutely crazy, and it can belong to the same project. So we went with this strange combination of an homage to the '50s classical design, and this decorated skin, which is very like a Japanese kimono. Our international society is changing, so we have to find new models, and this has to be reflected in our design."

The Dora was also the product of Palomba's informal and friendly relationship with the manufacturer. "I have a close relationship with the company," he says, "and we often talk about new projects. I'm very free, and when I have an idea, I go and I say, I have this idea, can we see about making it? It's very important for me to have a very flat and very simple relationship with the clients, who are generally sometimes my friends, too. So we talk about other things, not just about jobs, and sometimes ideas come from talking about other things." In the case of the Dora, part of Palomba's goal was to create something new and unique. "There are hundreds of pieces in roto-molding plastic," he points out. "The sales people were asking for something—always sales people ask for something they don't have. And so we say, if we have to make a Zanotta piece with roto molding, it has to be totally different from what is on the market."

From this multitude of ideas, influences, and impulses, came the Dora, with distinctive "flower tattoos." Palomba looked at several patterns, including stripes and oversized polka dots, before settling on the natural pattern. "I can say that I was thinking of having something that looks like fabric directly on the surface. I makde some sketches, then I saw some Japanese décor, and I said that I would like to do something like that, put a kimono on a '50s arm chair. Flowers, well, flowers are always a positive object," he points out. The pattern is created directly in the mold itself by having some parts of the chair polished and others matte. The Dora is also available in a lacquered, highly polished version without the pattern, but Palomba prefers the "tattoos."

The shape of the chair was designed not only as a nod to an earlier aesthetic, but also to provide optimal comfort for all-season, all-weather seating.

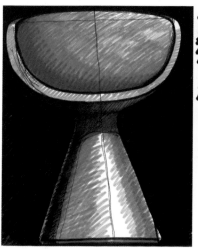

⌃ Early sketches by Roberto Palomba show the variety of patterns he considered before settling on the flower for its inherently positive associations.
Credit: Roberto Palomba

⌃ Palomba wanted his Dora chair, which can be used inside or out, to have a fat, sensual shape, as well as harken back to design influences of the '50s, as depicted in these early sketches.
Credit: Roberto Palomba

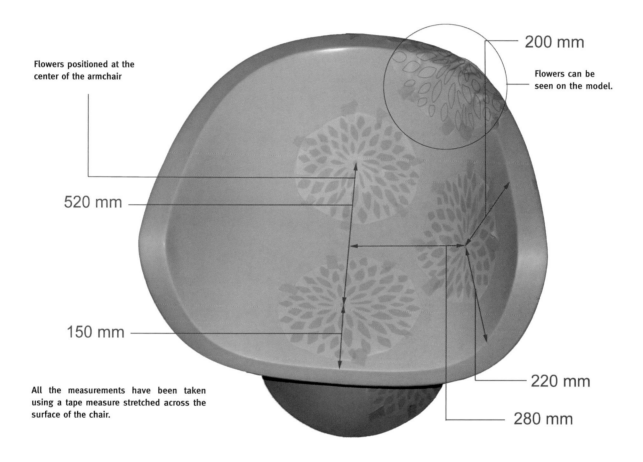

Flowers positioned at the center of the armchair

200 mm

Flowers can be seen on the model.

520 mm

150 mm

220 mm

280 mm

All the measurements have been taken using a tape measure stretched across the surface of the chair.

"When you make a thing in plastic, it's a continuous shape, and you always have to think about it like a ceramic or glass object, things that can be done only in one piece," Palomba notes. "It's very easy when using plastic to make a soft and sensual shape. I would like it to look fat and comfortable, but, when possible, the design has to also have a good price and be very comfortable." In addition to meeting these criteria, Palomba is pleased that the Dora is so versatile in both its pragmatism and aesthetics. "If you go around and look at this piece, the shape changes continuously," he points out. "You have lots of points of view. And this armchair can also be put outside, in the open air."

The chair's comfort resulted from rigorous testing of prototypes. "We were very careful with this," Palomba emphasizes. And also as important: nontechnical sit test. "It was very funny because in

⬡ Top left: One of the most interesting qualities of the Dora chair is how its shape changes subtly as you move around it—as shown in this computer rendering—while it retains the essence of its inviting nature. *Credit: Palomba Serafini*

⬡ Top right: Another computer rendering places the chair in human scale and shows the subtle shimmer created by the contrasting texture of the tattooed skin. *Credit: Palomba Serafini*

⬡ An early prototype focuses on the dimensions that create the extremely comfortable bucket shape of the seat. The pattern of flowers is also made more apparent. *Credit: Palomba Serafini*

the company, I discovered when they make armchairs, there is a man who is, I don't want to say fat, but he's a big man. When we make a model, we have to make a test with this man. When I arrive with the model, at the beginning, he arrives, and I was thinking it was a test to try and break it," Palomba recounts with another of his frequent bursts of laughter.

The chair also underwent some other, completely unplanned testing at an exhibition in the Salone del Mobile. Someone unintentionally placed one of the chairs over a light in the floor, turning the Dora into an impromptu lamp. This happy accident was then repeated intentionally to create softly glowing chairs throughout the exhibition. In addition, Palomba reports, "We left some chairs at the show and the people were playing a lot with them. What was very nice was the relationship with the babies. They were playing with them, climbing up and down, or putting them on the floor and using them like a big toy or creating a little car or something with it. I see that this kind of shape attracts the baby, and this was a good test."

Reflecting on the Dora chair's development, Palomba feels that it is both a bit of a departure in execution but also a continuation of an important design concern. "I think with this object, there is something that I've never done before: a very strong inspiration with a classic object. Generally, we try to make objects that are more original, I would say. But I don't feel this work is like something wrong, because the main research was to create an object that worked in this way. This is what I asked of myself in the beginning, I asked myself to do this, it was not imposed to me, it was not something that happened, it was something that I decided to do."

This is a lesson Palomba also emphasizes to his design students at the university in Milan, where he teaches. "I say always the same thing when I talk to students," he notes. "I say that they have to think before they draw. It's up to you, you have to dig very well inside of you and choose your own way, and you say what you really feel to say." Thinking about the contrast between the iconic designers of the era that helped inspire his Dora chair, he notes, "In university today, they don't want to be a designer, they want to be a famous designer. But when you are creative, you have to say what you really feel, and you can't mind if you will be famous, because then you are just a marketing man. This hurts the younger generation. They just want to be a superstar, and this is totally mistaken. Design is something you have to take care about. We can't make objects just to make our glory."

Facett Chair, Ronan and Erwan Bouroullec "We used the machine to make a kind of **clothes** for the sofa," says Erwan **Bouroullec** of the Facett collection. "It's a **bridge** between clothing and **origami paper** folding."

The Facett collection is made of quilted foam and fabric with an industrial sewing machine more typically used for mattress manufacturing.
Credit: Paul Tahon and Ronan Bouroullec

The machine to which he is referring was something he and his brother, Ronan, discovered on the factory floor at the furniture manufacturer Ligne Roset. "It was in the center of the factory and was a very big machine, and most of the time, I was just passing by and it was not being used," Bouroullec recalls. "I asked what this machine wais." It turned out to be an "incredible sewing machine" that makes mattresses. Ligne Roset is not generally in the business of making mattresses, but was using the machine approximately one week a month. Bouroullec found out that making mattresses "is an incredibly simple job for something that can do so much more." The discovery of the machine coincided with, and made possible, an idea the brothers had for a new kind of sofa. "The idea was to make a full-form sofa," he says. "It doesn't have any visual structure. It's just a shape covered by the fabric." Once they discovered this machine, they had to dust it off and reconsider the potential of what they had in their midst. "They had to learn how to use and program it in a much more complex way," Bouroullec says. "They even had to buy another part for the machine."

Making the Facett was a process of hands-on trial and error. "We made some really early drawings," Bouroullec says, "kind of imprecise drawings of what we might want to do, and we made many small prototypes, but we didn't really draw it. We went to prototyping quite quickly," he notes. "Our first decision was to choose a fabric and use the sewing machine to make a kind of sandwich between fabric and foam," Bouroullec says. "The sewing has two roles: when you repeat all the parallel lines on the surface of the sofa, you give much more stiffness to the fabric, so that the fabric/foam acts like cardboard. Sewing also makes a gap and can be used as a kind of folding line."

They quickly discovered that there are unique challenges when you try to sew rather than build a piece of furniture. "The work became very precise, which is why I speak of clothing and tailoring," Bouroullec says. "As soon as we had to make a transformation about the height of the seat, angle of back, or height—all the usual dimensions you adapt in prototyping to make it comfortable—every time we even had to make a two centimeter change, we had to redraw the entire clothes." Eventually, they were able to create flat patterns, similar to those used by dressmakers, for each piece in the collection. "There are like thirty surfaces," Bouroullec explains, "and all the surfaces came from one or two flat parts. Everything is flat like origami at first. Then, you make these lines that are rejoined with a second sewing process. At the end, we needed to have a perfect fit between the fabric/foam and the inside form of the sofa. The shape of the sofa is faceted, like a diamond," he continues. "There are all these triangles and perfect geometrical shapes that all answer to each other."

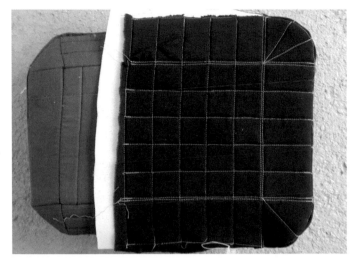

⬡ Top left: The stitching lines also designate where the material is to be folded, or more accurately, "tailored," and how it fits to the furniture. *Credit: Paul Tahon and Ronan Bouroullec*

⬡ Top right: Early prototypes were made by hand to gauge the proportions needed to configure the geometry of the facets that give the furniture its unique look and feel. *Credit: Paul Tahon and Ronan Bouroullec*

◁ Small paper models show exactly where the machine needs to sew lines for both quilting and folding of the fabric/foam material. *Credit: Paul Tahon and Ronan Bouroullec*

▽ Once all the dimensions and angles are worked out, a pattern not unlike those used to make clothing is created. *Credit: Paul Tahon and Ronan Bouroullec*

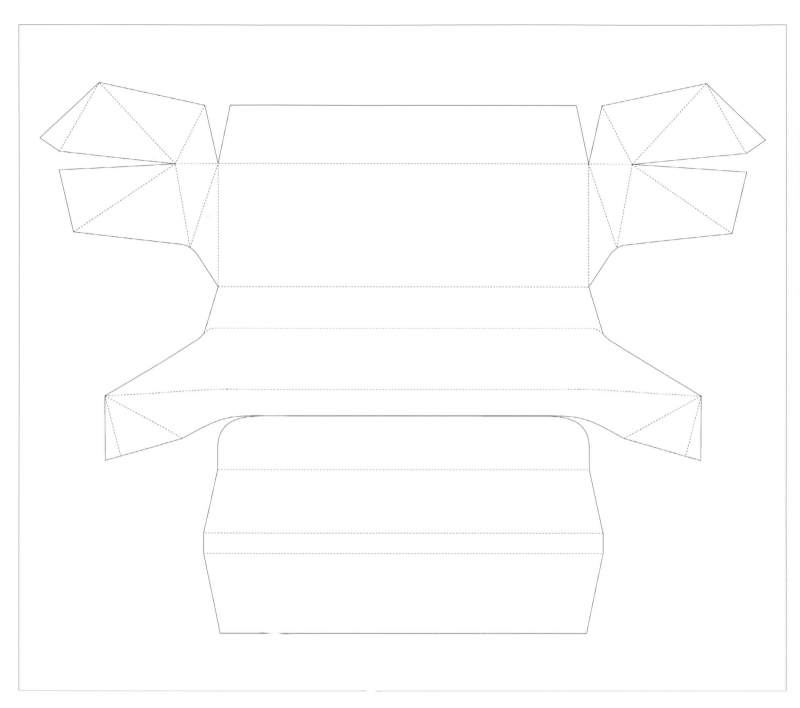

A pattern for the Facett Sofa shows which stitching lines will also be fold lines, much like a piece of origami.
Credit: Ronan and Erwan Bouroullec

Each piece in the Facett collection is made with a quilted, tailored, zippered cover of foam and fabric, which can be removed for cleaning.
Credit: Paul Tahon and Ronan Bouroullec

Opposite: The complete line of Facett furniture can be used together for modular versatility and flexibility, especially in small spaces.
Credit: Paul Tahon and Ronan Bouroullec

The most challenging aspect of the manufacturing process was creating the arms. "It was interesting to manage with the design of the armrest, to make it in such a small dimension," Bouroullec says.

Once made, these quilted "clothes" fit precisely over a wood and plastic internal structure. "You can take the cover off to wash it," Bouroullec notes. "It's very practical. There are two zippers on the back to remove it."

The original sofa is now part of a complete line that includes a loveseat, chair, and ottomans in two different sizes. They are also making some quilted "carpets" of the same sandwiched foam-and-fabric concoction. All the pieces are available in a wide range of fabrics with contrasting or complementary stitching. They create a versatile collection, particularly for people who want deep, extremely comfortable, movable furniture that fits into a compact space. "With the footrest," Bouroullec says, "as soon as you put it in front of the armchair or sofa, you have a really wide chaise lounge. You could almost sleep on it. It's perfect to be with a child or watch TV. The fact that you don't see any structure, you see only fabric, it gives a lot warmness to the sofa," he adds.

The Facett collection has been very well received, Bouroullec notes. "People really understand and like this haute couture, incredibly well-finished surface. There is some kind of value that people understand very quickly. They understand that behind it, there's a lot of work, and don't mind if it's from someone or from a machine. What is really different is the way we have been using the sewing, the shape, no feet—this is all quite new," he says. "But what is not especially different is that we have an idea at the beginning and we try to push the idea as far as possible. This collection has a very strong point of view."

On this project, like every other they undertake, Erwan Bouroullec worked hand-in-hand with his brother, Ronan. "The first thing is that we always work together, so there is no project that comes from me or my brother," Erwan says. "Everything is codesigned. Sometimes, the work is like a Ping-Pong game, and other times it's like a boxing game," he explains. "It depends upon the mood. Sometimes, it's easy and natural, and sometimes, we don't agree, and it can go quite far into disagreement before we find a solution." When asked if they have different strengths they bring to the process, Erwan answers with a hesitant and equivocal "yes." "But they are things that are not particularly understandable for someone who does not know us closely," he explains.

Flow Chair, Monica Förster At first, Monica Förster thought it was a **joke**. An email arrived that said simply, "**Hello**, we are **Seglas**. We have seen you on the **Internet** and would like you to design a **chair** for us. 3,000 chairs, **please**. Looking **forward** to hearing from you."

The Blue Auditorium at the Cartagena Cultural Center in Cartagena Spain, designed by Josè Selgas y Lucia Cano Arquitectos, features the Flow Chair designed by Monica Förster to conjure a feeling of water and waves as a reflection of the building's seaside location.
Credit: Josè Selgas y Lucia Cano Arquitectos

Assuming this was just a tease from a colleague or friend, Förster laughed and forgot about the note. Then, a few months later, she received another email from this mysterious Seglas. This time, it was an electronic holiday card. Förster took a moment to look at the recipient list and noticed her name appeared among those of many other well-known artists and designers. She found herself thinking that perhaps this Seglas was no joke after all. She responded to the first inquiry and discovered it had come from Seglas and Cano Architects, a leading Spanish architectural firm in Madrid, who were developing a major cultural center in Cartagena, Spain and wanted her to design the seats for the auditorium.

"They sent me ten different images of the model for the center," Förster recalls. "It was a very exciting, really a fantastic building that used many different materials and was very modern in its expression." As if this were not interesting enough, Seglas also told her they wanted her to work with new technologies and materials to create the best auditorium chair ever made. And, she would have the opportunity to work with Poltrona Frau, an Italian company known as one of the premier manufacturers of auditorium chairs in the world.

"Because the building was situated very close to the harbor of Cartagena, I knew I wanted to work with the feeling of water," Förster says. "I started looking at different ways of doing this and tried to think of how to make a chair, that when they were all closed, would look like waves or a waterfall, with reflections and all the rest."

The resulting effect is both understated and elegant. "I designed an organic chair, with a quite simple shape," Förster continues, "that when folded down, the armrest becomes like a wave, and when you close it, the armrest softly bends into the chair, which also means that the chair takes up less space than is typical for this type of chair."

To further enhance the flowing feeling, Förster was trying to achieve, she suggested working with three slightly different shades of blue. "Each chair is a different color," she points out, "put together in a pattern that Is not random but is organized in a clever way to create shapes with the color so it's not so clear what the pattern is, but it creates a feeling of movement within the building." The architects loved this idea, and decided to do one auditorium in red, another in blue, and have the chair bases match the color of the rubber flooring. Förster points out, "The

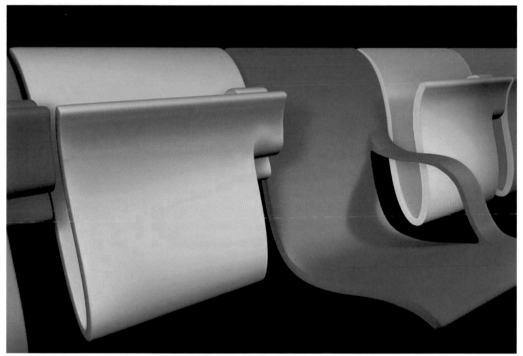

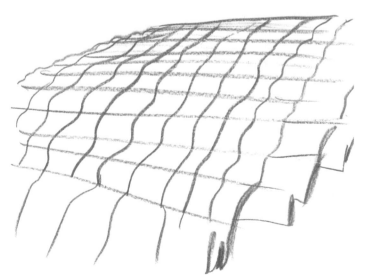

 Top: The Cartagena Cultural Center in Cartagena Spain, designed by Jose Selgas y Lucia Cano Arquitectos, makes a modern statement that inspired the simple lines of the Flow chair. *Credit: Josè Selgas y Lucia Cano Arquitectos*

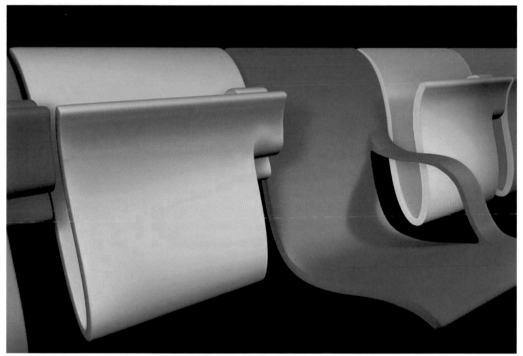 Above: The architects used a mix of materials to create a modern statement that inspired the simple lines of the Flow chair. *Credit: Josè Selgas y Lucia Cano Arquitectos*

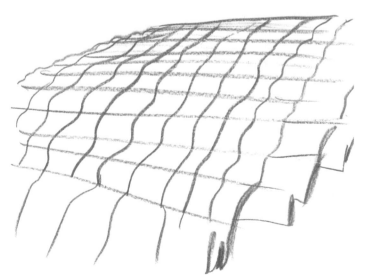 Left: An early sketch illustrates the feeling of flowing water, while only suggesting at the form the Flow auditorium chair would eventually take. *Credit: Monica Förster*

idea is that the base of the chair will be the same as the floor, so the base will kind of disappear. It will feel like the chairs are floating. It's like the chairs will fly."

Then it came time to see how—and if—these chairs could be produced. Förster describes what happened: "I was working on this idea, and I made a couple of models to take with me and present to the people at the factory. A colleague of mine said that they'd never be able to produce my idea, and forced me to make another solution with an armrest that didn't fold. The shape was the same, and he said that I'd have to present this other idea when they told me the first one wouldn't work. So when I showed my model to the fabricators, their foreheads wrinkled up, and it got very quiet for a bit. Then they congratulated me, but said it would be very challenging, which is an Italian way to say that's it very difficult. You never get 'it's not possible,' with Italian manufacturers; it's always 'challenging.' So we talked about it for a few hours, went out for lunch, and when we came back, they discussed some solutions, and I offered to think about alternatives. I thought maybe now would be the time to show the other model, which I had hidden in a box. They looked at the second version and sighed with relief. I thought that we'd be making this one. But what happened was the next day, Silvano Bonfranceschi, who is head of product development at Poltrona Frau, came back and said that he'd spoken to some folks and decided that they liked the first one better because it's more interesting—a novelty— more unique. So they thought about different solutions and decided to make the more difficult chair."

Another aspect to the fabrication challenge was simple durability. As an auditorium chair, it will be used by hundreds of thousands of people, opening, closing, sitting on the armrest, possibly standing on the seats. Ultimately, what Poltrona Frau made is an upholstered chair on a metal frame with injected molded polyurethane foam for cushioning. As far as creating the folding armrest, even Förster isn't sure how that's been achieved. "There's a lot of secret technology in the armrest that I don't know about," she says. It has to be soft to fold, and then when it's out, it needs to be rock hard. It folds like a piece of paper, and that's the really tricky part." The single armrest for each chair is made in two modular pieces, but constructed to look perfectly seamless.

Förster points out that knowing she would be working with such an innovative and experienced manufacturer encouraged her to push the original design. "I have to say," she says, "that this project would not have been possible with many producers because it is so difficult. Not all of them will have the resources. But I knew Poltrona Frau could take on a challenge like this." She continues, "In fact, they put so much pride into achieving this design and to overcoming the challenge. They did a great job in developing the chair. It's so important when things go into production to not let go of the original idea and to keep the poetry within the object or piece of furniture."

⬦ Top: Monica Förster also designed the fabric for the Flow Chair upholstery, creating a pattern of shiny blue over a matte background. The textile was produced by Väveriet in Sweden. *Credit: Monica Förster*

⬦ Above: An early prototype of a single Flow Chair shows the folded armrest, which is made in two pieces, but looks like only one. Silvano Bonfransceschi, head of product development, at manufacturer Poltrona Frau, stands next to the chair. The final product has a base that matches the floor so the auditorium appears to be made of chairs that float. *Credit: Monica Förster*

⊗ The Flow Chair is not a single object, but an entire auditorium of chairs upholstered in shades of blue that have been arranged in a subtle pattern to suggest undulating waves of water.
Credit: Monica Förster Design Studio

⊗ In another version, Förster suggestsed the Flow Chairs be given the additional benefit of lights in the back to indicate which seats are unoccupied. The manufacturer is currently looking into the feasibility of producing this option. *Credit: Monica Förster Design Studio*

Flower Offering Chair, Satyendra Pakhalé "We usually think of materials and what they can do for us. We **think** that **materials** are for one kind of **thing**," says industrial designer Satyendra Pakhalé, speaking of his **Flower Offering Chair**. "You never think of ceramic and a chair."

⊘ Combining the age-old, multicultural art of ceramics with some decidedly high-tech production processes and innovative joinery, the Flower Offering Chair is a ceremonial object of welcome.
Credit: Corné Bastiansen, EKWC

Pakhalé got his chance to find out what ceramics are capable of—and to push the material into new territory—when he was invited to a residency at the European Ceramic Work Centre (EKWC) in the Netherlands. The centre offers artists, architects, and designers the opportunity to live and work on site for three-month stints, where they can explore and avail themselves of studio space, workshops with complete facilities, and the expertise of skilled technicians and craftsmen. Pakhalé points out that they often invite people who have never worked in ceramics as a means to spur innovation. "Not being a ceramicist," he points out, "you don't know the limitations, so you're willing to try new things, which lets you go further. I do have a lot of respect for this process, perhaps one of the most magical yet age old innovations of humankind." He continues, "I wanted to use ceramics to create a piece of furniture as a symbolic object. This is an important thing because ceramics is one of those materials that has a long history; as long as the Earth has been here, ceramics have been here. But it's also a very high-tech material. This is the paradox I was working with."

Pakhalé worked at EKWC on two different occasions, separated by more than a year. His first residency involved working with staff to develop designs and models; the second was focused more on the technical aspects of making the chair work at full scale. Part of his goal was always to create something that could be commercially produced on at least a limited scale. "The object has to be multiplied to become a valid object," he says. "Then it will be a valid design in terms of produce-ability. As an industrial designer, my goal is to make a serial production."

From the beginning, he did not envision a traditional use for this chair. "This is not a chair to sit in front of your computer for eight hours a day," he points out. "The Flowering Offering Chair is more a chair as an object to welcome people. The typical setting will be in a lobby or front desk of a hotel. It becomes a ceremonial object, something like a universal, friendly gesture. You offer a flower to someone you like. Design is not only about cut-and-dried function; it's a psychological function to welcome someone as well."

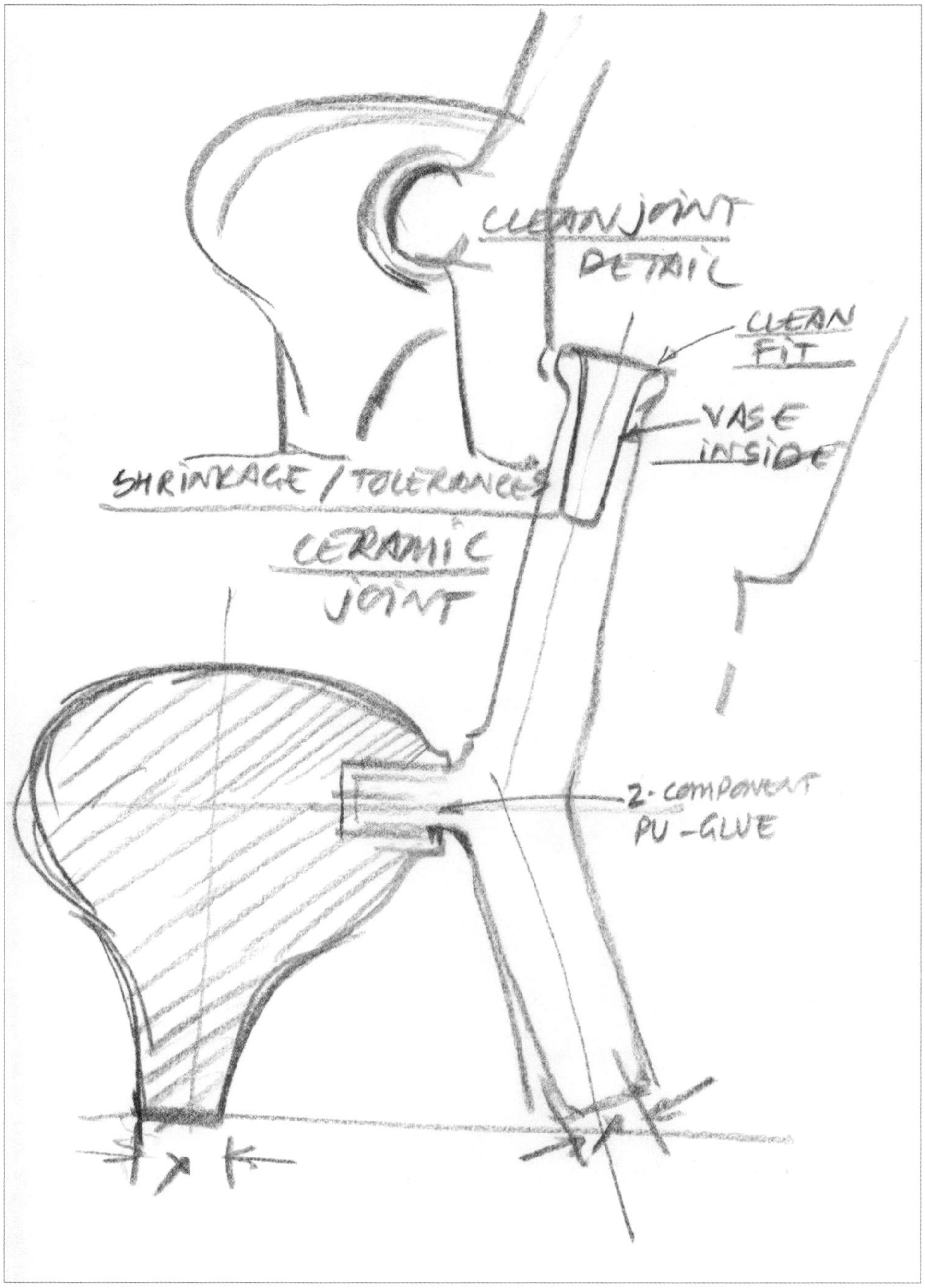
CLEAN JOINT
DETAIL
CLEAN
FIT
VASE
INSIDE
SHRINKAGE / TOLERANCES
CERAMIC
JOINT
2-COMPONENT
PU-GLUE

Early sketches show respect for tradition—the seat is a thrown pot turned on its head—alongside the more modern requirements for a joint that will hold the two-piece seat and back together, and the simultaneously playful yet and formal touch of an integrated vase. *Credit: Satyendra Pakhalé*

A watercolor sketch by the designer imagines the Flower Offering Chair at an amusing and yet beautifully overblown scale, with birds happily accepting its offer of hospitality. *Credit: Satyendra Pakhalé*

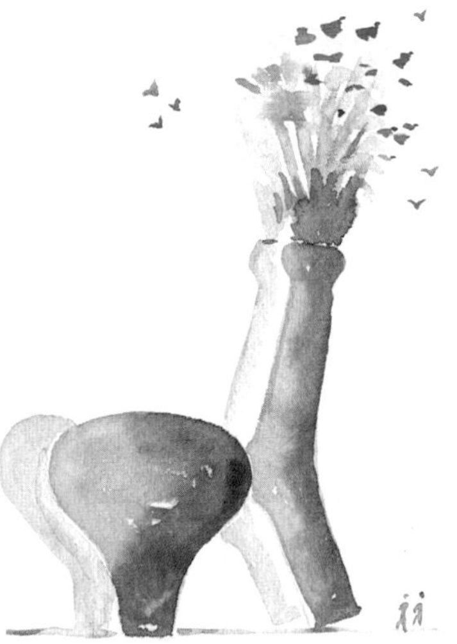

To create an object that was to work at so many different levels, Pakhalé and the staff at EKWC began with the fundamentals. "We went back to something very basic, which is throwing a pot," he says. "I don't know how to do that, but I found someone who does traditional pottery. It was an amazing amount of research into materials and the mixture of clay that would work for this chair. Ceramic is a very delicate and unpredictable material. Unlike metal and plastic, in ceramic there is an element of surprise. You make it, let it dry, and then fire it in a kiln, and in the firing process, anything can happen." And, many things did happen. Models of various sizes were made, clays were mixed and remixed, wall thicknesses were adjusted to allow for natural shrinkage of the drying clay, pieces were fired, and sometimes they came out beautifully, other times they cracked or became distorted. Then, back to the wheel and more pots were thrown. Once all these tests were completed, the team went to full-scale prototyping. Not only did the clay composition have to be just right, but because of different thicknesses in each piece, firing had to be calibrated very carefully. And then there was the joining of the back pieces to the seat. "At first, we put them together and then fired them," Pakhalé says. "But this made them susceptible to cracking and exploding. So I designed a special joint in ceramics by making the parts separately with a joint, and connecting them after firing with a two-component polyurethane glue. Fine-grained sculpture clay was used. The piece was placed on a shrinkage slab to allow equal shrinkage during drying and firing in order to avoid deformation or splitting."

Finding the right finish was also critical to making the most of the material itself. "I wanted to make it look very much like ceramic from close up or from a distance," Pakhalé says. "Normal glaze was not used because, being a chair and having a glossy finish, it could easily be misunderstood as a plastic chair, and I wanted to go away from that." After testing several different glazes, they settled on terra sigillata, which, according to Pakhalé, is Latin for "earth fitted with a seal." It is an ancient technique, used by Greeks and Romans, that applies a very thin layer of clay slip with a brush to the surface. "It gives it a satiny, glowing kind of finish, a very rich texture that's not gloss, not matte," he says. "I wanted it to look like a silk cloth."

◇ At the European Ceramic Work Centre (EKWC) in the Netherlands, a skilled ceramic artisan works on creating the first prototype for the chair. This part of the seat was created using a pottery wheel. *Credit: Satyendra Pakhalé*

◇ A technical drawing shows not only dimensions but also the various parts of the chair, including the removable vase and critical joint detail. *Credit: Satyendra Pakhalé*

◇ Below right: A technical drawing shows the detail of the joint, which proved to be the most challenging aspect of the product development. The chair parts were originally joined before firing, but they did not hold. This joint solved the problem: the pieces are made and fired separately, glazed with terra sigillata, and then glued together. *Credit: Satyendra Pakhalé*

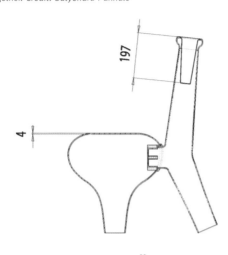

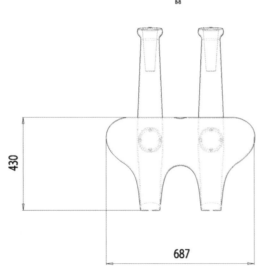

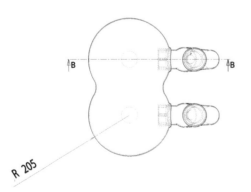

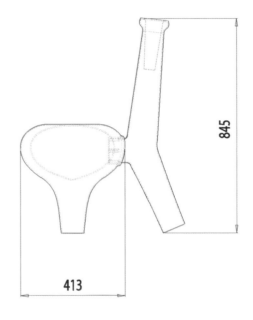

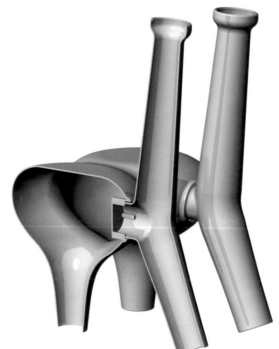

The next phase, critical to the chair's ultimate viability, was to find a way to produce the piece in some non-handmade quantity. "It took quite some time to search to find a ceramic workshop that could make the special mold," Pakhalé says. "The mold is made of plaster of Paris, one for the seat and one for the backrest with a special metal fixture to turn these huge molds in the slip casting process. The two parts are identical, so they can be made from the same mold." As an added bonus, the vase in the back sections can be removed for cleaning after the flowers have faded. While Pakhalé doesn't expect to ever make thousands of these chairs, the fact that he can make dozens is important. He wants an object that, while ceremonial, still lives in the real world. To this end, he points out that not only is the Flower Offering Chair extremely sturdy, but it can be used indoors or out.

Although Pakhalé forced the ceramic material and traditional processes into untested and innovative areas, the clay pushed him right back. "The ceramic material itself is very surprising. It's very hard to control," he notes. "For a person like me, who is a control freak, I need to control every single detail. I have a very clear picture in my mind, and with every industrial design project, I know how it all fits together. If you have a concrete idea, you can get it in 3D software right away and make it as you want it. With ceramic, you can't do that." And as satisfying as the final product is, with all its whimsical/symbolic, ancient/modern, high-tech/high-touch notions blended together, Pakhalé is ready to take what he's learned from this project into new materials and new products: "Right now, I am working on high-tech ceramic products for everyday use, a kind of engineering ceramics they use in aeronautics and space research. But I don't believe in being in love with one material for the rest of my life," he says. "I need to move on."

⊗ The back and bottom sections are loaded into the kiln for firing. Supports are put around each piece to help them retain their shape and minimize the potential for cracking. All parts are made with slip casting, then fired, and joined with polyurethane glue.
Credit: Satyendra Pakhalé

⊗ The first master model, made according to the 3D CAD drawings, was used to create a Plaster of Paris mold that will allow the chair to be made in quantity, rather than by hand.
Credit: Satyendra Pakhalé

⊘ The designer enjoys a moment of rest in his "ceremonial object" after several years of work, punctuated by two residencies at the EKWC, innumerable prototypes and tests, many cracks and explosions, and finally moving the chair into industrial production.
Credit: Corné Bastiansen, EKWC

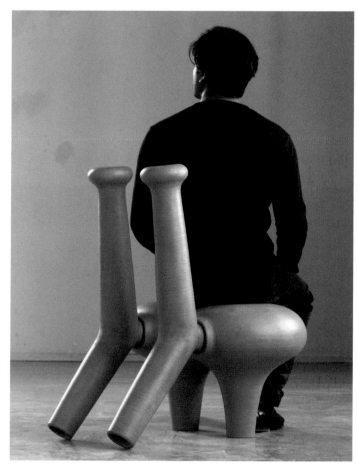

Fresh Fat Chair, Tom Dixon

"The personal **touch** has gone so much out of **design**," says Tom Dixon. "Most designers are not **involved** in the manufacturing at all. They do **something** on the **screen**, **someone** else cleans up the **drawing**,

The Fresh Fat Chair is made by arranging hot strands of extruded Provista PETG co-polyester over a mold and then allowing it to cool into a web of more than 40 pounds (18 kg) of plastic. *Credit: Ashley Cameron*

then someone else does the model and it gets sent to a manufacturing facility. This project was multidimensional."

The Fresh Fat Chair—and the table and bowls—collapse all these steps into a single, spontaneous piece of design performance art. Dixon subverts the industrial process of plastic extrusion by taking the hot polymer strands as they come out of the machine and draping and weaving them over a rough mold where they cool into the shape of furniture. The Provista PETG co-polyster plastic solidifies into a glistening structure that looks as delicate as a glass house but is actually solid and stable. "They're all individual," says Dixon. "The makeup, or pattern, is variable according to how it comes out and according to the people who are making it. Everyone has different handwriting."

The Fresh Fat line of furniture is the result of a competition to design a window for the upscale department store, Selfridges. Dixon says, "I actually made a small factory, which included a plastic extrusion machine that threw out hot, plastic spaghetti. There was an activity where designers were invited to come along and make unplanned objects from this stream of plastic. It was fascinating to see how people react to making an object. This project brings together craft and design. I've always been interested in craft and making things myself by hand or just for fun. I think this is absent from most people's lives. Designers are facing the computer and not the actual object." For Dixon, the immediacy of this process is a central part of its allure. "I love machinery and industrial processes but also making things by hand. There's nothing nicer than having an idea and completing it in a day. I think in modern man, that's impossible to achieve these days. Most people are involved in only a part of the process. There's something really nice about seeing the completion of an object."

Dixon also sees this way of manufacturing as a portent of things to come. "There's a logic to this," he explains. "My view is that shops today are where people come to buy goods. The IKEA model has been the future, where customers are forced to go to a warehouse. The next logical step is that they go to the manufacturing floor where they actually participate in the creation of the goods." For Dixon, creating products in the way he makes the Fresh Fat furniture has distinct benefits for retailers and consumers. "I moved the factory into the retail store. The dream scenario for retailers is to hold absolutely no stock and just produce the item when the customer pays for it. You don't over- or understock, but are just making to order. One day, you'll be able to react only to what the customer wants instead of what you think the customer wants. This is a reflection on the future of shopping, and the ideal situation for the retailer."

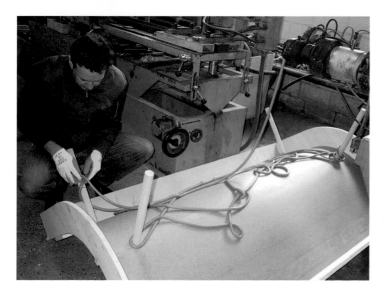

As the hot strands of plastic material come out of the extrusion machine, they are draped and shaped over a mold to create the form of the chair. *Credit: Gideon Hart*

Each Fresh Fat object is made individually by hand, so the patterns created express the unique "handwriting" of the person manipulating the plastic. *Credit: Gideon Hart*

Tom Dixon takes the hot plastic direct from the extruder and spreads it out over a very simple mold that is a rough inverse of the chaise lounge he is creating. *Credit: Gideon Hart*

After the initial success at Selfridges, Dixon has taken his extrusion machine on the road and set up his unique brand of design-theater at a Renaissance church and the Victoria and Albert museum. "It's taught me a lot about making things and the added value of objects," he says. "It's taught me something about the psychology of design. I will be using more industrial machines and diverting machines in my work. I think the future of design in general is to involve the customer more in the process."

For his Fresh Fat line of furniture, he experimented with a few shapes before settling on two chairs, a table, and bowls in two sizes. "It's been surprisingly successful considering it's an experiment," he notes. "People are surprised you can sit on them. At first they treat them very gingerly. They think the chair is made of glass because they're not used to seeing plastic used in this way. They treat them with respect, but this is something incredibly tough and hard to break."

Which is yet another somewhat subversive pleasure for Dixon about this chair. "There's something special about being able to use plastic," he says. "As a young designer, you don't really ever get the chance to make something in plastic because of the high tooling costs. And then there's the issue of, is plastic a throw away product or not? We're using forty to fifty pounds of plastic in the chair, which means you can't throw it away. You're in a position where you've got this thing that's almost as heavy as you can carry, so it's no longer disposable; it's a precious item. The

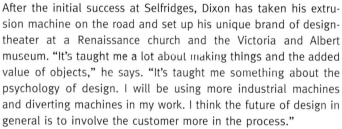 Left: The Fresh Fat Chairs come in a more upright dining version, and a more reclined easy chair. Dixon says the process of collapsing creation and manufacturing into one step reflects the future of retail. *Credit: Gideon Hart*

The plastic can be woven into any shape, but the Fresh Fat line features a series of connected circles and ovals that creates a rippling effect over the surface of the product. *Credit: Gideon Hart*

truth is that plastic is a petrochemical, it is a precious material, and it should be treated that way," Dixon points out. "People normally see it as a disposable material. I just try to generate larger shapes, and use the plastic in a very permanent way."

Because the chairs are made one-by-one, Dixon can scale production up or down as needed. "This product is somewhere between industry and craft," he notes. "It's not a supremely practical chair. It's very heavy. It's not that we're going to sell hundreds of thousands of them." But after all, these chairs are about the quality of the process more than the end product. The Fresh Fat has even brought new pleasures to the people on the manufacturing floor at the extrusion factory. "They look on this as slightly mad in the beginning, and then they start enjoying the process a bit more," Dixon says. "We've had some great times in the factories where we're liberating them from what becomes a very dull job watching plastic tubing come off the line."

Or perhaps it's just Dixon's enthusiasm that is contagious. When asked what was most surprising about the process, he says, "It was the joy of making things again. It was seeing people who hadn't actually made something for ages, responding to the unknown. This machine is just throwing out hot plastic that you have to manipulate with gloves. You can't really predict what you'll make, you can only try to form it. It's like having a first go on the pottery wheel; it's a little out of control. There was something so nice about the freedom and the immediacy of it."

◇ The Fresh Fat collection includes two chairs and a coffee table in clear plastic, and two different sized bowls in clear, vivid red, or black. *Credit: Gideon Hart*

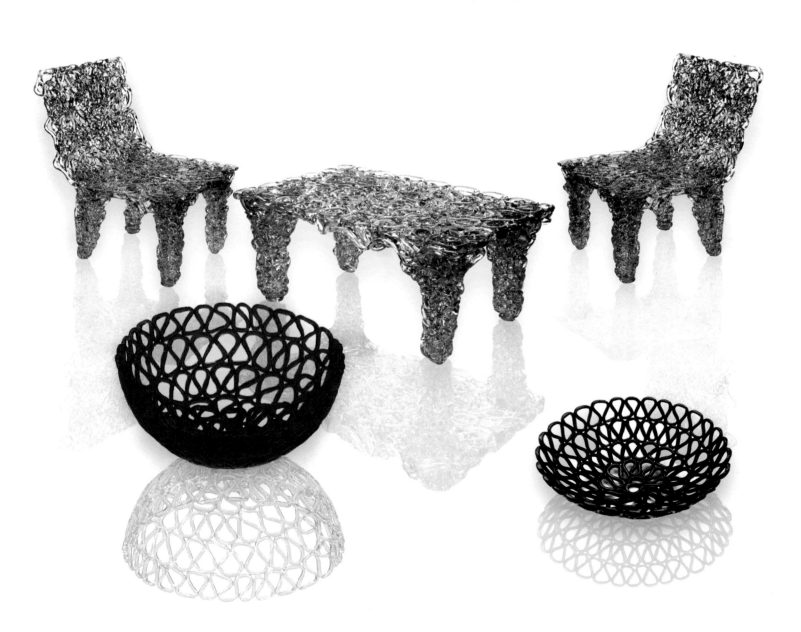

Glide Chair, Christopher Deam

"I was sitting in one of the standard-offering gliding chairs, and it was **hideous**, but it was so **comfortable**," says Christopher Deam. "I couldn't get over the beauty of the mechanism and **the movement**. I was really **intrigued** by how to create that **beauty of movement**."

⊘ The Glider as reimagined by Christopher Deam reinvents the classic porch chair and makes the signature soothing-motion mechanism center stage. *Credit: Lolah*

⊘ Opposite top: A page from Deam's sketchbook shows early efforts to resolve two critical aspects of the chair design. "On the left, I was trying to work out how the pivoting/gliding mechanism might work. On the right, I was trying to figure out an elegant base configuration. In both cases, I used a fairly generic seat set-up to be determined later." *Credit: Christopher Deam*

⊘ Opposite bottom: In an early technical drawing, Deam suggests using colorful climbing rope to support the seat. "But, because the manufacturer also makes yachts, they wanted to use materials and techniques indigenous to boat building, including sailing line." *Credit: Christopher Deam*

⊘ Deam dropped computer renderings of his glider chair into photos in an effort to show the chair's indoor/outdoor versatility and that "a rocking chair could be 'domesticated.'" *Credit: Christopher Deam*

What brought Deam to that particular moment was his wife's pregnancy with twins, which necessitated "the requisite pilgrimage to the baby furniture store." Deam found it intensely intriguing that such a lovely and comforting movement came in such an ugly package. "What I didn't like was that the way the chair worked was not evident," Deam notes. "They even put skirts around the bottom of the chair to hide the mechanism. So I wanted to do a beautiful, modern version of a glider because I felt there had to be a market for people like myself that were looking for a pleasant rocking chair in a modern idiom. The second objective was that I felt hiding the way it worked was a disservice. So I wanted to, in the design, give evidence of how the gliding was accomplished."

Deam first did a little research into both the mechanism itself and the history of the glider as an American icon. "On the traditional seats, the big problem was that it's a very clumsy, complicated mechanism that isn't integrated into the structure of the chair," he discovered. "There is a base, a seat, and a linkage that connects the two, but it doesn't really contribute to the overall form of the chair. I felt the linkage should be the form, should give the chair its identity." Deam also found out that gliders were created as an interior version of the porch rocker. This peculiarly American invention was made by people who simply nailed curved pieces of wood to the bottom of a chair and put the contraption where they could enjoy the soothing motion as they watched the world go by. "People loved the movement," according to Deam, "and wanted to domesticate it. But having a rocking chair indoors was considered gauche, so they started experimenting with a chair that would sit on the floor and not crush the cat's tail. And so, the glider was born."

In order to create his mechanism-evident rocker, Deam could not simply expose what was hidden on traditional gliders. "We had to reinvent the mechanism quite radically," he says. "A typical glider chair works on a trapezoidal linkage. Imagine a trapezoid, and each corner is a pivot, and when you move the top or bottom you get the gliding movement. We ended up rearranging that geometry, slicing it in half and rotating it." Deam makes it sound simple, but he quickly points out that it took many experiments to get the motion right. "We started by making trapezoidal models to study the linkage and the movement. They didn't look like chairs, but were made of paper clips and foam core. It took a lot of experimentation to get a linkage that would appropriately determine the form of the chair. Eighty percent of our efforts were spent on figuring out a linkage configuration that we liked."

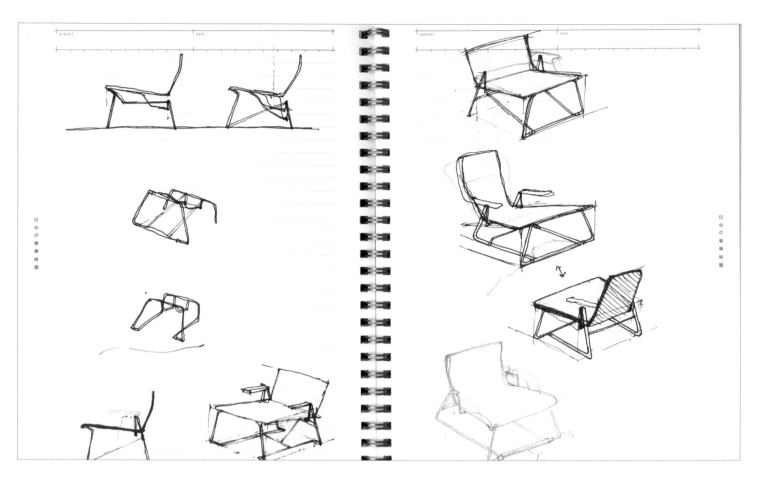

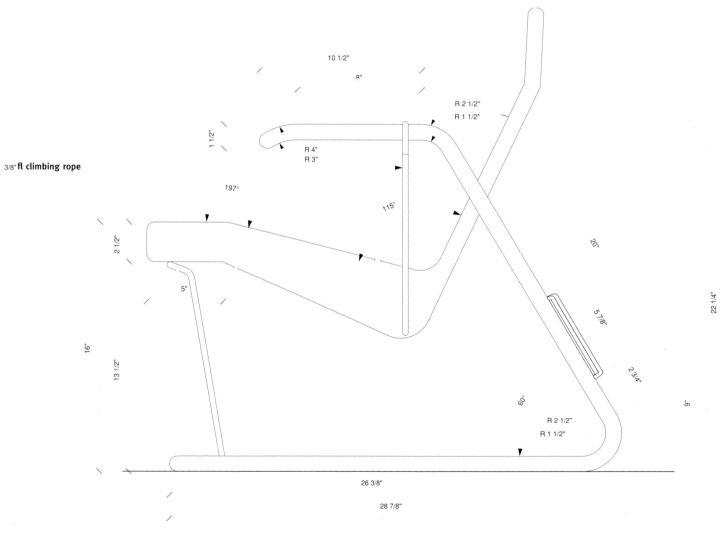

3/8" fl climbing rope

10 1/2"

8"

R 2 1/2"
R 1 1/2"

1 1/2"

R 4"
R 3"

197°

115°

2 1/2"

20°

5"

22 1/4"

5 7/8"

16"

2 3/4"

13 1/2"

9"

60°

R 2 1/2"
R 1 1/2"

26 3/8"

28 7/8"

side view

The next step was to find a manufacturer. He showed some of his designs to friends in Milan who ". . . scoffed at it. Europeans would never have a rocking chair in the home. It is distinctly American, and it became immediately apparent that I needed a North American manufacturer."

What he found instead was a Canadian luxury yacht builder. "They wanted to get into the furniture business to utilize all their unique manufacturing techniques," Deam says. "Fiberglass, stainless steel tube bending, and high-end wood work. These started informing the visual language of the chair. I wanted to show their strengths and superior craftsmanship."

The result is a chair with a fiberglass seat, hand-carved wooden arms, stainless steel legs, and a gliding mechanism made of spliced rope. Deam explains how it all comes together: "The way I design is I try to make the fewest moves possible. And so I knew I needed a support at the armrest level, I knew I needed a pivot at the front leg, and it became connecting the dots between the two with the fewest possible bends, so the structure seemed as clear and legible as possible. My aesthetic choice is that things are clear, legible, and where nothing can be reduced from the composition."

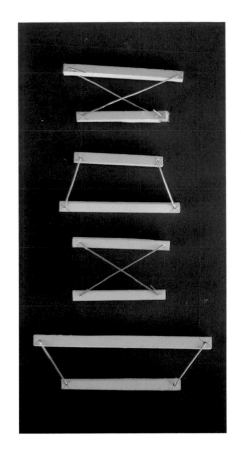

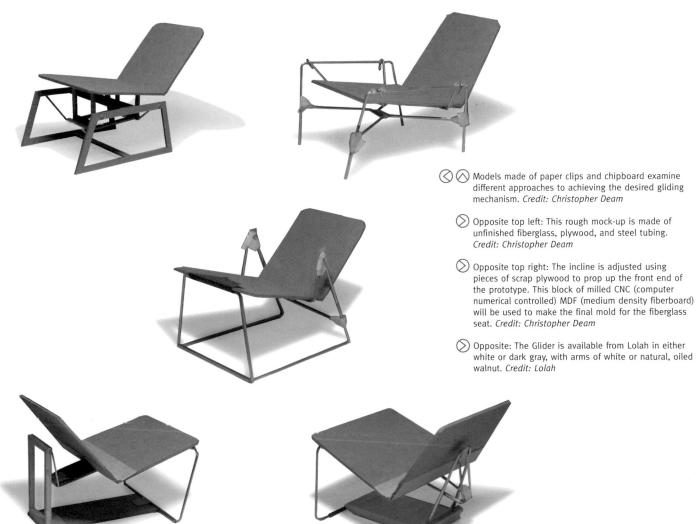

◁ ◌ Models made of paper clips and chipboard examine different approaches to achieving the desired gliding mechanism. *Credit: Christopher Deam*

▷ Opposite top left: This rough mock-up is made of unfinished fiberglass, plywood, and steel tubing. *Credit: Christopher Deam*

▷ Opposite top right: The incline is adjusted using pieces of scrap plywood to prop up the front end of the prototype. This block of milled CNC (computer numerical controlled) MDF (medium density fiberboard) will be used to make the final mold for the fiberglass seat. *Credit: Christopher Deam*

▷ Opposite: The Glider is available from Lolah in either white or dark gray, with arms of white or natural, oiled walnut. *Credit: Lolah*

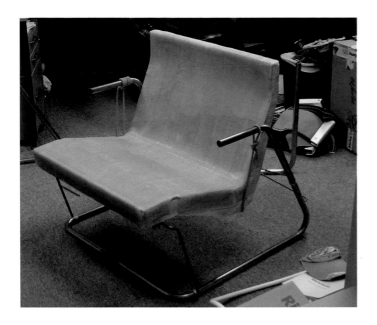

The seat is made from fiberglass, shaped in a two-part mold. "It's what they call monocoque construction, so it's a hollow form," Deam points out. "Our goal was to utilize a fiberglass shell and also give comfort through posture and less through shape. It was really important to me to get the inclinations correct, the angles between the seat and the back and what angle relates to the floor. You can have a fiberglass seat, and it can still be comfortable. It was a really careful study. We did full-scale mock-ups of different inclinations to make sure we got it right." The seat is finished with more fiberglass to hide the seams and then gets a coating of high-gloss resin. The chair is supported by legs in the front, while the back is suspended by the rope that runs in a continuous loop between the arms and through the seat. "It's very much a handmade object," Deam points out.

For Deam, the fact that the chair works is a straightforward result of his design process. "I approach design from a really human-centric position," he says. "I take the user experience as the generator of pretty much everything. I'm interested in structural clarity, evidencing the way something works, and making sure that it feels essential, that nothing is extra, nothing can be taken away." He pauses and adds, "At the same time, I try to allow for the idiosyncratic in my work. I'm not afraid of peculiar outcomes." Laughing, he says, "And this has been called a peculiar chair. I accept that. It's not trying to be, per se, elegant. But we ended up there. We tried to make it as elegant as we could, but it's not the generation of the idea."

Lazy Chair, Patricia Urquiola

"This is how ideas come," Patricia Urquiola says of her design process. "You **fall in love** with **something** and then you keep **trying** until you find a way to use it."

The Lazy Dining Room Chair completes what has become a family of chairs designed simply to enhance day-to-day living. *Credit: Fabrizio Bergamo*

In the case of the Lazy Chair, the material she fell in love with was a synthetic honeycomb fabric used for terrain embankment filters. Urquiola not only found the dimensionality of the material visually interesting, but its functional properties allowed her to make a chair that was weather resistant, extremely light, and reduced fabrication costs.

"My aim," Urquiloa notes, "is to domesticate industrial material and create objects that are interesting, pleasing, appealing. The material is important, but I don't think the use of a new material can guarantee, on its own, the newness of a product. The job of the designer is to give emotional meaning to materials in the context of concrete, practical applications."

The practical application for the first in the Lazy line was to create a comfortable, flexible patio chair with one position for sitting and another for lounging. Urquiola explains the chair's essential quality: "It's for the moment. You sit outside for a bit of conversation. Then the Sun comes out and you become lazy. The chair becomes lazy like you."

The chair's manufacturer, B&B Italia, was so pleased with the Lazy, they asked her to make something for indoor use. "They wanted to do something very elegant, but also to add a bit of irony, make it a bit contemporary," Urquiola says. She began her process by sketching various options for a high-back dining room chair. Ever mindful of the real-life application of her designs, she points out, "Sitting at a table, we are all so elegant. But in our contemporary times, this can be too severe, too bourgeois. There's a new way of living and eating with friends. I wanted to be conceptual and a little bit provocative from the very beginning. I wanted to do the thing that is not any more in fashion. All the designers now are making low back dining chairs. So I do the high back, but in a modern theme." The formality of the high-back chair is lightened by the sensuality of the shape, almost like a slender-shouldered, ample-hipped woman. In addition, the chair's metal wire frame allows it to flex with a person's movement, so it's extremely comfortable.

With the outdoor and high-back versions of the Lazy chairs complete, a family was beginning to take shape. A low-back chair was added, then an armchair, and finally a stool for the kitchen. "You need a papa, mama, etcetera," Urquiola says. "We created them all over the course of a few years. You need that time and mental space to create the whole family." All of the chairs are based on a

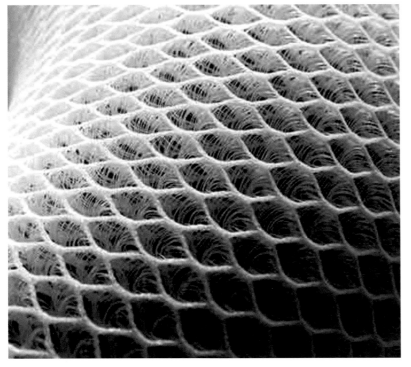

simple, wire frame structure: a "wire spaghetti" Urquiola calls it. The interior seating also has removable fabric coverings that can be washed or replaced to give the chairs a longer, more flexible life. Urquiola reports that the fabrication and manufacturing was quite straightforward. "This product went quite quickly," she jokes, "Just like the Lazy name says, it went the easy way."

All teasing aside however, Urquiola points out the importance of paying attention to every detail, especially the final upholstery and fabric. "The skin of a product must take a lot of care because it is the last layer, the one that is in view. You can't leave that part to someone else," she says. "If I design the dress, I also want to design the jacket."

But Urquiola also knows the value of collaboration. "I am not afraid of the brief," she says. "A brief gives a frame to the fantasy." She goes on, "Design is a long process and working with a company there are a lot of limits and compromises, from commercial concerns to marketing. They propose to you the problems, sometimes they think the problems are too big, sometimes they help you resolve them. But you have to pick and choose which problems you will accept. You must understand when you say no, why you're saying no."

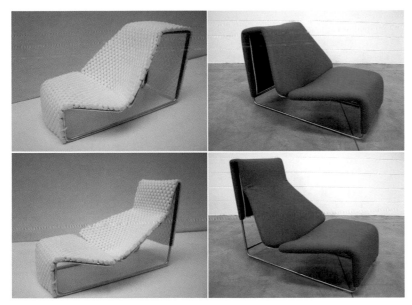

Urqulola also feels that self-awareness is critical to getting an end product that is true to the original design sensibility. "I am now beginning to be an adult, and know myself, and know how to use myself to get things done," she says. "I like to inspect, design, take time to get to a conclusion that we agree about. Because, you see, I am not so easy. But I try to be half of the day funny and sweet, and the other half of the day a little more demanding. Of course, you have to accept compromise, but one or two compromises. And your 'no' must be more seducing than your 'yes.' It's much more difficult to say a good 'no' than a good 'yes'," she points out.

Urquiola relates in a very personal way to her creations. She not only expects the Lazy line to grow—"perhaps one day we do uncles and brothers that are part of the family," she says—but she also has high expectations for the specific contributions her designs should make.

Top: This honeycomb fabric is normally used in the building industry to retain embankments. Because it is weatherproof and allows water to flow through, it was a practical solution for an outdoor chair, the first in the Lazy line. *Credit: Fabrizio Bergamo*

Side by side comparisons show prototypes and final versions, including the two back positions, of the Lazy Llounge Chair. *Credit: Fabrizio Bergamo*

The Lazy Chairs are made with "spaghetti" metal frames that flex when someone sits or moves, enhancing their comfort. *Credit: Fabrizio Bergamo*

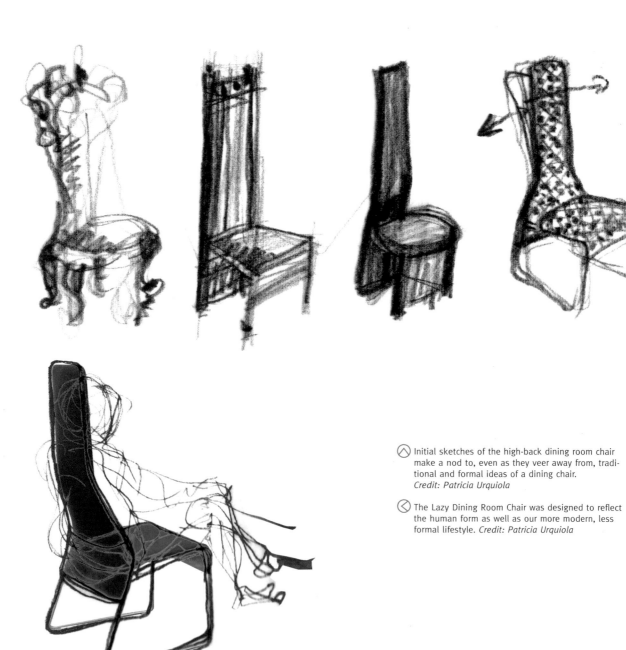

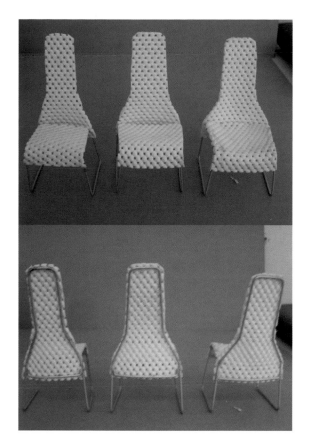

For Urquiola, design is about creating products that enhance our lives. "You provoke in the creative dimension," she says, "always to get something. But the product itself does not need to be provocative; it must be easy for life. We designers are not people who are changing the world. I am moving with my society, trying to get the most contemporary way, but I know the limits of my work. Products should give you an idea of something new, but they should also give you confidence." She concludes, "You need to have products that you can live with, your eyes can have a comfort with, and they can help with you with living."

⊗ Scaled down models of the dining chair were used to refine the proportion and line. The high-back design was chosen as a nod to tradition and a provocation to the current trend towards midback dining chairs.
Credit: Fabrizio Bergamo

⊗ The entire Lazy family offers a chair for every part of the home, from the dining room table, to the kitchen, living room, and out on the patio.
Credit: Fabrizio Bergamo

MT Series, Ron Arad "I wasn't so keen to do this," says Ron Arad. "I'm against doing things in **rotational** molding **because** it's a very **slow process**."

⬡ By slicing into a chair made by rotational molding, Ron Arad reveals the hollow core. Adding a contrasting color to the inside skin makes new use of the technology. *Credit: Ron Arad Associates*

But the manufacturer Driade had asked Arad to work with them on a project, and they wanted to work in rotational molding. Arad was resistant for a variety of reasons. "It takes about thirty minutes between pieces," he notes, "where with injection molding, every few seconds you get a new piece. Rotational molding is a bit like baking a cake. You have to heat it up, open it, and take it out. It's favored by young designers because the tooling cost is a lot lower; its a fraction of the cost of injection molding, so if you are not anticipating doing a hundred thousand units a year, but only a few a year, rotation molding makes more sense," he explains. "For that reason, because it had street credibility with young designers, manufacturers started to look at it. It makes each unit more expensive, but the whole process is cheaper. It is industrial, but semi-industrial. Rotational molding has some cautiousness built into it. It's a dumb process." But, Arad concedes, "It has its charm."

As Arad went ahead with the project, he uncovered something intrinsic to the rotational molding process that intrigued him: the pieces are hollow. "I wasn't excited until I made sketches of pieces you cut into. That gave me the opportunity to reveal another color that is on the inside. If I didn't cut the shape that came out of the oven, I would never see it; you would never know it existed. This is sort of the justification," he notes. "You have to find something more interesting and exciting about the process, and I think we did."

The MT series that emerged includes a chair, a rocker, and a sofa. Each is defined by a sensuous shape and a side cut that reveals the hollow inside of the piece, which features a contrasting color. "The themes that emerged are the cuts," says Arad. "So it's like a skin, an envelope. There is no illusion of volume, just the skin makes the chair, and it's a two-tone skin—an inner and outer that gives you the chance to choose colors."

Arad begins his design process with drawings—but not in the conventional sense of the word. "I came up with the shapes with a pencil," he says and then quickly adds, "I'm telling a lie. I draw directly on the screen with a light pen, so all my sketches are drawn on the computer screen. I have a very big screen and I hardly use paper anymore," he explains. "It's a horizontal screen, and if you see prints you won't know it's not done in watercolor, crayon, or acrylic. I've been using it for a few years," he says, "and I preach to all my friends to do the same, but for some reason I have not converted anyone really. I like it because I come from drawing, and it beats drawing. I like it so much, I went electric just like Bob Dylan did in Newport," he quips.

Arad uses a light pen to "draw" on a horizontal computer screen. He values this high-tech tool that allows him to utilize his drawing skills, while creating images that appear to be painted.
Credit: Ron Arad

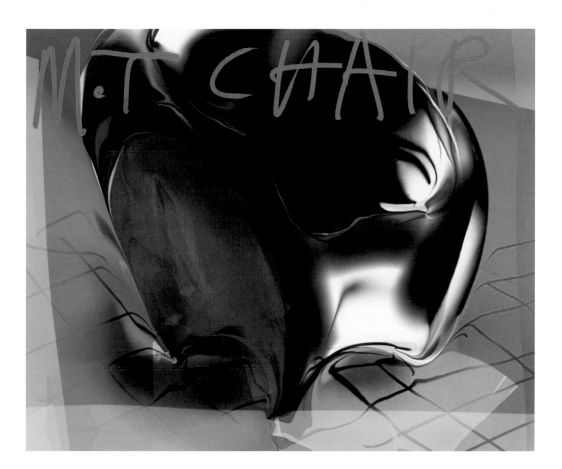

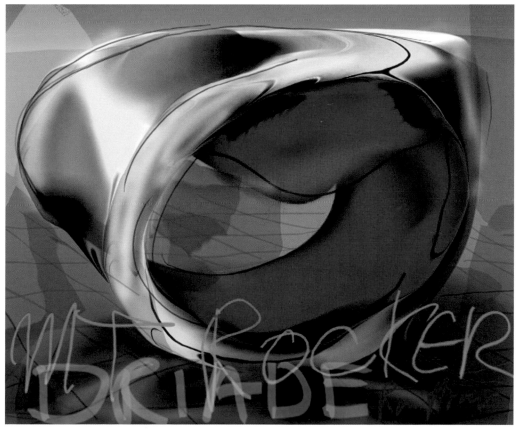

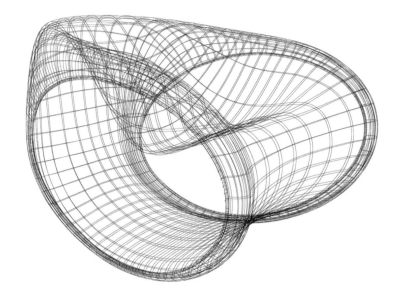

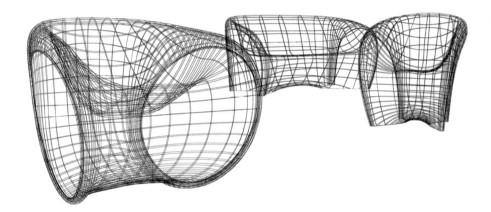

A wireframe 3D computer rendering of the MT rocker will be used to create the model that will, in turn, be used to create the mold. *Credit: Ron Arad Associates*

Wireframe computer renderings show the entire MT line of chair, rocker, and sofa, including the hollow core that openings in the side of each piece will reveal. *Credit: Ron Arad Associates*

Once the shape is drawn, Arad turns things over to designers probably too young to understand his reference to Bob Dylan's 1965 plugged-in performance at the Newport Folk Festival. "My studio is full of whiz kids," he says. "We turned my drawing into a 3D model on the computer. That virtual model was used to create a real model, then it was used to cut the tool, and then they make the piece," he explains. "It is made as a container. There is just a different pigment in the inside," he says. "First, you do the outside color, then you continue with the inside layer, and then they cut the sides with a very sophisticated cutting process that leaves it polished."

As for the colors, Arad says, "This is my least favorite bit, when you finish a job and you have to choose colors for people you don't know, to go to places you don't know. There are no bad colors."

When asked how he came up with the shape of the MT, Arad insists on the functionality of the piece and the practical concerns of the process. "You have to think when you design something you want to make the least number of parts for the mold, so all the shapes should release easily from the mold without undercuts. That implies some morphology." When asked if the shape was influenced by other design periods or a desire to reflect some natural mood, Arad bristles a bit. "I wanted to do a chair. I don't use words like organic. It's all about sitting on it. It's a chair. It has to sit well. Everyone is entitled to their own associations.

But it has to do with process and materials. I was never going to do a retro piece or a futurist piece. It's just what I drew." And the result of that drawing pleases him specifically because it works in such a straightforward way. "It doesn't apologize for itself," he says. "The rocker rocks, the chairs are very nice to sit on, they look nice. It has something to it that others don't. They're very friendly creatures, no if, ands, or buts about them."

And the name? It refers to an earlier product, the Empty chair. "It's a little empty, but you can't call it Empty," Arad explains. "So it's almost the same. It's like text messaging language."

The process of creating the MT series has not changed Arad's feelings about rotational molding. "I feel the same as I did before," he says. "It's not that I don't like it. I just don't want to do another one in a hurry. It has its place." But he adds that the goal is always to find some inventive way to use whatever process is in front of you. "There's no point in doing something unless there's something new to do," he says. "With every process, your duty is to find out what else can you do with it. Reluctance is a good place to start with anything. Because you have reasons why you are reluctant, and when you accept it, you have all the reasons to overcome your reluctance. It's like people you don't like at first, and then you like them a lot; it's much better than people you like at first, and then go off of later."

In the factory, the mold for the MT sofa is finessed by shaving and sanding to perfect the shape. *Credit: Ron Arad Associates*

The models for the MT rocker and chair will be used to create a rotational mold, a process Arad likens to "baking a cake."
Credit: Ron Arad Associates

The MT rocker, along with the companion chair and sofa, are all made from rotational molded polyethylene, which makes them appropriate for indoor or outdoor use. *Credit: Ron Arad Associates*

Muu Chair, Harri Koskinen Friends of Industry

"What I try to do here is to avoid all frills and **not-needed** bits and parts. And to be **honest** to the material and to the **category**," says Harri Koskinen.

The Muu Chair is a study in Finnish pragmatic simplicity and Italian wood craftsmanship. *Credit: Montina*

Opposite top: Sketches of the Muu Chair show the purity of line and suggestions for joinery. *Credit: Montina*

Opposite bottom: Computer renderings show various incarnations of the Muu concept, including a bench made simply from joining two armless chairs together. *Credit: Friends of Industry*

"I'm not going to make any icons, but when doing a chair, you really have to do a chair. I'm not trying to do a kind of art piece or celebrated, unique thing. My interest lies in practical and useful solutions." He pauses and then adds, "But every now and then, I think I happen to achieve good results with aesthetics." Apparently, Koskinen achieved just that with his Muu chair, which was awarded the prestigious Compasso D'Oro, only the second Finnish designer and one of a handful of non-Italian Europeans to ever garner this recognition.

The honor is even more rewarding given that the Muu almost didn't get made. Koskinen recalls that after meeting the creative director of Montina, he was invited to make some proposals to them. "I presented two concepts, one of which was the Muu collection. At the meeting, of course, it was very exciting for me, we were all quite happy. But I got a message after a couple of weeks that they don't have any interest. I was surprised after such a happy meeting, but they were like, you never know, maybe you can come back sometime." A year passed without any mention of working together, and then Koskinen got another, this time, welcome surprise from Montina. They called out of the blue and asked him to come check some prototypes they'd made from his drawings. And to hurry, as they were going to launch the collection at the next Salon di Mobile.

The simplicity of the Muu chair is quite captivating. "The main approach," according to Koskinen, "was to use wood in a very minimal way. So the idea with the frame and the structure is that with the minimal use of wood, we achieve a very stable construction. I happened to find a solution that is really kind of omnipotent from all directions. From all the angles, it is an interesting piece, and that was my approach."

Although Koskinen had made renderings to show to Montina, he had not specified any particular materials. "They were made out of solid whatever material. The idea was to make them out of the wood, but I didn't define it on those images and I didn't make any further kind of proposal about how all the joints needed to be done and so on," he notes. Montina provided him yet one more surprise when they showed him the prototypes. Koskinen was stunned at the beauty of the manufacturing, specifically at the joining. "They are really skilled and the craftsmanship is amazing so it was kind of fantastic to see the pieces," he says. "It was really fantastic to understand that they are capable to do like I thought. It's a kind of celebration to solid wood."

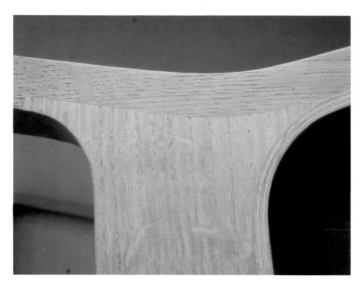

⊘ The plywood seat, side supports, and back are connected with an elegant joint that is tapered at one end and squared at the other. *Credit: Friends of Industry*

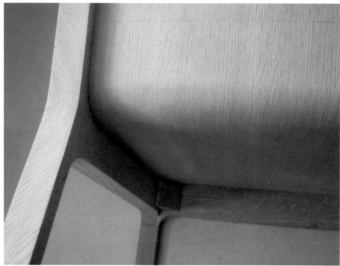

⊘ Even the underside of the Muu Chair receives equal attention to detail with a single piece of bent plywood swooping down from the back to the seat. *Credit: Friends of Industry*

The final version of the Muu is made out of oak. "The first pieces which we made," Koskinen notes, "they were with kind of white lacquer on top of the oak, but that was because on that specific year, they had a white image of Montina, so every piece of their furniture was white. Now they have natural or painted versions. I like the natural oak because I'm a fan of honest materials and to have the materials look like they are." Koskinen points out that some of this affinity for wood comes from his early training. "My background is that I used to study craft design, so I really did my hours in workshops, and I have made several things by my own hand out of wood." The chairs are made of a solid frame, with seats of molded oak plywood. "It's a very normal process how they handle the wood," says Koskinen. "Cut, grind, sand." In addition, Montina is also offering versions with saddle leather or felt seats.

Koskinen designed a table at the same time as the chair and thought originally of them as pieces for the home. Again, he was in for some surprises about the multitude of ways and places the chairs are being used. "I was seeing it more as residential use, like a dining room chair. They are low chairs, so I see them in a lounge kind of contract use, as well. But in Finland they're using them in a church or a kind of chapel, too. And then another idea when designing those chairs, the top view is very rectangular, so you can have a massive bench when you have them in a row. You can connect them if you want to."

As for the name, Koskinen explains: "Muu, it's a Finnish word and it means something other, something else. But on the other hand, it's quite international, I think. The cows they are saying, moo.

Partly, I can say that it's also kind of a short word. There are other words that are similar, but they might mean something else. For example, puu in Finnish, that is wood, but it sounds like something else not so nice. And even in Italian puu means something different. Muu works nicely," he concludes.

Looking back at the unusual process of development, Koskinen is naturally pleased that it all turned out so well. "The whole collaboration with Montina makes me happy," he says. "Or laugh in a way. I'm really happy that we managed to do this out." He notes that the Compasso d'Oro award also recognized the power of this joint venture. "The reason they gave it to me was kind of understanding the Scandinavian design and combining it with Italian craftsmanship. I hope that people can see that not much is really needed to make this chair. The joints are so beautiful, and it is really all the small details that make the whole chair."

Having good humor, remaining flexible, and taking the long view about product development is something Koskinen learned early in his career. When asked how he happened to name his company Friends of Industry, he responds with a story about a meeting he had when he was just starting out as a furniture designer. "I happened to meet one Italian manufacturer, and I was eager to work with him. I went to him and said it would be interesting to collaborate. He looked at my portfolio, and said he liked this stuff, but he would prefer to work with his friends. So I set up my business and gave it this name. I worked for five years, and that same director came to me one year ago, and didn't recall that we had met before. I am waiting for the situation where I can tell him. He will be happy to hear this, I think."

The almost childlike simplicity of the Muu Chair belies the high level of hand craftsmanship and elegance of design that garnered it a Compasso D'Oro at the Salon di Mobile. *Credit: Montina*

Osorom Chair, Konstantin Grcic

In an act that would prove **prophetic**, Konstantin Grcic named his **mashed**, wire-framed computer image **representing** a kind of public seating Osorom, which is the **manufacturer** Moroso spelled **backward**. "It is **quite** contradictory to what they usually do," he notes.

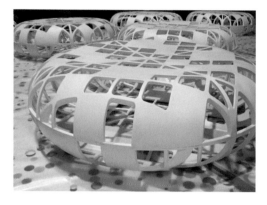

The Osorom as it came directly off the tool, the day before the official opening of the Salone del Mobile 2005, where it was introduced. *Credit: KGID office*

Opposite top: The original computer rendering of the conceptual Osorom chair, an idea that was never supposed to be built, and almost wasn't. *Credit: KGID office*

Opposite bottom: A paper cut out shows the grid pattern that distinguishes the Osorom. Closed areas are sized for sitting. Several studio assistants try it on for size. *Credit: KGID office*

"A few years ago, Moroso furniture celebrated their 50th anniversary by inviting fifty designers and architects to submit ideas about furniture linked to rapid prototyping. All we had to do was send digital data, and they'd create 3D images and put the design ideas into an exhibition," he recalls. "This intrigued me because I thought, we design a beautiful thing, and send to them, and don't concern ourselves with how it's made." Grcic glibly describes the result of this exercise as a "squashed piece of a round thing with holes in it. I saw it as a seating island for public spaces, where comfort was not a prime issue. Just as a place to rest."

However, the perverse name of the product seems to have unleashed a whole long process of contradictions. To start, Moroso fell in love with the design and decided they wanted to make this completely unrealistic item real. "When they first said they wanted to make it, I didn't take them seriously," Grcic says. "I thought it was impossible and that would be the end of the story." But Moroso didn't give up. "That's one of the great things about the Italian furniture industry," Grcic notes. "It works because of people who have a real passion for these kinds of things, and they have an attitude that everything is possible. They say, 'We just make a few phone calls and we'll find someone who will agree to make it.' Which is exactly what happened," he recalls. "We were on the manufacturing floor, someone started making some calls, and half an hour later, this guy appears, who looks like Einstein. He lives in a village down the road and builds rally cars for off-road racing, working in fiberglass. He looked at the piece and said, 'Yeah, it's not a problem.' In Italy, they have a belief that if it's beautiful and they want to make it, they will."

However, after about ten days, all beauty aside, 'Einstein' decided he couldn't make the piece after all. Then a relative of the owner of Moroso, known by one and all as Uncle Marino, said he would do it. "And the thing is," says Grcic, "he did. Single handedly, he made the first prototype. He used a kind of electric jigsaw to cut out the holes from fiberglass. It was quite crazy. He produced this 3D full-scale prototype of my little computer CAD drawing. Of course, Uncle Marino doesn't use the digital data; he took the dimensions and then drew the grid by hand and cut out the holes. It shows how someone who is skilled and has an educated and trained eye for design—he's been working with designers his whole life—had a sensitivity for what I had in my mind, and he was able to translate it into this full-scale thing."

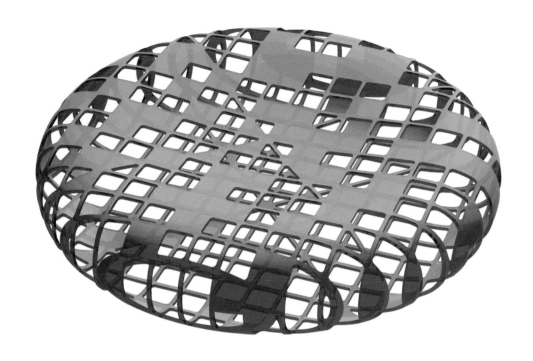

Once again, Grcic thought he has reached the end of the line with Osorom. Moroso showed it at the Milan Furniture Fair as simply a beautiful, one-off, object. "They just wanted to say to people, 'We went through all this trouble to show you a prototype because we think it's beautiful. It's the kind of thing we believe in'," says Grcic. "But then, at Milan, people really liked it and asked about producing it, and the ball started rolling faster and faster and became impossible to stop," he continues, in amazement.

Finding the appropriate material was critical. The solution arrived in the form of an Italian engineer and inventor named Bertoglio. He had just created a plastic called Hirek that is porous on the inside, and has a smooth surface on the outside, similar to human bone. This quality allows it to be injection molded in a wide variety of widths. "Normally," Grcic notes, "you injection mold plastic very thin, up to 4 or 5 millimeters ($\frac{3}{16}$"), not up to 50 (2"). But since this material is spongy on the inside, it's less heavy and has great structural integrity. In addition, you can injection mold with relatively low pressure, which means the tool can be made from aluminum rather than steel, which reduces the tooling cost substantially."

Once this problem was resolved, another followed soon on its heels. Grcic continues the story: "There was a bit of a bottleneck, as the man who had invented this plastic also claimed sole rights to use his own material and technology. When we asked him to work on it, he had 100 other commissions. He was overwhelmed, and for days and weeks, we would try to phone him, and no one could trace him. Moroso had paid him up front money to buy the aluminium that had to be specially tempered, brought from the US. . . it probably had to be tempered only during the full Moon!" Grcic says, laughing. After almost a year, they decided to move

on. "There was a point when we started to work with an engineering office to make a study of this piece and see if there was any other technology or material in which it could be made. They found certain solutions, and we found suppliers that could make tools. We were still talking about injection molding with more conventional plastics. Then one day, Bertolgio calls and says he's now ready and he will have tools ready in two months. We had totally crossed him off our list, and he calls and says everything is now possible. It was a very strange, emotional, and heated debate trying to figure out what we are going to do now. Do we trust in this guy who had messed us around for a year and was just an outrageous character? His system is the smarter one, but as a person, he was a really risky factor. The engineering model was a less smart solution, but probably a safer one. In the end we all decided to go with the smart technology and the crazy guy and hope it would work out. And the miracle is that ever since that phone call, he kept every promise he made."

The final Osorom piece is made of two identical halves that are then put together. The pattern of holes is, according to Grcic, quite arbitrary. "You look at it from above and project a square grid on it, and then decide to punch some holes out and keep some filled. There's no rule or system, other than we've kept patches of places filled because this is intuitively where you would sit down." The production model of the Osorom was shown at the 2005 Milan Furniture Fair and Grcic reports that in fact, it is actually quite comfortable to sit on. "This Hirek material feels very soft, has a smooth touch, and a beautiful temperature, which matters with material. Also, because it has quite a span, it flexes just a little bit. It feels good." After all these years of tumultuous development, that simple satisfaction is probably the best reward.

⊗ Uncle Marino uses a jigsaw to cut individual pieces from a monolithic piece of fiberglass for the first—and what was supposed to be the only—Osorom chair. *Credit: KGID office*

⊘ Shown here is one half of the tool that is used to create the production model Osorom, made of a unique, Hirek plastic that has a structure similar to human bone. *Credit: KGID office*

⊘ The cutting lines of the distinctive, but "arbitrary," grid pattern were hand-drawn—and then hand cut—onto the original fiberglass prototype. *Credit: KGID office*

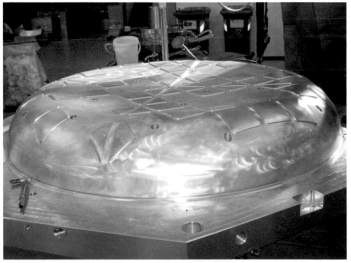

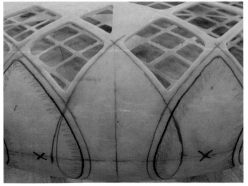

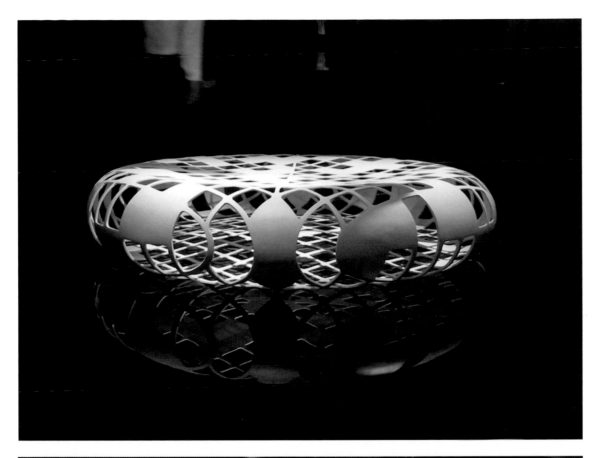

⬡ Top: The original, preindustrial production version of Osorom, presented at the 2003 Salone del Mobile, where it was intended to be a one-of-a-kind, one-off object of beauty and curiosity. *Credit: KGID office*

⬡ Another view of the original Osorom shows the scale and open structure of the seating piece, which was the source of many production challenges. The discovery of Hirek plastic offered the combination of strength and lightness Osorom required. *Credit: KGID office*

Sfera Chair, Claesson Koivisto Rune "He wanted us to do something that had a **connection** between the West and Japan. We **needed** to mix these two **cultures**," says Ola Rune

The Sfera chair is made from stainless steel into which thousands of holes have been cut to create a leaf pattern that not only results in a beautiful surface, but also casts delicate shadows. *Credit: Ricordi & Sfera*

of Claesson Koivisto Rune, speaking about the client who commissioned both the Sfera chair and the building that inspired it. "We found the old tradition of putting bamboo screens in front of a house to screen the sunlight very interesting."

The Sfera was designed to be a café chair in a "culture house" CKR was designing in Kyoto, Japan. Rune explains, "A culture house means he has exhibitions, restaurants, a shop for design, and a book shop. It's a privately owned culture house, but it's open to the public." The architects Mårten Claesson, Eero Koivisto, and Ola Rune found a stunning means to incorporate not only East and West, but also the contrasts of shadow and light, as well as natural materials and modernity into their design. "If you go in a park," Rune says, "the leaves casts shadows, and it's very diffuse. It's not very sharp, because they move all the time. It's a very beautiful kind of shading." He continues, "You have the sunlight, but also the shadow at the same time. This is the feeling we wanted to have inside the house." The architects decided to encase the entire building in a screen inspired by the subtle play of light and pattern that they observed in nature. But instead of bamboo, they chose a much more high-tech material: "We made this leaf pattern in titanium steel," Rune says. "We punched holes in the steel, and it creates fantastic shadows inside the house. And then at night, it becomes the reverse, and you see the light from inside shining through to the outside."

When they set out to design an outdoor chair for the building's café, they decided to incorporate the same punched-out leaf pattern. "When no on is sitting on the chair," Rune points out, "you have the same sensation of the shadowing of the leaves on the ground."

CKR incorporated yet another aspect of Japanese culture by using an origami-inspired folding technique as a means of fabricating the chair. Working with paper models, they realized that they could take a flat sheet of metal and fold it into the shape of a seat. "It looks like a hexagon from top, like a kimono, when it's spread out," Rune says. "It's really beautiful flat." In order to produce the chair in quantity, they needed to find a company that could cut holes in metal to create the leaf pattern, and then also fold and weld the metal into the appropriate shape. They turned to a company that makes large ventilation systems. "They'd never made a piece of furniture before," says Rune, laughing. "They thought, of course, that we were really crazy. They used one machine to cut holes with the laser, and then, they trimmed it down with another machine to make it smooth so you don't cut yourself when you sit down," Rune explains. "Then they needed to be able to fold it. They were very clever, the way they do it. It has two triangles that are open, and when you start folding, it comes together at the angles. You fold it and then weld it together, but the two welds are underneath the seat so you never see them."

A man-made pattern of cherry tree leaves was transferred to sheets of titanium and then illustrated by punching different diameter holes in the metal. *Credit: Ricordi & Sfera*

Unlike the building screen, which is made of titanium, the chairs are made of stainless steel. Not only is titanium very expensive, but according to Rune, "The titanium was too thin and too weak when you cut out the holes. And, it flexes too much for a chair." Using stainless steel allowed them to make the chair "quite generous in size. And you sit very comfortably, because the metal makes it flex just enough," he points out.

The legs of the chair are made of straight tubular steel. "It's like a normal chassis," says Rune, "but they needed to follow the top in proportion and have the right angles and such. We tried that ourselves in a one-to-one paper mock-up, so we knew what it would look like."

Because the chairs are handcrafted in a labor intensive, many-step process, "They can't do more than two chairs a day," says Rune. "They become a rare thing, which I kind of like." He pauses and then adds, "But I'd also like everyone to have one." In addition to being used in the café, the chairs are being sold in the shop at the culture house. "People see the chair and love it and want one," Rune says, "but then they see the price and pause and have to think about it," he laughs.

Top: The Sfera building and chair were inspired by concepts and contrasts of light and shadow, East and West, traditional and modern, inside and out, as illustrated by this model. *Credit: Ricordi & Sfera*

The titanium façade of the Sfera building was inspired by both traditional Japanese bamboo screens and the natural play of shadow and light created by leaves dancing on a tree. Hundreds of thousands of holes perforating the metal filter sunlight and create patterns in the building interior. *Credit: Ricordi & Sfera*

Rune values the opportunity to design a building and furniture that reflect and enhance one another and make a unified artistic statement. "It's very natural that you do both architecture and design," he says. "Not for all the projects, but when you have the time. For us, it's easy, because when we do architecture, we get inspiration to do design, and vice versa. It's a nice privilege to do both." However, he points out that there are important contrasts when approaching these different design projects. "Both a building and a chair have a meaning and a function," Rune feels, " but the chair is so close to your body, it really needs to be perfect, or else you'll dislike it. The architecture in this case was quite straightforward. It was so perfect when we got the idea of the metal sheets for the building that it was easier to do the building than the chair," he continues. "Just to do this chair, took about two years. This chair took longer than the building itself."

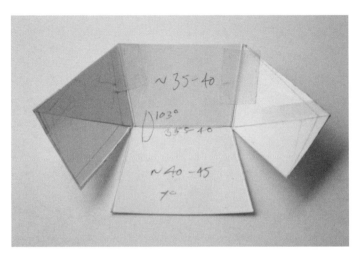

⊗ Inspired by the Japanese art of paper folding, the Sfera chair was designed to be a 3D structure created by folding a precut 2D piece of metal.
Credit: Ricordi & Sfera

⊗ Working with 1 mm ($\frac{1}{32}$") -thick stainless steel, a laser is used to cut the outline and the thousands of holes that make up the leaf pattern in what will become the Sfera chair. *Credit: Ricordi & Sfera*

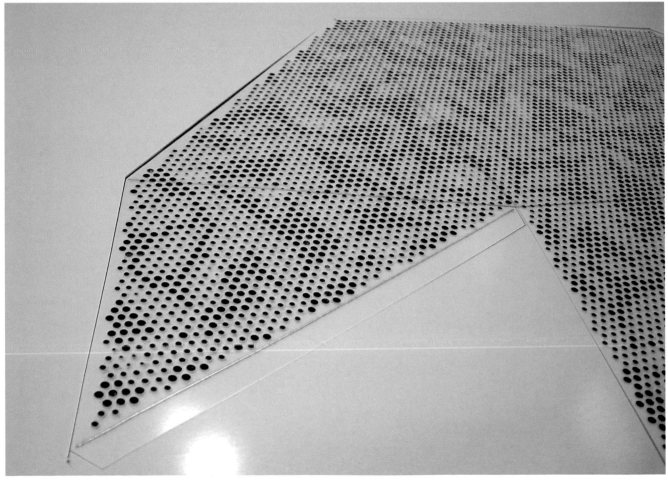

⬦ Top left: A technician bends the flat piece of precut metal along five fold lines to turn it into the shape of a chair. The stainless steel is not only durable, but has just enough flex to make the chair especially comfortable for sitting. *Credit: Ricordi & Sfera*

⬦ Top right: Two welds along the underside of the chair hold the piece together while presenting a seamless side to the user. In addition, two small plates are welded to the bottom to attach the supporting leg structure. *Credit: Ricordi & Sfera*

⬦ Above: Two chairs—the output of an entire day's work—begin to take shape, with the leaf pattern and three of the five required folds in place. *Credit: Ricordi & Sfera*

Stradivarius Chair, Matt Sindall

"I knew the **ply-wood** had this **energy** in it, in these **layers**," says Matt Sindall. "I **didn't** really **know** what the **result would be**,

The Stradivarius Chair is created by using a five-axis router to cut a seat shape into layers of plywood, which harkens back to the rings inside a tree trunk.
Credit: Baptiste Heller

but I knew some interference would be the result of cutting into plywood with a machine and forming it. I didn't realize quite how complex it would be. It was quite a surprise."

Ever since he carved a wooden fish as a nine-year-old boy, wood has always fascinated Sindall. "I'll never forget it. I was doing it for a school project and I could see the fish, I could feel it." When he became a furniture designer some years later, he rekindled his love affair with the material. "As a furniture designer, wood is one of the first materials you come across, and you discover that it's not inert, it has a life, and age, and history behind it." The internal rings that carry the personal life history of a tree are particularly inspiring to him. But, he didn't want to cut down a tree just to be able to cut open the trunk. So, for the Stradivarius, he layered and then cut into high-quality plywood to mimic the look of the original tree.

He began by drawing on the computer to render the stratum and the shape of the seat, both of which were developed more by feel more than by measurement. "I think when you make pieces of furniture," says Sindall, "You understand the relationship between the curve and the human body. With other pieces that I have sculpted by hand, you're not looking at the curve in a stylistic sense; you're imagining a hand grasping an object or your back resting against the backrest—you're seeing the relationship of the body and the form." As sensual as this approach may be, Sindall doesn't only rely on, but actually relishes working on a computer to make his ideas real. "I love having the opportunity to experiment with materials and machines and the use of computer, which I believe is not just a cold, inanimate object. It can be harnessed in such a way that you can arrive at very animated sort of vibration, in a way. I've got this tool, I've got this program, it seems very inert and cold, but what can I do to make it live?" he continues. "We came full circle because the result is quite a natural looking object. It looks like it was cut out of a tree trunk, but it's not. It's not natural because the wood has gone through its whole product lifecycles and come back to a trunk of wood."

The Stradivarius was a one-off creation made for an exhibition. Sindall used both technology and the skills of a group of high-end cabinetmakers to make the seat. "To achieve it, I have to work with a computer program to create a 3D object in virtual space. This information is then transferred to a machine, a five-axis router that receives the computer-generated information, and transfers it into coordinates," he explains. "The block is assembled of different layers of very good quality plywood which was assembled in different layers. And then the machine's got a drill bit that takes the material out. It's a really beautiful thing to watch. It's extremely precise, down to $\frac{1}{10}$ of a millimeter ($\frac{1}{320}$")."

⊘ The stories told by the rings of a tree and the sensual beauty of objects sculpted from wood were the initial inspiration for the Stradivarius Chair. *Credit: Igor Ternet*

⊘ A wire frame drawing "shows the transition between the tree cross section and the object. A wood block becomes an object just with the cut," according to Sindall. *Credit: Matt Sindall*

⊘ A computer drawing shows an alternative shape that could be made with the same layering and milling process used to make the Stradivarius.
Credit: Matt Sindall

The numeric milling process uses a computer drawing to direct a router to cut in any of five different axes. Used in woodworking applications like cabinetmaking, Sindall used the technology to create a piece of furniture that is more sculpture than chair.
Credit: Matt Sindall

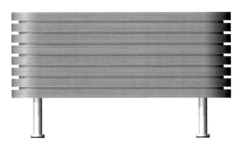

A computer-generated image shows further details of the chair, including the exterior serration in the layers of plywood and the metal feet picked up at an IKEA store. *Credit: Matt Sindall*

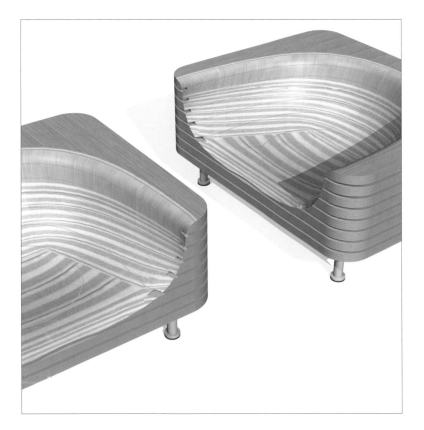

⊘ The router leaves a subtle layer of grooves in the surface of the wood. The craftsmen were about to sand the interior smooth when Sindall happened to stop by, and in the nick of time, asked them to leave this extra, textural detail. *Credit: Baptiste Heller*

It is this convergence of the natural with the technical in order to mimic the natural that Sindall finds so interesting. "My main preoccupation when I design a piece of furniture is not really concerned about comfort or style in the sense that it's about a formal object," he says. "Over and above the fact that it's a functional object, I'm trying to bring out other elements, other stories. I don't really want to ram these down people's throats, it's very much up to the observer, the person who sees or uses the object to make up his own mind. You give people signs, or messages hidden in the surface and the treatment of the surface that brings out their own impressions, their own themes about what an object is or what a surface is."

The feet, however, have a much more prosaic story to tell. He picked them up from an IKEA furniture store. Sindall saw the feet on a piece of kitchen furniture and wandered around the store all morning before finding them as an individual item for purchase. "They're stainless steel feet with a nice proportion," he says. "It's slightly antidesign. I saw them, and I liked them. There's no point in redrawing something that you can find. I like the diameter of the stainless steel tube. For the size of the chair, this very solid mass of wood on these very fine legs creates this sort of finesse."

For all his interest in surfaces, and all the surface interest in the Stradivarius, Sindall contends that he's not "100 percent happy with it. I'm not happy with the outside because I think it's detracting from what's happening in the surface. In a way," he says, "it's too designed. It's confusing the message. I think it would have been interesting if I'd wrapped it in a brightly colored laminate so the levels of plywood were not seen on the outside. It would create mystery." But Sindall accepts that this dissatisfaction is inevitable. "Designers suffer from being designers in a sense," he says. And the piece, like any project, has other lessons to teach him. "When I started, it was all about the outer surface, the skin," he says. "But this has woken up something in me, gotten me thinking about what's going on inside, in the core of the object. This is what it's given me. There's a whole world to explore in the core of a piece of furniture."

And sometimes, the world conjured by a particular furniture object has it's own, inherent and straightforward sweetness. Says Sindall, "I always come back to a Mille Feuille pastry. I love that pastry. When I see one, I have to buy one. This piece keeps coming back to that. When I look at it, I can almost taste the pastry."

Supernatural Chair, Ross Lovegrove "I don't want to do dumb, boring **rubbish**! I just don't want to **live my life** that way," Ross **Lovegrove** exclaims. "I want to look back and think I've been involved in things that have **some sense** in them."

The Supernatural Chair by Ross Lovegrove uses advanced techniques in polymer technology, tooling, and manufacturing to achieve a soft skin with a strong core and a lightweight structure with strength and stability, in an affordable, commercially viable, stacking chair.
Credit: Alessandro Paderni, Eye Studio

The Supernatural is his answer to a perceived need for "sense" in a plastic, stacking chair. "Right at the beginning I've personally always wanted to do a really good plastic chair," Lovegrove says. "I don't do many chairs. But I like the idea of doing things that reflect the culture of the day. If you look at everything I do, they're very technologically innovative. There are a few chairs on the market that did pioneer polymer technology. But I always felt that there was a missing link, a chance to produce a chair that has the visual stability of a four-legged stacking chair, but with something organic, a more liquid form that reflects the material."

Lovegrove has been working with polymers for over twenty-five years. He also has a long-standing relationship—and friendship— with Moroso. When Patricia Moroso told him they were ready to do their first polymer chair and they wanted him to design it, he was thrilled. "They're a relatively small company, so for them to invest in a full-blown, gas-injected, polyamide injection-molded chair is a big undertaking." Lovegrove continues, "It was a massive responsibility on my behalf to do something fresh, new, culturally iconographic, but at the same time, something that would have really great commercial potential. Something that respected both the process and the material. It was a wonderful opportunity that allowed me to exercise the maximum of my professionalism."

The technology provided Lovegrove with new possibilities for both design and commercialization. "With the advent of injecting gas into certain sections of products, you can remove material to make them lighter, and also, in a way like bones, you make them stronger," he points out. To find an open, airy, asymmetric pattern that pleased him and would maximize the potential in the manufacturing process, he generated at least ten, digitally-produced patterns. "Imagine if you stretched a piece of balloon and then you got someone to stick a pin in it, or heat it at points, so it will stretch and a hole will appear that will gradually open," Lovegrove explains. "That's a form of tension that I've tried to put into the aesthetic of the chair. If you look at a leaf that's been eaten away, it's kind of like that. It's a manmade product, but it has a sense of true nature."

This idea of allowing organic forms into the design vernacular of a plastic object is carried throughout all parts of the product. "What one is trying to do," notes Lovegrove, "is to incorporate the bioengineering of it so it feels natural, so it feels as one. If you look at the back of the chair, the strength is generated out of the back leg that blends into the neck, and then it diminishes. It

A sequence of images shows how the plastic flows into the mold, starting at the center of the seat, where there will be a hole in the final product. The colors reveal how the material cools as it collects. Lovegrove says, "It's a bit like frostbite. The problems usually happen at the tips." *Credit: Moroso—SPM*

starts as a leg with a very particular dimensions, then that section changes orientation, and then diminishes around the back of the seat, of the chair." This design is not only visually alluring but is also expected to add comfort to the chair, allowing the legs to remain stiff and stable, but giving the back some flex.

The technology also offered other options that enhanced the sensual aspects of the chair by giving it internal strength and a more smooth surface quality and ability to hold color. "What's beautiful about the chair, is that it has two different densities in the same chair," Lovegrove explains. "There's a higher concentration of glass in the central core and less glass in the skin. To get added strength you need more glass, but it's transparent and doesn't allow you to produce darker colors because you'll see the stratification. And the glass will migrate to corners, which causes some variation in the color. So we've created a skin with a lot less glass in it, like 40 percent in the core and 10 percent in the skin. We can control one material density internally and one externally."

For all his fascination with the opportunities technology offers him to realize his design visions, for Lovegrove, it's all a tool that he keeps an arm's length away from the creative act. He designs by sketching. "I always buy these particular sketchbooks, which have become a bit legendary, now. They are made in Venice. When they run out, I go to Venice and get more. Any excuse to go to Venice!" he laughs. And then adds, "The thought of drawing something that has meaning on anything else, it just hurts me." To get his sketches into digital form, he relies on technical design staff in his office, with whom he works closely, but also from a comfortable distance. "I don't touch the computer and I probably never will," he says. "Because it's not intuitive and I'm always on the go and I don't want to depend on a power source to create. Also, pressing a square key to make a shape doesn't link for me. The drawing, which is a deeply personal act, is becoming ever more valuable," he notes.

The Supernatural Chair comes in two versions, one with perforations, and another with a solid back. Both are made from the same tool, by just switching out a single separate steel insert. To Lovegrove's understanding, this is the first time two chairs have come from the same mold. "I don't think anyone thought of it before. It might be as simple as that," he says. However, this added versatility is part of his sense of responsibility as a designer. "I'm very much interested in extrapolating the most from the least in whatever I do," he points out. "That's why my work looks trim, fit, and skeletal. With this particular chair, I'm trying to get a certain biodiversity in the product. If someone's putting up so much money—and from such a small company—I'm going to try and extrapolate the most from the least for them."

Lovegrove loves the integrity and possibilities of open-back version. "The intention of the perforations is to add a polysensorial effect from the chairs when light passes through to create shadows that enrich space and provide unexpected layers of beauty to architectural surfaces," he says. "This effect is increased by the layering of the chairs and their orientation, their variety of colors, and also when stacked because the experience becomes very three-dimensional, like sunlight through leaves on a tree." He also points out that this model was the most conservative of his proposals for a pattern, but necessary for production concerns. "It's important to push, but important to not go into territories that are going to cost people a lot of time and money or cause problems. I try to push it as far as I can, and then, by the time you pull back, you have something that has a greater acceptance. What I'm trying to do," he concludes, "is to give the product its maximum chance in life. That's my duty."

While Lovegrove eschews designing on the computer, preferring to draw by hand in notebooks he picks up in Venice, Italy, he works with staff members to turn his sketches into technical drawings. *Credit: Gernott Oberfell, Lovegrove Studio*

Bottom: These brilliant colors provide a heat map of the chair in production. "It's a bit like rubbing away layers on plywood," says Lovegrove. "You get a topographical surface mapping that's easy to read." *Credit: Gernott Oberfell, Lovegrove Studio*

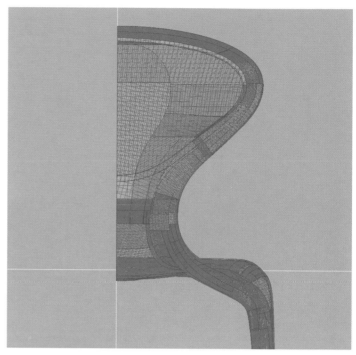

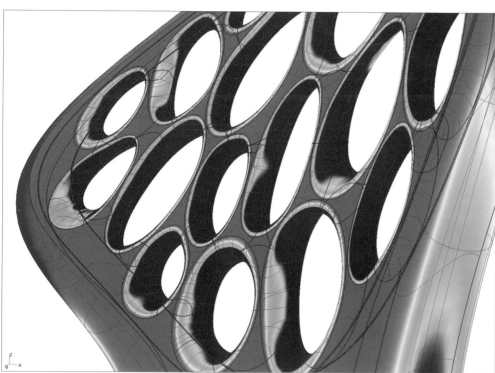

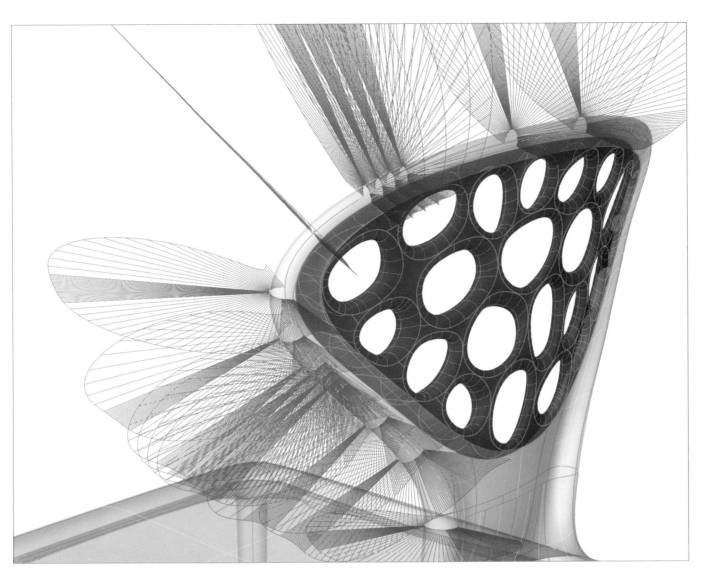

△ This technical drawing turns the Supernatural into a kind of butterfly by showing where external pressures will be applied to the chair.
Credit: Gernott Oberfell, Lovegrove Studio

◁ The holes in the back of the Supernatural—designed to look like pinholes in a stretched balloon or a leaf that's been eaten away—work aesthetic double duty by throwing a shadow pattern where the light sifts through. *Credit: Alessandro Paderni, Eye Studio*

Tilt Resin Chair, em [collaborative studio] "The furniture is really an **accident**," says Emmanuel Cobbet of the **Tilt** resin **chair**.

The Tilt Chair is made of translucent resin suspended over a metal base. It was inspired by a one-off table made for a gala event, which sparked the desire to find another design application for polyester resin.
Credit: Michael McCreary

Asked to design a table for the LA Dining by Design event, he and his em [collaborative studio] partner Mark Yeber decided to take a decidedly different approach to the charge of dressing a table for this gala evening. "We knew that every designer taking part would be decorative. We wanted to look not at what was on the table but the table itself," says Cobbet. They built a table made of translucent polyester resin in a mosaic of very warm colors. "We dressed it in vintage glass. Everything had to be transparent so it could be about the table. We lit it from underneath, and it looked quite stunning," he says. "Everyone went gaga over the table and asked what else we do. And we didn't do anything."

Six editorials about the table started to change all that. "We thought, okay, maybe we have something interesting here," Cobbet recalls. "We got really excited about pushing the resin in a new direction. The material excites us so much. We like the grain, the texture, the warmth, the coloring options, but we were challenged by the fragility. We use polyester resin, and that composition is as brittle as glass would be. So if you hit it with a hard object it would break. You can dance on it, but don't wear metal heels."

Cobbet and Yeber started considering the idea of a making a resin chair. Before beginning to design, they set out a list of objectives. "It had to look good as a product, but more importantly, the one who uses it had to look good in it," says Cobbet, who has a fashion design and marketing background. "No matter what you wear, the chair would make it for you. You're wearing your chair," he explains. "This is very important. Third, but not least, it had to be as comfortable as any other chair. I like the idea of introducing art to the chair, but we didn't want to push it to an experimental level."

Because resin is a cast product, and they couldn't afford rapid prototyping, they had the first prototype sculpted out of fiberglass. "The first one looked really odd," Cobbet says. To make adjustments, "we traced on it by hand, like I would do in fashion," he says. "It was kind of like a fitting, really. We'd go back the next week to see how much they took off. It took three visits to adjust it." Cobbet and Yeber also asked several different people to sit in the chair to test its comfort and proportion, and make sure it met this critical goal.

The open-back design was dictated by the sheer weight of the resin, which again, is comparable to glass. "Should the whole chair be closed, it would become a 75 pound (34 kg)-chair, instead of a 45 pound (20 kg)-chair," notes Cobbet. "It was an imperative to us to lighten up the chair. The process and material dictated that, but we're very happy with what it translated into."

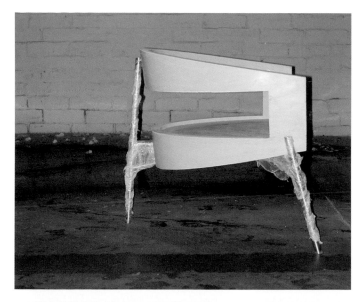

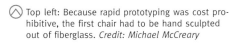

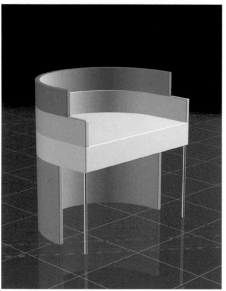

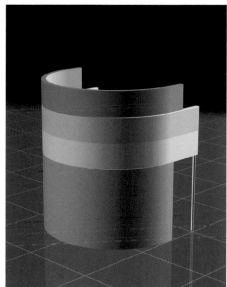

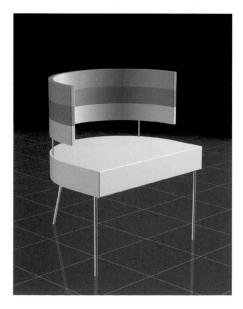

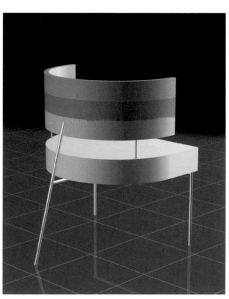

Top left: Because rapid prototyping was cost prohibitive, the first chair had to be hand sculpted out of fiberglass. *Credit: Michael McCreary*

Top right: To make adjustments, the designers drew on the fiberglass shell, much like a fashion fitting, to mark areas where more material could be removed. This is the final fiberglass prototype. *Credit: Michael McCreary*

A series of different studies was made exploring possible forms for the chair. Full-back versions were abandoned because the resin is so heavy: "It was an imperative to us to lighten up the chair," Cobbet says.
Credit: em [collaborative studio]

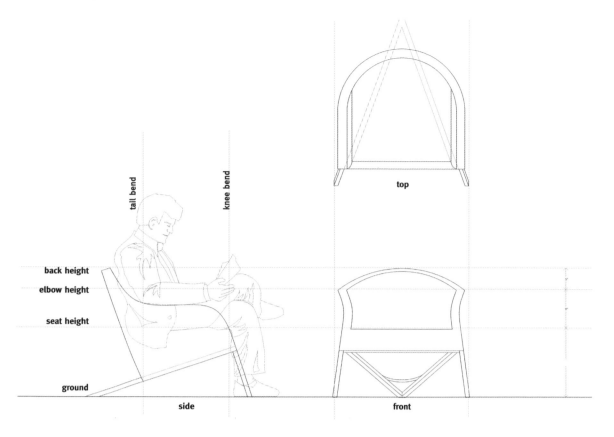

tall bend

knee bend

top

back height

elbow height

seat height

ground

side

front

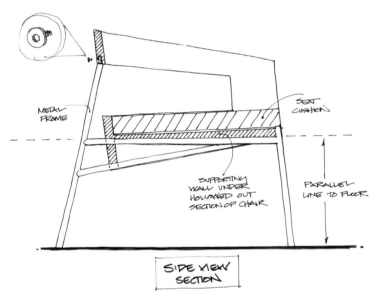

METAL
FRAME

SEAT
CUSHION

SUPPORTING
WALL UNDER
HOLLOWED OUT
SECTION OF CHAIR

PARALLEL
LINE TO FLOOR

SIDE VIEW
SECTION

Initial studies of proportion and shape show the distinctive three-leg design. While the drawing shows a comfortably seated person, the tilt in the final chair is much less pronounced.
Credit: em [collaborative studio]

Construction drawings show the extended V-shaped support that is mostly hidden underneath the seat but provides critical extra support to the heavy resin back.
Credit: em [collaborative studio]

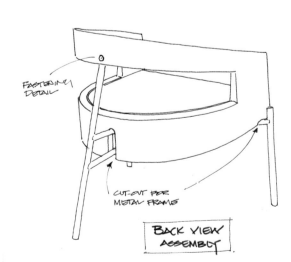

FASTENING
DETAIL

CUT-OUT FOR
METAL FRAME

BACK VIEW
ASSEMBLY

The chair is made in "one solid pour of resin," Cobbet explains. "The different colors are done in stages. If we do striping, we wait for one color to dry and then do the next. You have to time it right or otherwise the colors run into one another. It cannot be done by machine." The colors themselves were derived from the original table and the imperative that they enhance the person sitting in the chair. "We were looking at colors that, once lit, would sort of be flattering to you. If we did a blue table, at dinner you would look a little green," Cobbet says. So they chose colors lifted from the western sunset. The chairs can also be made in solid colors or up to four stripes. "We have a palette of twenty-five colors," Cobbet says, "I invite people to make their own palette. But it almost always comes down to what they've seen working already."

While the resin performs like glass, it is not self-supporting, so a structural frame was required. "We were looking at suspension rather than four legs where you can see where they're coming from and going to," Cobbet says. "Three legs give it the illusion of suspension. It seems very light." Two bars that extend vertically from the lower part of the back give extra reinforcement to the base. The legs come in either brushed or hand polished, highly mirrored steel and are permanently glued to the seat. Finally, a urethane sealer is put over the resin to help protect against normal wear and tear and make it resistant to oils and water. The chair comes with a thick foam cushion, made to order in any fabric. They are also making the chair in solid colored fiberglass, which can be used outside.

Getting the structure correct was the most challenging aspect of production. "I still don't understand why and how so many companies have difficulty in getting the angle right," Cobbet says. "I've been told it has to do with the coping of the metal, but I think there's an aspect to it that people don't want to think it through and they just want to do it fast. I wish I could find someone passionate about what they do, who could look at it and find some efficient way to achieve the result. As much as we battle with the imperfection of resin, there is a seductive quality to that. But there's nothing seductive about the difficulties of getting the base right," he says.

The resin material apparently seduces not just Cobbet, but everyone else who looks at the chair. "Resin has this warmth and grain," he says. "It's very attractive and tactile. The first thing people want to do instead of sitting in it, is to touch it." He points out that this is all part of their design philosophy. "We work a little bit like modernists did," he says, "using material and technology that are available today and doing the design around them. We like to look at the materials of today and use them to make designs that are relevant for today and tomorrow, without falling into the experimental. That's of no use to us. We live today, we'd like to use it today."

In addition to resin available in any combination of twenty-five colors, striped or solid, the Tilt Resin Chair (as shown here) is being made in an all-weather fiberglass version available in solid colors. *Credit: Michael McCreary*

Topografi, Jonas Wannfors "I wanted to do **something** that would feel **soft** and look **soft**, but be made of **harder** materials," says Jonas Wannfors of his **Topografi** seating system.

"I wanted to make something of an organic shape so it would feel soft to your body, but is not upholstered. It is hard, but shaped around your body so it feels soft when you sit in it."

The result of this original concept was an easy chair made while still in design school. The hard part of the chair was made of painted MDF (medium density fiberboard), between which Wannfors sandwiched pieces of felt. "The felt stood up a little bit, so that's what you sat on," he notes. He made this prototype himself, working with a metal manufacturer. "At first," he says, "they couldn't understand how it would turn into a seat from the drawings. But afterwards, they were excited." This prototype was displayed at a graduation exhibition as well as at the Stockholm International Furniture Fair. "After that school project, I wanted to see if I could use that idea for more complex furniture, for more intelligent furniture," he continues. "I wanted to create this system that would let you create your own seating."

The result of this effort is the Topografi modular seating system, manufactured by LYX. Three different modules can be combined in a wide variety of configurations to create anything from a single chair to a sinuous sofa of two-sided seating that goes on and on for as long as space allows. The system comes in indoor and outdoor versions made from thirty-four slices of water-cut and painted MDF or fiber concrete board. Each slice is separated by spacers and connected with a metal tube. To create a seat, you always need two end modules, but you can put endless straight or exchange sections in between. The modules are connected to one another with a small bolt. "It looks very uncomfortable because of all the slices," notes Wannfors. "The basic idea is that it looks very hard, more like a sculpture than seating, but when you sit in it, it feels very good and very relaxing."

For the Topografi, like most of his design projects, Wannfors began with a hand sketch. "I get an idea in my head," he says, "and I use the paper to get it down. Many times, only I can understand the sketches that I made." From there, he moves to clay models. "I do modeling in clay because it's impossible to understand everything with just the sketches. Many times it's difficult to see if things work three dimensionally just with sketching." He always includes computer modeling at the end of the process. "There are many benefits from it," Wannfors notes. "You can create presentation materials and advertising materials. And if you make a good computer sketch, it saves time later on. But I never start to sketch on the computer."

In the case of the Topografi, the computer was also used to work with human models to get the curves and the proportions just right. Wannofors notes, "We used full-scale models to check the seating curve and the profile for your back support." In addition to these practical considerations, the sensuous curves were created to serve aesthetic and design concerns as well. "I wanted to

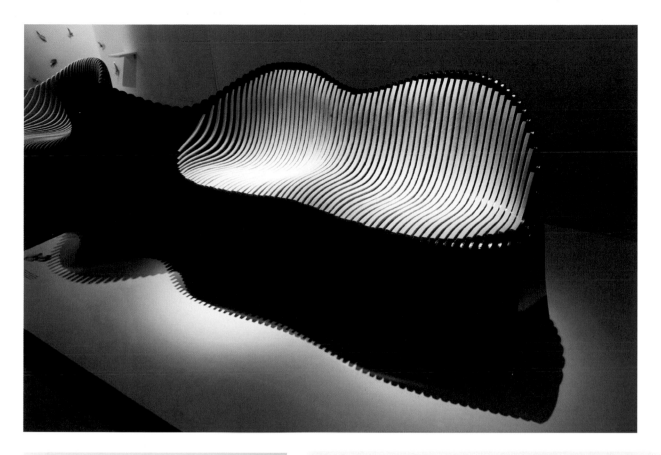

⌃ Top: The first prototype of what would become the Topografi was made as a school project out of concrete boards separated by industrial felt to create a seat of both hard and soft elements. *Credit: Jonas Wannfors*

⌃ Because of the complexity and variety of the shapes, clay modeling was essential to understanding how the component parts might work separately and together. *Credit: Jonas Wannfors*

⌄ Working off the idea of "creating a 3D object by using two-dimensional sheets," this computer rendering depicts the initial concept that eventually evolved into the Topografi system. *Credit: Jonas Wannfors*

create a really organic shape," Wannafors says, "that was as smooth as possible to be in contradiction with the different slices or the boards themselves that are square at the beginning. From these pieces, you cut shapes and create something very different from what you had in the beginning."

As a young designer, moving from his original concept to a commercially produced product offered Wannfors many lessons that even highly experienced designers find themselves relearning. "For a long time," he notes, "I wanted to keep the felt between the sheets. But along the way, I discovered that the felt pieces didn't do anything for the seating. And it was impossible to put it there, you couldn't take it away to wash it, and it was expensive." Repeating a piece of literary advice usually attributed to Ernest Hemingway, Wannfors says he had to "kill my darlings." Other concessions were made to practicality. "In the first prototype, I had a little different spacing, and then we adjusted it to make it more economical to produce. A little less material, a little more air," he notes. "The most surprising thing for me was that the things I didn't think would cost anything were the things that cost the most, and the things I thought would be expensive cost nothing." And Wannfors learned how long things really take to go from idea to reality. "When you're in school you think, 'Oh I made a prototype, it's completed.' But that's only a small part of it. You have to stay focused, you have to be there and watch everything so it turns out good in the end. You can't just turn it over to the manufacturer."

But some important efficiencies also came out of the process. "I thought that to create this modular seating, you make one seat and then another and something to put them together," Wannafors says. But in manufacturing, they found only four components would make a multitude of seating forms. "This was a good discovery," he notes. "I could make less pieces to make the whole system."

The Topografi can be seen as a kind of bridge that took Wannafors from his life as a design student to that of a design professional who now works in graphics, lighting, and furniture. Looking back on the process, he says, "Still, after all this time, I'm amazed at all the work, and I'm very satisfied with the result. Sometimes, you make something, and after five years, you think, 'Oh, that's not very good,' but this still feels fresh even though I've lived with it for a long time."

The Topografi also reminds him of an episode in his life when he had the freedom to be entirely focused on ideas. "When I look at this piece, it reminds me that when you're in school, you have so much time to develop things," he reflects. "And now, it's hard to get the time to just think and be creative and not go to meetings all the time," he adds with a good-natured laugh.

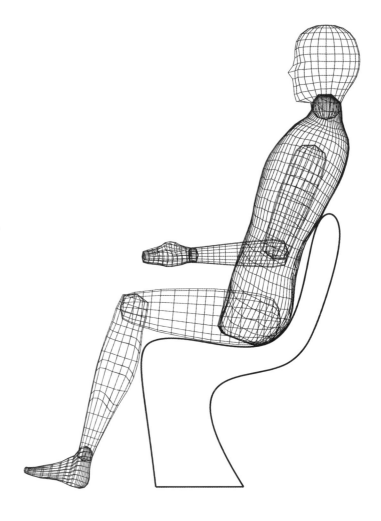

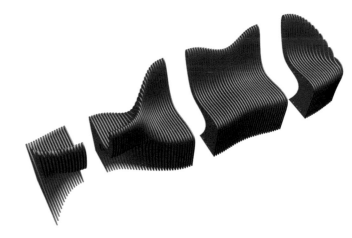

⊘ Top: Working with human models in the computer allowed the designer to finesse the curves of each module so he could achieve his goal of creating a comfortable seat out of hard materials.
Credit: Jonas Wannfors

⊘ A computer rendering shows the three modules— straight, exchange, and end—that can be connected in any combination to create a customized seating arrangement. *Credit: Jonas Wannfors*

The concrete and fiberboard pieces are cut with a water jet. By placing the shapes like a jigsaw puzzle, they reduce manufacturing waste. *Credit: Jonas Wannfors*

This Topografi configuration is made into a sinuous sofa with straight, exchange, and end modules of concrete fiberboard. The components are also available in thermocoated MDF (or medium density fiberboard). *Credit: Ingmar Lindewall*

Calder's Table, Ali Tayar, Parallel Design "I got tired of telling people I didn't have a **job**," Ali Tayar recalls, thinking back to his **few years** of unemployment in the **1990s**. "So, I just told people I had an **office**. But I didn't have any work. So, I started **sketching** furniture based on **structural concepts**."

Calder's Table uses no mechanical connections or moving pieces, but the simple force of gravity to create a connection between the supports and top.
Credit: Joshua McHugh

He continues, laughing, "Then, I would bring these drawings to friends, and look sad until they gave me money to make prototypes." This unusual approach to product development goes a long way towards explaining why almost all of his products carry personal names: each has been given the moniker of whoever helped fund their realization.

Trained as an architect with a heavy emphasis on engineering and structural optimization, Tayar describes his design approach as a ". . . playful investigation of the relationship between design and mechanical reproduction. Structural behavior is the other guiding component of my design work. I investigate structures with optimal ratios between load-bearing capacity and weight. I try to reconcile the often contradictory requirements of production processes with diagrams of the flow of forces." Tayar found working with furniture provided him an opportunity to play with—and then solve—various small-scale structural principles.

He recalls, "As I grew older, I started doing more work and having a real office, and sometimes I would get a commission where furniture was required, but often, I would think of a system that was interesting to me, and I would just have it made." Such was the case with the Calder's Table.

"It's inspired by the Barcelona Table of Mies van der Rohe," Tayar explains. This iconic design features a piece of glass resting on central, crossed metal supports. "The Calder table is almost an explosion of that table base, so instead of having this cross that turns into four legs, just imagine dismembering this space and putting it on four sides of the table," he continues.

Tayar always consults with a friend who is a structural engineer on projects like Calder's Table. "Sometimes, we do a full, structural analysis on the piece, or we discuss in concept if this thing might work. I have come up with things that will not work," Tayar reports. "But with this one, he said, I can't engineer it, but I think it will work. So we had to just make the piece. Short of making it, there was no real way to try it out." At the same time, another friend had a connection to a bronze manufacturing facility in Nepal. The support pieces that are the heart of the Calder Table were hand made in a sand casting in Kathmandu.

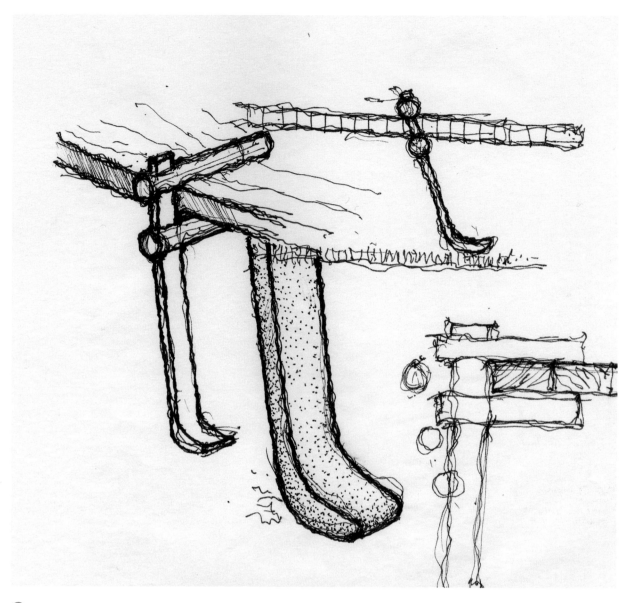

⬙ An early sketch outlines the shape of the Calder leg supports; however, the only way to find out if they'd work was to go ahead and make them.
Credit: Ali Tayar

There is a critical trick to how the Calder table functions, as there are no mechanical connections between the table and the legs. Tayar explains how it works: "The structural design is based entirely on gravity—there are no moving parts. The two rods are offset against each other. Essentially, two people have to hold the piece of wood and then slide the bracket in, vertically. As it rotates, it locks itself in one position. Depending on the thickness of the wood, there is always one, and only one, angle at which the bracket will rest. Once there are three legs, the thing is stable."

Describing the process of development, Tayar continues, "I would be lying if I said that there was just this one moment when it all came together."

Named after the son of the photographer who documents all his designs, Tayar says, ". . . at the same time, I enjoyed the fact that the piece evokes the other Calder's work." However, the weight of each support gives it a marked difference from the famous artist's mobiles. "Each piece is so heavy," Tayar notes. "They weigh 25 pounds (11 kg). They don't need to be heavy, but the fact that they are does help. Each one wants to fall down to the ground. The top prevents it from rotating, and as a result, it's kept at a distance from the floor. And, the curved leg always gives the impression of lying at the correct angle. Even if you used a thicker table top, you can't tell that the geometry has changed. The way

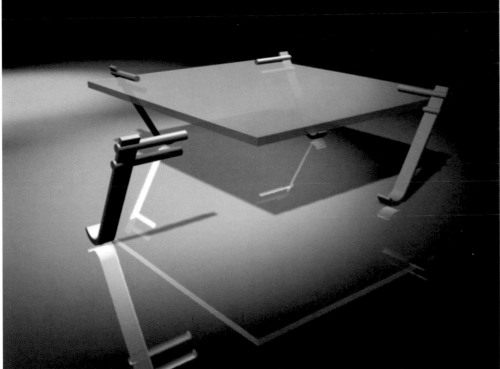

⊗ Top: While this computer rendering shows what appears to be a delicate balancing act of the Calder Table, the connections are actually very secure.
Credit: Jose Lew

⊗ Computer rendering anticipates the probability that gravity alone will allow the table to achieve stability when just three supports rotate into place.
Credit: Jose Lew

the leg touches the floor appears to be properly designed, even though a thicker piece of wood would change the angle."

When not doing their job creating a table, the bronze pieces still seem to contain some kind of embodied energy. "I generally don't like finding and reusing objects," Tayar says. "But the aesthetic of this piece is kind of like a found industrial object. Even alone, the brackets look like they must do something."

Tayar also takes great pleasure in the contradictions inherent in the particular production processes unique to Calder's table. "In general, my work is half inspired by structural principles and the other half by production processes," he reports. "I like very advanced processes, geared towards industrial production. But in this case, I had access to something that represents the first industrial revolution. It's interesting, in that we would develop 3D models and email the file half way around the world to someone I'd never seen, they would read it, they'd take these virtual models and create some kind of a mold, cast them, and then FedEx them back to me. The connections were twenty-first century, even though it was reaching back in time to a production process that's been around for thousands of years."

In keeping with this international approach, the few Calder tables that have been made have found homes all over the globe. One lives in Capetown, South Africa, another in Beirut, Lebanon, while two have settled in New York City, in the TriBeca and Meat Market neighborhoods.

Now that Tayar has been established in a real office for some time, he finds himself working on a wide range of architecture, furniture, and product designs. "I've been doing restaurants, lofts, and homes," he says, "and these projects are big, so this furniture design is not the main thing, but it's the thing I love most." Tayar points out that many of our most well-known designers felt the same way he does. "The reason Eames and other designers like him didn't design too many houses is because they liked to have control over the entire piece. If it fails, it's just a prototype when it's a piece of furniture, and you just make it better the next time. You can't say that to a client when you're designing their home."

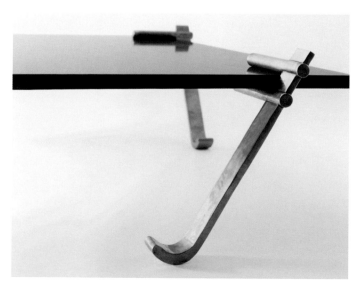

⌂ Top: The Calder leg supports are approximately 2" (5 cm) wide and 18" (45 cm) long and can be used on tabletops of up to 1" (2.5 cm) thick of almost any material or shape. *Credit: Joshua McHugh*

⌂ Tayar is especially pleased that the Calder table was created using high-tech methods to communicate half way around the world with people using ancient methods of production. *Credit: Joshua McHugh*

◁ The Calder leg supports were sand-casted in bronze by H. Theophile in Kathmandu, Nepal, utilizing one of the oldest manufacturing techniques known. *Credit: Joshua McHugh*

Float Table, Ana Franco

"The students **knew** from day one that if they were **selected**, this was not **something** that was going to be **exhibited**," says Jerry Helling, **creative director**

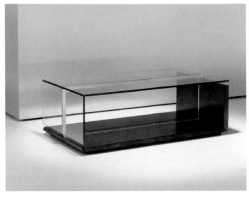

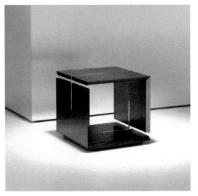

The Float Table, made of wood and glass connected by a sliver of metal, was designed by Ana Franco, while a student at the Art Center College of Design, and produced as part of a class sponsored by Bernhardt Design. *Credit: Lisa Adams Photography*

of Bernhardt Design, "but would be produced in the real world for market, and they would have the complete experience as if they had graduated and they were working for a client."

This idea of reality-dose-as-educational-opportunity started when Helling decided to get Bernhardt more closely connected with those who are on their way to becoming the next generation of professional designers; it grew into a bit of phenomenon for both the students and the company. "I have been wanting to be involved in the educational process somehow, some way, for some time," says Helling. "But projects with companies working with educational institutions are generally about competition, looking at the future, creating an exhibition, or doing one-off work. I talked to lots of students, and one day it hit me that what we could bring to the table that would benefit students most would be if we could provide a real-time, real-life experience of what it's like to work with a client and manufacturer." Helling approached Art Center College of Design in Pasadena, California not only because of its reputation for excellence, but because of the nature of its students. "The student body is a little older," he says, "and it's a very professional school. The practicality of life is stressed there in addition to pure creativity."

Working with David Mocarski, chairman of the Environmental Design Department, they created a two-semester course. The first semester took twenty-two students from research and concepting through prototyping a piece of furniture. According to Helling, "They started by researching the American furniture market. They saw what was out there, what people wanted. Then they researched our company because they had to design something appropriate for us. Then they started down the design process, doing broad-based conceptuals, refining that into computer models, and moving into small-scale modeling. Ultimately, their final task at the end of the first semester was to go out into Los Angeles and find full-scale prototyping. They only had to make one," he notes. "They had to do it because they learned so much in that process about what kind of accommodations had to be made to their ideas just to produce one."

This semester ended with a presentation of their prototypes to their client and patron, Bernhardt. The students knew that if their work was selected, they'd move into semester two, which would take their designs through the manufacturing process, all the way to market, and include lessons on marketing and public relations, as well as royalties. The results of this first class far exceeded Helling's expectations: "Our goal was to bring three products to market. I was prepared to take none, and originally thought I'd take five or six. We chose ten. We chose those we thought were most likely to be viable and marketable products."

◇ Foam core models helped develop the concept. "This was the first time I turned one of the 'leaves' upside down to form a cube," Franco notes. *Credit: Ana Franco*

◇ Franco's original concept was to create a table made of folded wood. The project evolved when designer Jeffrey Bernett came to class as a guest critic and suggested she try exploring other materials in addition to wood. *Credit: Ana Franco*

◁ The first full-scale mock-up was made in cardboard to check size and other details necessary for Franco to get her first real prototype made. *Credit: Ana Franco*

◇ For a prototype, Franco used welded plates on the metal strips to connect them to the wood. In production, Bernhardt used a much more ingenious method to make the connections totally invisible. *Credit: Ana Franco*

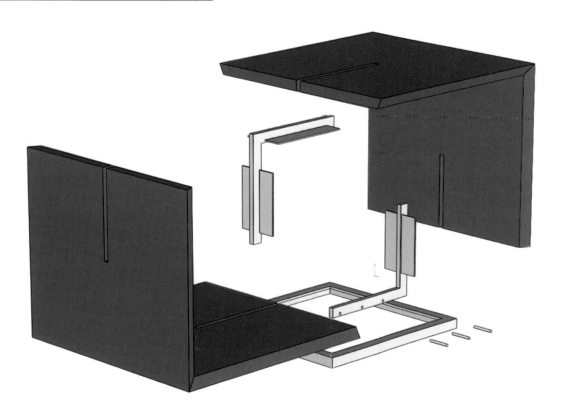

Franco's first prototype, the final assignment of the first semester, was constructed of veneered 1" (2.5 cm) MDF (medium density fiberboard). *Credit: Ana Franco*

In the Bernhardt factory, a CNC (computer numerical controlled) milling machine is used to cut the groove for the metal band in a piece of wood. *Credit: Bernhardt Design*

The table parts are secured with a process called polarization, whereby pins that are countersunk into the wood and run through holes in the metal strip are magnetized to create a completely invisible connection. *Credit: Bernhardt Design*

⊘ In the fully assembled table, the glass top appears to float above the wooden base, magically suspended by a slice of metal. *Credit: Bernhardt Design*

One of those chosen was the Float Table by Ana Franco. Her design process began by thinking about the client: "I started with words that describe Bernhardt. This was an opportunity to look at the company aesthetic, which is elegant, sophisticated, airy. I used these words to spur me onto to some ideas. Their products are also really architectural, and I thought this was a great opportunity to play with simple but interesting forms. We were told that Bernhardt uses wood, and it would be better to incorporate that, rather than asking them to do something they don't do. That was part of the lesson—to stick with the materials and process they already have ready access to."

Franco started sketching, making models, and fighting to find the right form for her ideas. At several points in the process, she was sure she wouldn't make the cut. "The brief was to do table or chairs, and I did both. I kept showing them and showing them, and I didn't get any bites," she says. Then things started to change. "Jerry liked an idea I had of folded wood connected with a sliver of metal. I kept struggling, thinking, this is the one he's interested in, and I should pursue this one, but I kept thinking it's too simple. This was the biggest challenge: to create something with a very simple form but still with one interesting gesture. One weekend, working with a model, I turned one of the folds over, and turned the table into a cube. My teacher said, 'Jerry will love this.'"

Jerry did. In fact, he points out that Franco's design of a table in wood, metal, and glass was one of the few that had almost no changes from concept to final production. But Franco had some

doubts along the way about whether they would be able to execute on her vision: "Jerry told me at the final crit that the table would never look as good in final production," she says. Then she quickly adds, "And he was wrong." She feels that part of the success of this college/corporate partnership is the unique energy students bring to the process. "To get chosen," she points out, "we were to push the boundaries, but not beyond what Bernhardt does. We brought a kind of gutsiness to it. We brought that kind of enthusiasm, where we wanted to challenge them, but with a cap on it. To me, more constraints make for better design."

Not only have these students had the unique learning experience as well as they financial rewards of seeing their work produced, but they have also enjoyed a surprising amount of publicity and awards. In addition to write ups in the *New York Times*, *Chicago Tribune*, and *Newsweek*, they received a profile in *Metropolis* entitled, "The Magnificent 7", and were given the Best New Designer award by the ICFF (International Contemporary Furniture Fair), as well as a Best in Competition prize and two gold awards in seating/sofa and lounge and tables/occasional at the NeoCon trade fair.

Naturally, Helling says Bernhardt Design is committed to continuing their investment with the students of Art Center College of Design. "We got a great experience, they got a great experience, and we got good products. So in taking a chance like this, the payoff was great for everyone. I've learned that you can take the risk, and it can work and be wonderful for everyone involved."

Low Down Table, Jeff Jenkins "If you look at the structure of instruments and how they're put together, the end result is always beautiful, and it hasn't changed much over time," explains Jeff Jenkins.

⊘ The Low Down Table is made, much like a musical instrument, so it can be tuned to keep the large slab of Sugar pine tabletop flat in any season, regardless of fluctuations in temperature and humidity. *Credit: Aldo Tutino*

⊘ Opposite: In this series of sketches, the simplicity of the Low Down Table is made apparent. Constructed of two matching ends, a single plank of wood, and a support beam, along with a removable felt cover, the table was meant to express the essence of modernism with a "low-tech" idea. *Credit: Jeffrey Jenkins*

"Successful furniture is about connections, and how you bring materials together," he says, "and I started to think about how to translate that structural language of instruments into furniture. It's a bit of a structural experiment for furniture."

The Low Down Table's apparent simplicity belies a hidden and unique feature: it can be tuned, much like a musical instrument. Jenkins points out that with most types of wood, a solid slab such as he's used would warp and possibly crack over time and with changes in the atmosphere. While the Low Down is made from a solid plank of western or sugar pine, a wood that has a low moisture content, that helps it remain stable, it will expand and contract. But when it does, a few twists on special mechanical fasteners underneath the table let you readjust its shape, just as you might tighten or loosen the strings on a guitar. "This wood will move only minimally, and it will happen at the corners," Jenkins explains. "Fasteners you can adjust are inserted in the underside and connected to the underlying frame, so you can tune it like an instrument. When summer comes around, and there's lots of humidity, if you see the corners start to cup, you can adjust those with a few turns and it will bring the corners back down. It works through tension. There are two fasteners in the center and four at the ends. With this structure, you're able to control it without overcontrolling it and forcing the wood to do what it doesn't want to do."

All this is achieved without altering the clean, uncluttered lines of the table itself. "What we've done is reduced the parts to essential elements," says Jenkins. "It's a plank, a beam, and space frames that elevate the beam off the floor." However, even a table this lucid does have its manufacturing demands. "The biggest challenge is locating that pine in a consistent form," says Jenkins. "You can't just call up a supplier and say, 'Send me X number of board feet of this western pine.' You actually have to go to lumberyards and choose it. I try and use sustainable forestry resources and it's becoming less and less available because so much of it has been consumed."

The pine is finished with a beeswax linseed oil that is not harmful to the environment and won't build up a hard, lacquered surface. Because the wood is fairly soft, and because he simply likes the material itself, Jenkins has added a pad of gray felt to the top of the table. "This is a material you wouldn't typically see

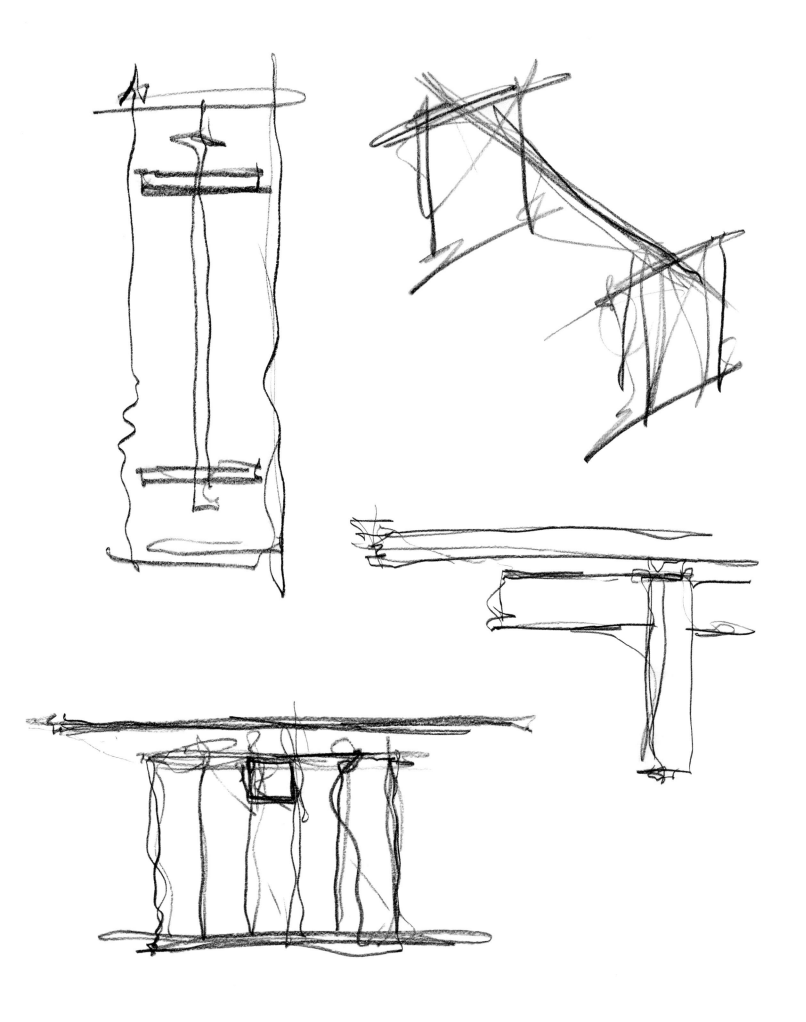

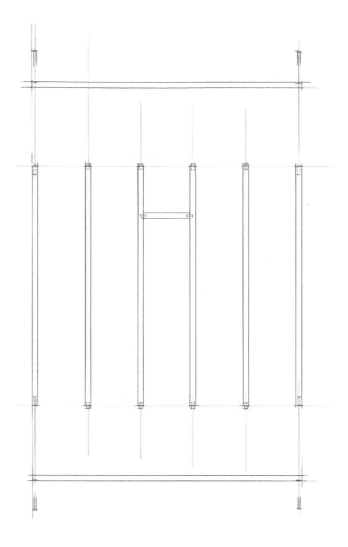

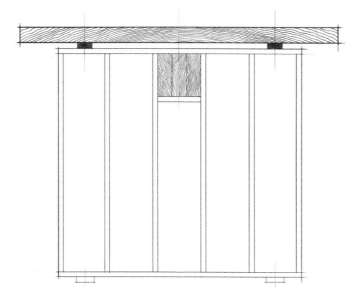

⊗ This exploded elevation of the leg frame assembly explains how the entire frame bolts in compression on just four corners. The rest of the connections are press-fit pins. Once the four corners are tightened, the frame becomes very rigid. *Credit: Jeffrey Jenkins*

⊗ A drawing of the side elevation shows how the frame connects to the wood beam and the top plank. *Credit: Jeffrey Jenkins*

exposed," he notes, "because it's an industrial-grade felt. It's normally used for cutting out die-cut gaskets and washers for machinery. You also have the option of rolling it up and not using it and just enjoying the wood surface. The gray felt offers a nice visual contrast to this soft yellow, buttery pine. It's a very natural color."

The tabletop is supported by a beam made of the same pine. "But the beam has been glued in such a way that it won't ever move," Jenkins says. "It's a lamination. The whole idea of the table is this central spine that's holding it all together. We approached it as a structural problem. How do you take a solid plank of wood—it sounds so primitive and basic—and make this long table supported by a beautiful structure?"

Part of this beautiful structure is achieved by the two, barred frames at either end. "The end pieces are a kind of visual contrast," Jenkins notes. "You have these thin, flat pieces contrasting with this big, solid timber of the spine and flat plank. I was also trying to create a formal geometry for the frame that was not material driven and reduce those flat pieces to be as thin as possible and still have a strong structure." While the plank, beam, and felt pieces are always the same, the ends are offered in either stainless steel or padouk, an exotic wood with a rich red color.

Jenkins points out that in addition to being easy to assemble, disassemble, and tune up as the environment requires, the table has yet another benefit: "The other beautiful aspect of the end result is that it's extremely lightweight," he says. "It's under 15 pounds (7 kg), not including the felt. You can just pick it up and balance it vertically on your fingertip. Which was another important part of the structural problem. "How can I make it as lightweight as possible in these materials?'"

Jenkins adds, "This is a very low-tech idea." Which was, after all, the point of the exercise. "So much of furniture is overdone," he says. "The world is full of these overstylized pieces that use excessive amounts of materials. If you look at bad furniture design, it just makes your eyes sting. Sometimes, you have to take a step back and get back to basics in terms of material and form, and take a philosophical stance." For Jenkins, this attitude is the essence of a modernist aesthetic. "I like to think of a quote by Paola Antonelli, curator of the Department of Architecture and Design for the Museum of Modern Art in New York. When she was asked 'How do you define modern?' she said, 'Modern is not about certain shapes. It's a certain attitude. Nothing is wasted intellectually.' I always think about that because that's what I'm striving for," says Jenkins. "Defining modernism through this low-tech structure and combination of materials."

The Low Down is easy to assemble and disassemble. The beam fits through each supporting end and the sugar pine top is adhered to the frame and support beam in six places with special fasteners that allow the wood to be "tuned." The felt top is added both to protect the pine and as a visual complement between the blond wood and shiny metal supports. *Credit: Aldo Tutino*

"What we've done is reduced the parts to essential elements," says Jenkins. "It's a plank, a beam, and space frames that elevate the beam off the floor." Along with an ingenious tuning device that ensures the simplicity always rings true. *Credit: Aldo Tutino*

Not So Soft Table and Chairs, Stephen Burks

"There **always** has been a kind of **joy** for me in assembling something and **understanding** how it works," says Stephen Burks,

The Not So Soft line by Stephen Burks is made with two different shapes of injection-molded polypropylene that snap fit together to create an indoor-outdoor-lightweight-floatable chair and table.
Credit: Miro Zagnoli

Semiassembled Not So Soft Tables and Chairs are packed at the factory. The parts were to be sold in packages of two that could easily be put together by the purchaser. *Credit: Readymade Projects*

explaining the Not So Soft Table. "The best, most successfully designed objects are those that are immediate, that communicate, in a way, their function, that say what they do.

I like how this table explains itself, and how it also explains the design process in a way. You get to choose how much of it you put together," Burks points out, "even if there is only one way to put it together."

The Not So Soft Table was an unexpected outgrowth of Burks' work with Mogu, a Japanese manufacturer of pillows filled with polystyrene pellets. During his year or so as international art director for the now defunct company, "I realized they were making things in injection-molded polypropylene. It has a higher oil content that holds pellets together and stiffens them, hardens them. I wanted to take a minimum wall thickness of material, and try to conceive a piece of furniture that could be made from a single molded part. This way," Burke continues, "the tool would be smaller, you'd use less material, and you could make the piece as big or small as you want. We had two months before the Milan Furniture Fair, so in two months we designed the Not So Soft Collection. The table reminded me, in a way, of Mogu's other products, but it was less soft." Hence, the name.

The very odd shape of the component parts for table and chair were a direct product of considering the practical issues associated with the manufacturing. "We knew it had to be a solid because of the strength issues related to the material," says Burks. "We couldn't do anything with legs because that would have been too fragile. We wanted to work from a solid base, and from that, come up and form a seat and a back. There's no formalism in it per se," he notes. "The rounded corners were softened basically because it seemed to fit the aesthetic."

Burks feels that although this process was entirely new to him, and he had never designed a chair before, the Not So Soft collection is clearly another expression of his design process and concerns. "I try to do what's right for my client," he says, "and I saw this as a chance for them to do something totally proprietary. The idea of taking a smaller part and making a bigger product is consistent in my work because I am interested in conveying the kit-of-parts nature of design. All products have a kind of assembly," Burks explains. "I think design can be communicative in that way and can engage the user in understanding and using the product. It's a way of making design accessible. The process is actually communicated through the form and the function of the thing. Not just the design process, but the manufacturing and assembly process as well. Some people interpret this as a playful nature in my work, others call it a kind of ready-made utility, but for me it's a matter of communicating the process."

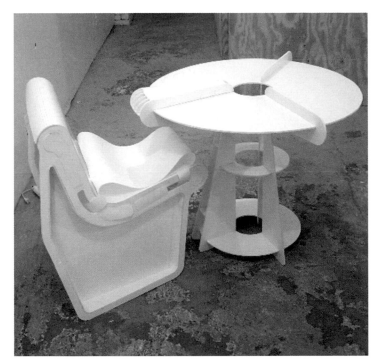

Burks and Mogu found a factory that was using injected molded polypropylene to make automobile bumpers. They had never manufactured furniture, but happily jumped into the project and made a mold for the parts to both the chair and table. "They cranked out a bunch of pieces, and we used them to make a circular seating arrangement and a circular table," recalls Burks. "They friction-fit together. They are designed for very little tolerance between the pieces and the material compresses a bit, so they push together with a very satisfying squeak. Four parts made a chair, twelve parts a love seat, forty-eight parts made a circular chair. The parts are actually curved, smaller at front and bigger at the bottom," Burks notes. "With the table, we did the same thing with a different part. Twenty-four parts make the table. It was a great thing—lightweight, outdoor, indoor, it floats. We didn't do color because it's much more expensive, so we did it all in black and white."

⊘ Top left: The basic outline of the Not So Soft Table and Chair take shape in these study models; however, manufacturing considerations and the commitment to use only two pieces eventually dictated that the table be made without legs. *Credit: Readymade Projects*

⊘ Top right: Injection molding tooling of the two parts required to make the Not So Soft products. The small nubs are where the pieces will be snapped together. *Credit: Readymade Projects*

⊘ The first prototype of the Not So Soft Chair. Only four pieces are required to create a stable footprint, and the final product is surprisingly lightweight. *Credit: Readymade Projects*

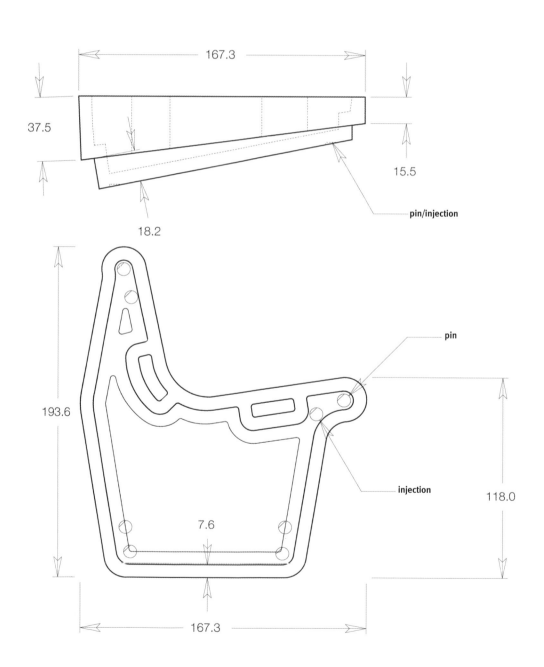

A technical drawing of the Not So Soft Chair component reveals the thin layer of material that is used, as well as the pins that allow multiple pieces to be snap-fit together. *Credit: Readymade Projects*

167.3

37.5

15.5

pin/injection

18.2

193.6

pin

injection

118.0

7.6

167.3

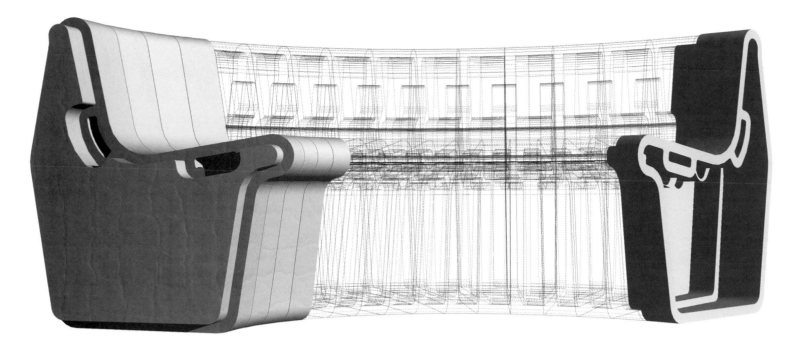

⊘ This assembly illustration demonstrates how four Not So Soft pieces create a comfortable chair, while adding a dozen more parts adds up to a circular bench.
Credit: Readymade Projects

⊘ The Not So Soft Chair parts fit together like an adult-sized toy, transforming itself from odd-shaped pieces of plastic into a multifunctional chair.
Credit: Miro Zagnoli

Burks recalls the thrill of seeing the parts come out of the mold. "There was a real sense of excitement," he says. "They looked at this thing and held it up—it weighs nothing—and the engineer went to piece it together, and he was so excited, he sat down and put his thumbs up." He points out that it was especially gratifying to take an industrial process that is focused on one particular industry and transfer its processes to a completely different industry. Plus there's just something fun about the Not So Soft. "It's really exciting to see people put it together," says Burks. "It's a kind of giant toy."

While the Not So Soft line was quite a hit at the Milan Furniture Fair, it unfortunately never went to full production because Mogu went out of business. Strangely, the company was a victim of their own success. They were not able to fulfill the massive quantity of orders they generated for their pillows, and also did not protect the propriety of their product, which was copied and knocked off endlessly by other companies. Burks is both wistful and philosophical about the unfinished piece of business the Not So Soft represents. "I think half of our work as designers is entrepreneurial," he says. "People don't want to admit that this business is speculative. You go out there with your suitcase and your vacuum cleaners, and say this is what I've got. Young designers all want to know how did you do this or that, and they don't understand that you just go and talk to people and you try to communicate that you have something to offer." Burks remains committed to the Not So Soft. "The design was very successful and it communicated what I wanted it to," he says. "It's potential was huge, but it's still a dream unfulfilled until I can find a way to get it out there."

Origami Table, Michael Wolfson "They were based on the **geometry** and forms that I deal with, **looking** into the ideas of movement and **motion**, which were developed by the **modernists**, the deconstructionists and other 'ists' and 'isms,'"

The Origami Table explores issues of motion and movement through folded plates of mirror-polished stainless steel that transform themselves into a dining room table with a dramatic cantilever.
Credit: Wolfson Design

says Michael Wolfson of the genesis of his Origami Table. "Their studies of movement and motion are still going on today."

In addition to these influences, the seeds for what would become Wolfson's Origami Table were planted a decade ago with a project that involved designing some chairs. But it wasn't until a couple of years ago that he dusted off some old sketches and began to look at how to make his more formal studies viable. "In the last two years, when there began to be a stronger interest in art furniture," he says, "this spurred me to go back and spend some time looking at furniture and see where it is in the culture." According to Wolfson, "The more extreme forms of art furniture are not accessible or desired by the public, and that's understandable. But you see that when extreme examples are produced, then they are eventually distilled down and accepted by the public, just like it is in the world of fashion."

When Wolfson first began looking at how to turn his sketches into a real piece of furniture, he worked with a complete novice on preliminary modeling. "I was visiting my family in the United States and had a young nephew help me cut out pieces of paper," he says. And then laughing adds, "But the study was so wonky that we just put is aside." When Wolfson returned to his London office, he brought in the professionals. "A few people in the office and I had a jam session and started looking at what this could become. It started evolving in paper models and clay and every possible instrument. We really did start from this non-functional piece. It was a sketch of angles and forms and crystals, and we started to impose a function on it," he recalls. "As the models began to develop, we realized it needed to have a certain scale so you could walk around it and see what it was and could be, because it looks different from every angle." And this is how these sketched studies of motion and movement and angles and planes began to take shape as a table.

Once a full-scale model was made, they began to make computer renderings. Wolfson calls the computer "a wonderful tool," before quickly adding, "But I don't use it. I enjoy watching what can be done," Wolfson says, "but I don't think I'd design from a computer." He says he "sits over someone's shoulders" while they transfer his work to technical drawings, and is quick to give credit to the rest of the crew in his studio, including Chris Glaister, Maxim Nilov, and Cian Plumbe. For the initial prototype, they didn't work with a structural engineer. "We started with just a feel for the material," Wolfson reports.

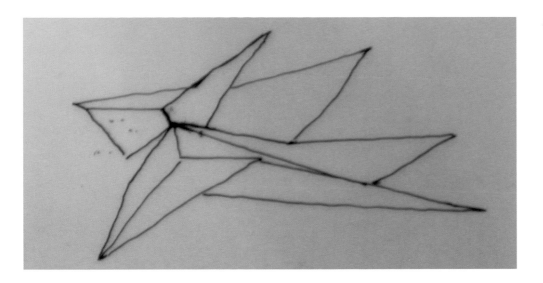

Sketches that explore the relationship between angles, planes, folds, space, and motion were the genesis of the Origami Table. *Credit: Wolfson Design*

Cardboard models in a variety of scales were used to explore both aesthetics and viability. The white chalk markings note areas that will need to be altered or revised. *Credit: Wolfson Design*

As the models progressed and got closer to what would become the final piece, the scale went from 1:10 to 1:6. And the white chalk markings became fewer and farther between. *Credit: Wolfson Design*

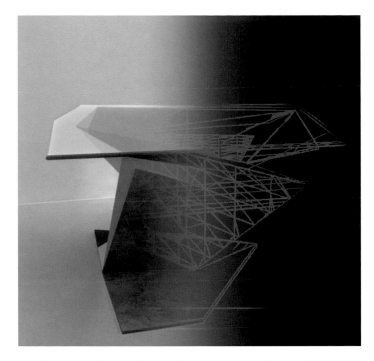

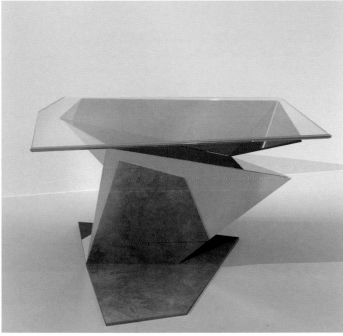

This "graphic abstraction" morphs a computer image of the table with the three dimensional model. Wolfson feels that this image "represents the movement that is meant to be felt by the composition of the elements." *Credit: Wolfson Design*

Because the Origami Table is so highly reflective of its surroundings and therefore difficult to photograph, this computer-generated image was made using photographs of the actual prototype and incorporating last minute design changes to provide an accurate representation of the final product. *Credit: Wolfson Design*

Opposite: Computer-generated three-dimensional models use colors and patterns to represent different fabrication elements of the Origami Table, which is made from a number of metal sheets that are laser cut, and then folded, glued, screwed, and welded together. *Credit: Wolfson Design*

The material used is mirror-polished sheets of stainless steel. "There is a basic, unfolded diagram sent off to laser cutters," Wolfson explains, "and it's basically six or seven pieces that are cut off. There's a whole diagram for the manufacturing of it. Certain lines are etched by the metal worker where it's folded so you get the forms of these folded plates that are put together with laminating and glue." Wolfson points out that there is very little welding, just a few screws, and that the piece does come apart. In addition to the mirror-polished plates, there are other pieces with an acid patina. "It creates a dark blue-brown effect," Wolfson notes. "I hand apply it with sponges." The base plate is made of mild steel, which is a standard, carbon steel. "The base plate receives the main body of the piece," says Wolfson. "It's kind of like a slipper that is screwed to keep it in place. We needed a big base to balance the strong cantilever of the table." The piece is finished with a glass top and weighs several hundred pounds. Wolfson finds this fact an interesting irony, given that his intention was to explore issues of movement. However, as a large dining room table, Wolfson doesn't see it moving around much in real life. He does envision it surrounded by other pieces of furniture that are simple and have clean lines. For example, he suggests, "Very pale leather chairs with slender legs. I would not exaggerate a piece like this," he continues. "It's so strong. It's all mirrored and any light on it is magnified."

While the Origami Table is an art piece, and as such not likely to go into full-scale production, Wolfson is considering finessing his design to make it more practical. "We're looking to make a variation that would be much lighter, made in a translucent material," he says. In addition, "We've revised the design to allow for a little bit more structure. We've also decided to increase the thickness of the metal on the subsequent pieces. I'm going to drop it off with a structural engineer to have a look at it from a structural as well as production aspect to make it easier to put together," he notes. And as much as he loves the aesthetics of the Origami, Wolfson says, "I don't really like the impractical aspect of it. Ideally it would be a little bit lighter. I don't like the idea of having things trucked into a gallery."

In general, Wolfson sees the Origami Table as a natural extension of his design concerns. "It's very much in the style I carry out," he says. "It's just a much more extreme example." At the same time, designing furniture like the Origami Table gives Wolfson the opportunity to explore. He says, "I have two hats. I do classical interior design, but I am equally passionate about the more contemporary work I do." He points out that commercial work allows him to be more cutting edge because, while people may not be interested in living with designs that are on the vanguard, they are happy to see experimental or challenging pieces in a restaurant or other commercial venue. He also insists that these two sides to his design life do not affect each other, maintaining that they are two very different, but deeply felt passions. And then he pauses and says he does hope to someday find a project that will give him the opportunity to blend the two.

Shell Table, Barber Osgerby

The Shell Table is the only logical conclusion to Barber Osgerby's twin **fascinations** with a **humble** material and a **pared-down** aesthetic.

The Shell Table is an expression of Barber Osgerby's "fascination" with plywood's strength and humble character. *Credit: Lee Funnell for Ikoson*

"We love working with plywood," says Ed Barber, "because it's somewhere between working with regular wood and with plastic. Like plastic, you can mold plywood into certain shapes, but unlike plastic, it doesn't deteriorate as it ages. In some cases, it actually looks better as it ages."

The other idea the designers, Jay Osgerby and Ed Barber, had in mind was to create something as lightweight—both literally and aesthetically—as possible. "We were intrigued with the strength of plywood. Even though it's thin, when you fold it, it becomes very strong. The Shell Table puts that principle into practice," Barber continues. "By just folding the top over the leg, you get a very simple line and each component is very strong, but very lightweight."

The designers' collaboration with manufacturer Isokon began informally. Because the studio was next to a plywood factory, they often found themselves running into the Isokon folks, who happen to know a lot about making furniture out of plywood. From casual discussions on the nature and possibilities of the raw material, they decided to develop the table together.

"The great thing about plywood," Barber points out, "is that you can experiment with cardboard beforehand because it performs in a similar way. So there were no hidden surprises."

Getting the elegant lines and pared down look turned out to be a process of reduction. "We ended up using a thinner plywood than we started with," Barber says. "We realized that it was unnecessary to have it so thick, so we thinned it down." They then continued this process of taking away for the remainder of the table parts. "You need enough material to affix the top to the leg so it's strong," Barber points out, "but not so much that it detracts from the lightness of the top. We just kept making the leg thinner and thinner until it became unstable, and then we put some back."

In addition to the gentle curves and airy feel, the Shell Table is marked especially by the unusual openings in the corners. This unique element came about, like so much of the design, by simply letting the material have it's own way. "When you fold the plywood down," Barber notes, "you can't make a neat joint. So we decided to just make a statement out of it, and that became the statement of the table." Through the tried-and-true process of straightforward trial and error, they came up with a shape for the openings that was "pleasing" according to Barber. "This is quite often the way it happens in design," he continues. "We knew there'd be a hole, but we didn't know what shape it would take, and by the time we were done, that was one of the nicest parts of the table."

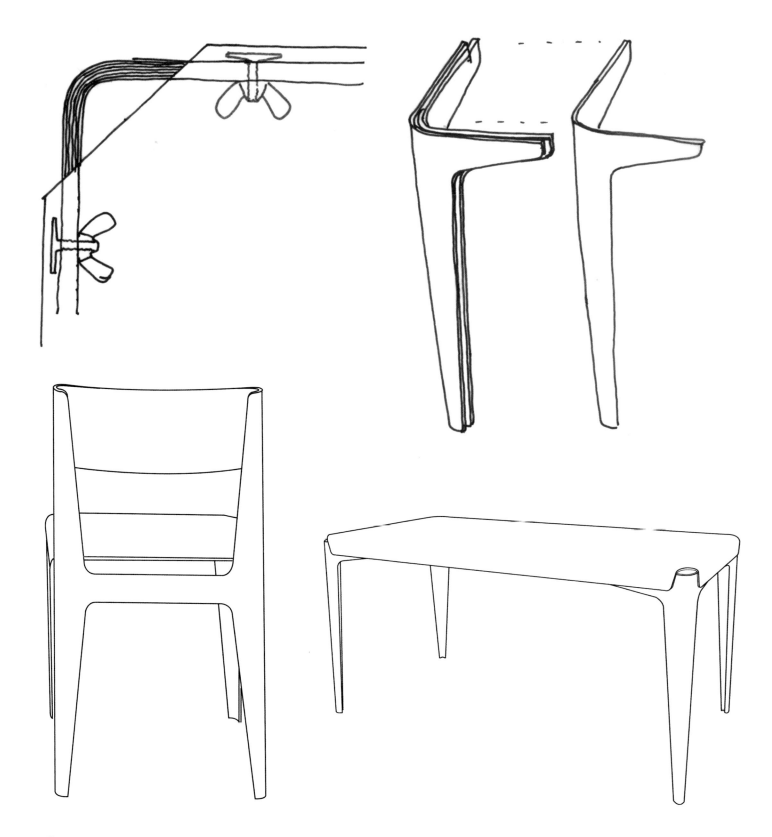

⊗ Top left: A preliminary sketch shows one way to connect the top to the leg structure. Ultimately, the designers settled on an option that combined gluing and a mechanical fix that is invisible. *Credit: Barber Osgerby*

⊗ Top right: The leg was designed to use as little material as possible and still offer a stable footprint for the table. *Credit: Barber Osgerby*

⊗ Above : Barber Osgerby uses Vectorworks and Freehand to create computer renderings that are used to present their ideas to the manufacturer. These renderings express the essential elements of the design brief: "to design a table that can be used for both home and work with a minimum number of components, to keep production costs low and assembly easy."
Credit: Barber Osgerby

However serendipitous the development of the Shell Table seems, it is also a natural extension of the forms that inspire the designers. "What inspires us is not so much a finished product, but details of certain things," says Barber. "For example, anything that is designed for performance, there's an honesty about it. We really enjoy looking at boat hulls and plane wings. They are designed solely for function and because of that they look really stunning. If you can borrow these ideas, and put them into furniture, which is of course not essential and not purely about function, you end up with these really elegant forms." This reference found its expression most clearly in the shape of the table legs. "We could have made the leg straight," Barber points out, "but then there would have been this unnecessary material. Visually, when you pare the shapes down, you end up with these pleasing, almost aerodynamic forms."

The designers also made a welcome discovery after the table was made. Because the plywood has a bit of natural flex, the table is self-leveling, even on uneven flooring. When asked if they planned it that way, Barber laughs and acknowledges that it was simplye a "happy coincidence."

Making the matching chairs was simply a natural extension of the process of making the table. "We just made loads of mock- ups to get the curves and angles just right, to get the comfort," Barber notes. "It's really the only way to do it, actually." Both the table and chairs are made of several parts that are glued and then bolted together. And because Isokon is making them in limited quantities, each piece is hand-finished by a master carpenter. They are available in birch plywood, as well as solid colors. "In theory, you could have it in any color. If someone wanted a zebra pattern," Barber quips, "we'd say no. But any flat color? We'd make that."

There's a pleasing inevitability to the Shell Table and Chairs. Barber points out that this is not an affectation: "Of course, we experimented with cardboard mockups and such. But this was one of the few things we've designed where, once the first one was produced, it was like, 'Okay, that's that.'. It just had this kind of personality of it's own. It didn't need days and days of changing and experimenting. It just felt right."

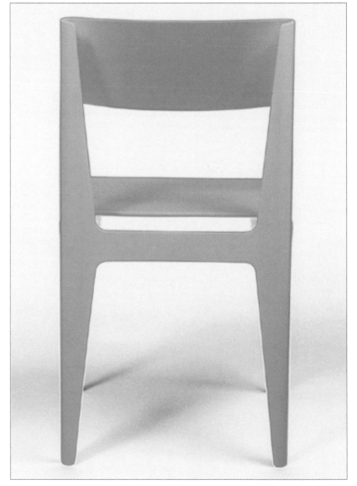

 To create comfortable chairs in the same language as the table, the designers made several mockups to get the curves and angles right.
Credit: Lee Funnell for Ikoson

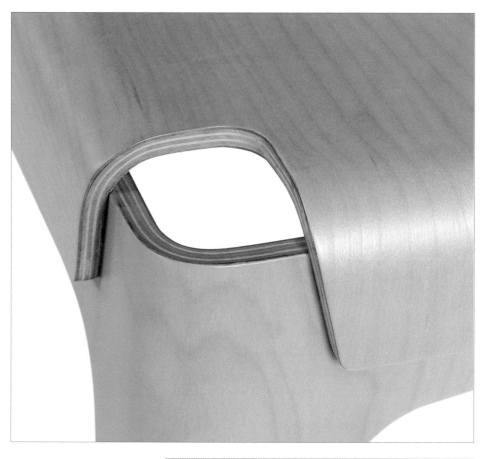

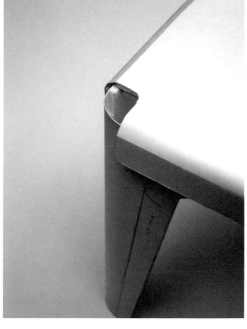

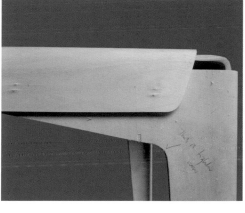

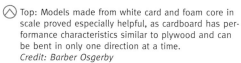

⬦ Top: Models made from white card and foam core in scale proved especially helpful, as cardboard has performance characteristics similar to plywood and can be bent in only one direction at a time.
Credit: Barber Osgerby

⬦ An early prototype shows how the lines of the leg and top meet one another; note the scribbling on the wood that asks to pare down the silhouette even more. *Credit: Barber Osgerby*

⬦ Top: The distinctive hole in the corner of the table was a design decision that evolved out of necessity; because there was no way to bring the two pieces together without a hole, the designers decided to make it an essential aspect of the overall aesthetic.
Credit: Barber Osgerby

⬦ The slender shape of the Shell Table's leg was derived simply by paring back and paring back until the designers reached instability, and then adding in just enough material to make the table self-supporting.
Credit: Barber Osgerby

Solid Series, Patrick Jouin

"When you design a **chair**, you know the **technology** you will use," says Patrick Jouin. "You know if you design one in steel, or **plastic**, or wood, so before your **pencil touches** the paper, you have in **mind** all the constraints of the **technology** you will use to produce the product."

The Solid Chair has been made using stereolithography, a technology that uses a laser beam to create a single object by building up layer upon layer of hardened polymer. *Credit: Thomas Duval*

"When you design an object," he continues, "you will always have someone else who will come in the process, and say, 'Sorry Patrick, you can't do it like this because our machine won't do this.' So I change it. I don't want to, but I have to find a solution. Or the manufacturer will say, 'I can't sell this, the market will not accept.' But this time, there is no technical constraint, and no one in the middle of the process. It's now a pure idea; not cooked, but raw. Which is why it looks so incredible."

Jouin is referring to the freedom he found when he began creating functional objects with a process normally used for rapid prototyping. Jouin first became familiar with stereolithography when he was designing a decorative object for a Las Vegas bar. "To make the model," he says, "it's very hard to describe for the mill worker, so it's best to make a prototype. It's all about the power of the 3D programs and 3D rapid prototyping. After I saw the pieces materialize, now I knew very well the process and I see a great opportunity, not to manufacture, not just to design an object you look at, but to make something you really use—a chair, or a stool, or a table."

While rapid prototyping has been available in various forms of technology, new advancements in stereolithography made Jouin's vision possible. "There was no machine to manufacture a big object like this when we started to design," Jouin notes. "The mammoth machine was just being made to produce larger objects in stereolithography. It was the coming together of this new technology that allowed an ultra freedom with shape, which is totally new for a designer."

Stereolithography is a process that quickly turns a 3D CAD file into a physical object. It works by tracing laser beams over the surface of a vat of liquid photopolymer. The laser instantly cures one slender layer of the photosensitive polymer resin at a time; each layer adheres to the previous one, thereby creating the object. Jouin uses a low-tech metaphor to explain this high-tech process: "I can describe it also another way, very simple," he says. "You will print an image with your laser printer, okay, and each time there is a very thin layer of powder or ink. If you put the same page again and again in the machine, every time there will be some ink that will go on top of the other layer of ink, and if you do it thousands and thousands of times, you will have a real 3D piece made of ink."

⊻ Top: A rendering of the Solid stool depicts how stereolithogrpahy allows a designer to go directly from a 3D CAD drawing to a product, without molds or traditional manufacturing processes. *Credit: Thomas Duval*

⊻ Bottom: In stereolithography, a laser cures the surface of a vat of photosensitive polymer resin; the next layer adheres to the first and the object is built like a sedimentary rock. *Credit: Thomas Duval*

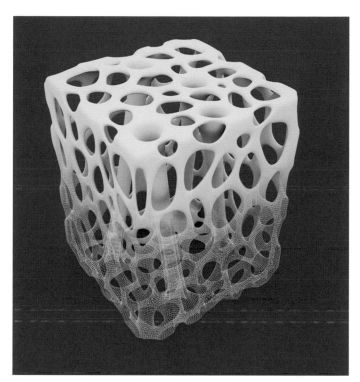

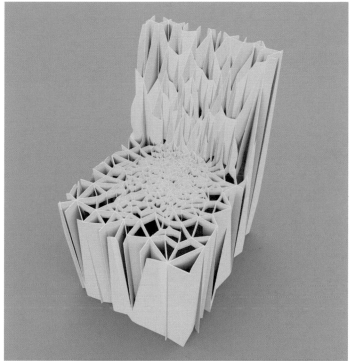

⊼ Top: Too fragile to put into production, this prototype of the C1 chair shows how stereolithography allows fantastic structural ideas to be the guiding design concern. *Credit: Thomas Duval*

⊼ As the laser hardens each slender layer of polymer, the whole piece is lowered into the bath where the next layer is carved out of the liquid. *Credit: Thomas Duval*

⊘ The C1 Chair seems to have been neither built nor manufactured, but simply grown.
Credit: Thomas Duval

The organic rather than built nature of the process forced Jouin to rethink how he designs. "The idea wasn't to design an object, but to invent a structure and how they grow. It's really linked to nature," he says. "When a tree grows, even if it has no brain, it will totally react to the environment, it will look for light and water, and it will adjust its shape with the condition. And so, the idea was for the ribbon chair, I have on the floor a number of grasses and they grow, and they want to take the shape of a chair at the end. When they are 17.5 inches (45 cm) from the floor, then they become a seat, then they become a back, and then a leg. But they are too fragile," he continues, "so, some other grasses come and grow and support them and triangulate the structure."

The ribbon, or Solid Chair is just one of several objects Jouin created using stereolithography. He points out, "The technology is not very simple to understand, but as a designer, you have to understand it very well to design something interesting. Because, if you really look carefully, no craftsman can do it. It's impossible." He quickly corrects himself, "Nothing is ever impossible, but it will take the genius of a sculptor to work for thousands and thousands of hours to do one object. This is almost impossible. But the machine can make anything I want. Maybe it's not comfortable, and I can't sit on it, but if I want, I can do it."

For Jouin, stereolithography forces a rethinking of several key assumptions in how we consider design styles. "All modernity is based on the reaction against the bourgeoisie, the luxury, everything made by hand and craftsman," he explains. "And this time, you can do something super complex or not complex at all—it's

up to you, the machine does what you want. This technology is more for complexity. And this is the important point, because now complexity is not antimodern. Because it is a machine that is producing this complexity."

It is this convergence of idea and technology—and the immediacy it offers—that intrigues Jouin. As he explains in a small booklet he published, "What this experiment shows, above all, is the telescoping of design technology and production technology. It is part of a general trend towards immediate materialization of the object: the amount of time separating the idea—which used to be nothing more than a presage, a vague specter of the thing—from the three-dimensional object is shrinking. Soon, no one will be involved but the designer and the machine—the design process will immediately plug into the production tool."

Jouin says working with stereolithography has been "a break for me. Because I was more working on the skin and the surface of objects and this time we are working on structure. Sometimes I discover with this project that I am more free than ever. I show to myself that I can do what I want. And there is no barrier." Again, he pauses to correct himself. "There is always a barrier. It was beauty. I always tried to make something beautiful, and this time I didn't care." After all, with this means of collapsing the time it takes to move from idea to final object, paradoxically, the final product matters less than how it came about. "It's an adventure," Jouin says. "I am more happy about this, to discover something new. After this, I am less interested in objects; it's more the process, the adventure, than the result."

The Solid Table uses triangulation of the various ribbons to create a structure that is solid enough to stand up and support a glass tabletop.
Credit: Thomas Duval

The rapid prototyping process used to fabricate the Solid Chair allows the designer to create pieces in any form, without considering the usual limitations of more typical manufacturing techniques.
Credit: Thomas Duval

Laurel Bench, Mark Goetz, TZ Design "This project began, as most of my projects do, with a **particular** need," says Mark Goetz of his Laurel Bench.

The Laurel Bench by Mark Goetz for Bernhardt Design brings the classical proportions and leg design of ancient Chinese lacquered tables to a seat that that seems to invite a passer by to take a rest.
Credit: Bernhardt Design, Lisa Adams Photography

Opposite bottom: This color sketch, which was hand drawn and then digitally colored in Photoshop, emphasizes the elegant curve of the Asian parawood, as well as the substance of the monolithic leg extending from front to back. *Credit: Mark Goetz*

"The need, identified by Bernhardt Design, was to develop a bench for architectural settings, specifically hotels, hallways, any kind of business environment." He pauses before adding, "And then, my sort of hopeful and less verbalized intention was for it to find it's way into people's homes."

Once these basic parameters had been identified, Goetz looked to the distant Far East for inspiration. "A lot of my designs have an element of old and new," he says, "and recently, I've been very interested in the notion of very ancient shapes. I think it's interesting that pieces from ancient history have a sort of truth and freshness about them. For this piece, I was looking at Chinese antiquity. I was looking at some Chinese altar tables, often seen in black lacquer. They have a quality that lets objects put there be presented beautifully. The other thing I love about these tables is that they don't have four legs, but they go into space as long planes. I'm interested in elements that are found in ancient objects but are also relevant and current today."

This focus on presentation and leg shape became central design influences. "Instead of taking objects like a bowl or a candle and putting the object on a table, I thought of the idea of presenting a very soft and comfortable cushion. The intention of the bench is like two hands presenting this cushion to the person who might sit there. That has been a theme through some of my furniture in the past, the idea of creating a piece that actually welcomes the sitter and invites them to sit down." He adds, "One of the really relevant points of the piece is that you're used to seeing a bench with four legs, but in this, the solidity and massiveness is achieved by this monolithic leg going back."

In order to realize these ideas, Goetz takes himself through a uniquely physical process of sketching. Instead of using pads of paper and a desk, he places oversized sheets onto the wall of his studio and sketches oversized. "I like to think of working not using just my hands, but to sketch by using my whole arm and upper body because I actually want my arm, as it draws my intention on the wall, to go through a complete gesture." Goetz explains the significance of the result: "Because it's full size, I'm able to achieve something that at the beginning is very bold. I work with very broad lines, with a broad tip magic marker. What I'm trying to do at first is, in a way, draw a mark on a sheet of paper on the wall that captures the feeling and gesture that I want for the piece." Goetz compares his experience with the vertical surface to what he imagines happens on the street. "One of the things I love about graffiti—and I hate many things about it—is that when people create graffiti, they're creating these lines very rapidly. They're very fluid, they have a lot of energy, and the line is coming right out of their expressions. They're not thinking or planning their line; it's just coming right out. I try to have a feeling, and let it just happen on the wall."

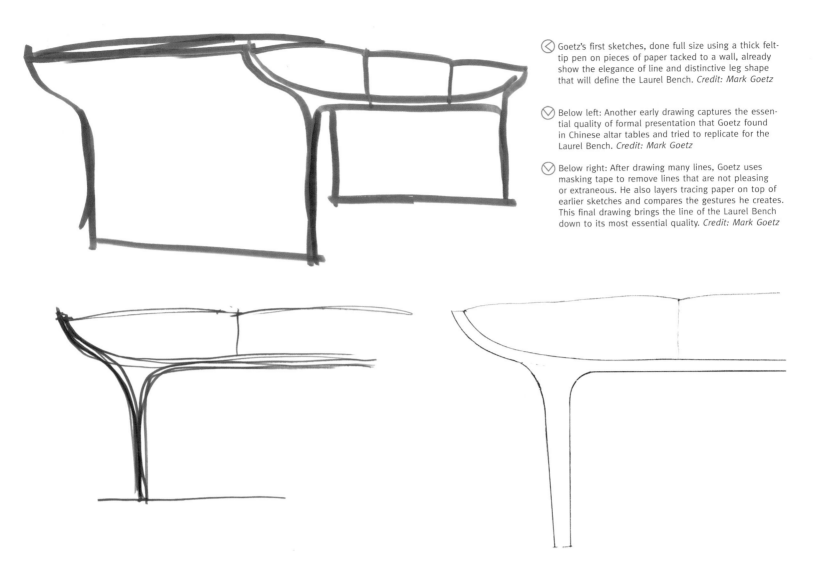

⊘ Goetz's first sketches, done full size using a thick felt-tip pen on pieces of paper tacked to a wall, already show the elegance of line and distinctive leg shape that will define the Laurel Bench. *Credit: Mark Goetz*

⊘ Below left: Another early drawing captures the essential quality of formal presentation that Goetz found in Chinese altar tables and tried to replicate for the Laurel Bench. *Credit: Mark Goetz*

⊘ Below right: After drawing many lines, Goetz uses masking tape to remove lines that are not pleasing or extraneous. He also layers tracing paper on top of earlier sketches and compares the gestures he creates. This final drawing brings the line of the Laurel Bench down to its most essential quality. *Credit: Mark Goetz*

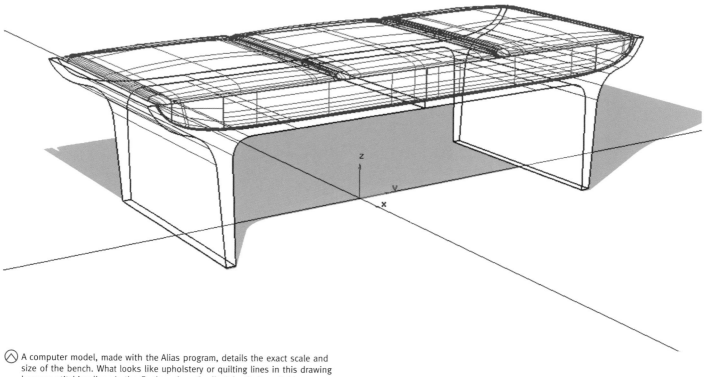

A computer model, made with the Alias program, details the exact scale and size of the bench. What looks like upholstery or quilting lines in this drawing become stitching lines in the final version. *Credit: John Switzer Kohler*

Goetz lays down line after line, and then goes back with tape and masks out the ones that aren't working. "In a way, I sculpt out the line I'm looking for," he says. Then he applies layer after layer of tracing paper. "I try to draw a smaller line, and I ask myself if what I've just drawn is better than the one below. If it is good, I keep the one on top. I go through about ten of these, and the final result is one thin pencil line," he explains. "Some objects, like this bench, are perfectly described as a line for their form. This one is really about the lines as they present themselves in front view and then extrude their way back into the form."

From the pencil line, Goetz makes a cardboard model. "What I'm looking for is taking that line and bringing it into three dimensions. That's when I work with proportions and how as a three-dimensional object, it communicates its function." Goetz points out that there are two other critical components to his design process: trust your feelings and take lots of breaks. "I'll do a drawing, go have lunch, and then ask myself if it's still feeling like I thought it was. The same thing with models. I will build it and then I will evaluate it another time. I try not to generate work and evaluate work at the same time or the same sitting. If you scrutinize your work as you're creating, you don't create anything. You shouldn't be too hard on something that's just sprouting as an idea."

Goetz knows he has the proportions right when the model suddenly looks viable. "It's happened many times that someone has walked in and tried to sit in a model because we're not used to seeing something that's so believable. This is the point where it becomes very exciting, where you can say, Wow! This is going to be real. Once I'm convinced of that, then we put it in the computer and it just keeps looking better." Goetz also points out that working in full-scale models saves money for the manufacturer;

because he's already gotten the scale, proportion, and details dialed in, they can make fewer prototypes.

The final Laurel Bench is carved and shaped from ten pieces of solid parawood, an indigenous Asian hardwood. And Goetz is very clear who gets credit for the ultimate beauty of the final piece. "The one element that isn't talked about much and should be is that I get wonderful direction from Bernhardt, not just technical, but creative direction as well. We have worked together for so many years, that I will often design something to a certain level, and the last 10 or 20 percent, I will rely on input from other people who make the furniture. This might result in a piece that's easier to manufacture, has some beautiful details I didn't' think about, and most often it will result in a perfecting of the proportions." While Goetz prefers the Laurel bench to have the high contrast of very dark wood with a very light-colored cushion, the piece is available in ten standard colors and any custom finish.

And the name of the bench? "We all responded well to Laurel because it's not only a tree, but to me, it has a noble quality about it." It's also important to note that Goetz's secret hope for the Laurel bench ultimately came true. "My greatest satisfaction of the piece is that it's getting ordered a lot for people to put in front of their beds," he reports. "I find that to be one of the greatest compliments. It tells me that people are not just responding to it out of respect, but they have a very personal attachment to the piece that they'd bring it into their homes and then have it right in front of their beds. With all that I go through in my process, I'm trying to put some of myself into the design, some emotion and feeling that I have about the piece. When I hear that people feel very strongly about the piece, or they've become attached to it, or have these strong personal feelings about it, that tells me that I've succeeded."

A paper model is made to full scale. Goetz feels strongly that a sensually accurate model helps a piece of furniture suddenly come alive and become real in the designer's—and sometimes, potential user's—minds. *Credit: Mark Goetz*

The Laurel Bench is offered in a variety of finishes and upholstery options, but Goetz is partial to the high-drama of the high-contrast between dark wood and a light cushion, as shown here.
Credit: Bernhardt Design, Lisa Adams Photography

Park Lane Bench, Björn Dahlstrom, Dahlstrom Design

"I've always been quite **interested** in the public space," notes Björn Dahlstrom. "I think it's quite **fascinating** when you have a lot of **people** who don't know each other sharing a space

The wood and metal Park Lane Bench offers an "island in the park" that makes a welcoming and expansive gesture to the public. *Credit: Nola*

and furniture in a museum or someplace. It's like experimenting with what kind of a space you need for when you sit next to people you don't know."

When he began to design the Park Lane Bench for Nola, Dahlstrom turned his attention from interior public spaces to the world outside. "I thought of the bench as sort of an island in a park or the city environment. Instead of creating wooden armrests at the end of the bench, I wanted to do something that made a gesture outwards. It gives you a little bit of space to put your bag down but also to shield you from the environment." Dahlstrom began his sketching directly in the computer, creating strong horizontal lines that swooped around at either end, almost like a running track. The strength of the gesture reflects Dahlstrom's early career in design. "Many of my works start with some kind of graphic idea. I started out as a graphic designer, so it's very important for me to make communicative and quite strong graphic pieces."

One of the Park Lane's unique features is an elegant combination of wood and metal. While this contrast creates visual interest, it was also done in response to pragmatic concerns. "Sweden is quite a cold country," Dahlstrom points out, "and doing something from pure aluminum is not practical; it's too cold to sit down. You need the wood to have a nice material to rest against. The aluminum was good to use for the bent part. It's quite a harsh environment, so if you used bent wood for the outer part, it would get destroyed by the weather. You have too much stress built into the wood material, and sooner or later it would pop out." The two elements also add to the graphic statement that is so important to Dahlstrom: "I like that when you follow one of those boards, you have wood, and then it translates into aluminum and then it's wood again. Then, when you see the bench from behind, in a backlight, it's like a silhouette. It's all black, and you don't see the change so it becomes even more of a graphic image."

While the shape of the final bench is stunningly close to Dahlstrom's original computer sketches, there were a few design and production details to be sorted out when the piece was considered full scale. "We did have to do some tests to try the seat angles and such," Dahlstrom says, "and we had to change some things to get it comfortable from the angle of the seat to the back, and the angle of the seat itself." Then came the more challenging part. "When that was finished and we were happy with the comfort, we did the geometry for the aluminum parts, and that was actually quite tricky," he recalls. "This is quite a big aluminum piece. Of course, also the mold is quite big and costly, so we had to really think in a good way to make it not so costly. What we did was make the aluminum part the same, just turn it 180 degrees. So

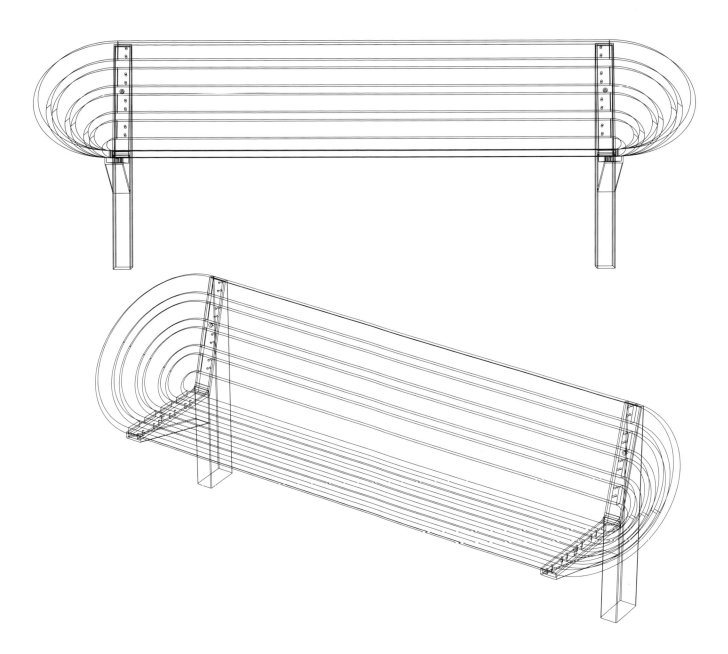

there are four different curves and each piece looks exactly the same from both sides," he explains. "Every mold has two halves, and then you have these very tricky parting lines, and you have to have them in just the right spot to get them to separate. My studio did it together with Nola. They have great experts as they do quite a lot of aluminum casting."

The back supports and feet are made of a single beam of steel that can be anchored to the ground in a park and has been given a surface treatment so it will look similar to the aluminum. Dahlstrom chose to have two rather than four legs. "I wanted it to be a little bit floating," he says. "The leg goes from the back straight down, so the seat is floating, which gives it quite a nice silhouette," he notes.

The seat and back will be available in a variety of wood, according to client requests. In addition, Dahlstrom notes that in Stockholm, park benches are traditionally dark green: "They are quite nice and we just did some computer sketches that show what the Park Lane would look like if you painted the whole thing green,

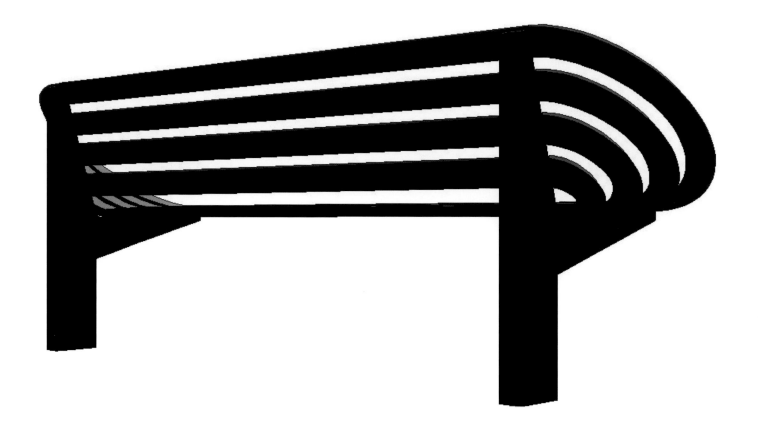

⬡ Top: A screen grab from the 3D modeling program shows the beginning of the structural details, such as the angle of the seat and relation of the seat to the back. Two steel supports create legs that can be anchored to the ground, and yet give the bench a feeling of floating above the earth. *Credit: Dahlstrom Design*

⬡ Above left: The curving end pieces were made of cast aluminum to provide strength in weather extremes. Each end piece of four curves is a mirror image of the other, allowing them to use one mold for both. *Credit: Dahlstrom Design*

⬡ Technical, three-dimensional drawings, created by Dahlstrom Design and the manufacturer, Nola, are used to get every detail exactly right so there are no mistakes when making the very-expensive molds. *Credit: Dahlstrom Design*

even the aluminum." The wood and metal parts are invisibly attached to one another with screws in the backside. "There are a series of holes in the aluminum, and there is an overlap on the wood. So on the side you're sitting or resting your back on, you don't see any screws," Dahlstrom points out. "You screw it all together, then you put it onto the leg structure, so all the screws holding the wood are not visible because they're inside the leg structure."

One of the things Dahlstrom finds most pleasing about the final product is that its form creates a strong—and changing—graphic image from all angles. Dahlstrom's first foray taking what he learned from graphics into three dimensions happened with a toy. "I've always been interested in furniture design," he says. "I had the opportunity to do this by doing wooden toys. I did a rocking toy built on flat pieces of wood that people put together themselves. The flat pieces were exactly what I wanted to see about translating my graphic design into 3D products. I could work flat and have it put together in a kind of sculptural way. Since I was interested in furniture," he continues, "I started to do things for my own sake, like furniture for my own studio." In 1993, he exhibited a small collection at the Stockholm Furniture Fair, and the next year went to the Milan Furniture Fair. Now, graphic design makes up only a small percentage of his work, while the majority is in product, furniture, and industrial design. "I'm really happy with what I'm doing," Dahlstrom says. "When you do ordinary graphic design, it's on a flat paper, and you have a fixed view on things; it's supposed to be looked at 90 degrees to the paper. But in the case of furniture, as you move around the object, you see different patterns and details, and to me it's more exciting."

⊗ From any angle, the Park Lane Bench creates a powerful outline that reflects Dahlstrom's professional beginnings as a graphic designer. *Credit: Nola*

Rocks, Arik Levy "There was only the **urge** to create a new object," says Arik Levy of the **inspiration** for Rocks. "An object which has a **fascinating** appearance and represents the **contrast** between the **human being** and **nature,**

To its designer, this highly polished piece of metal in the shape of a rock represents a whole range of complexities in our relationship to nature.
Credit: Arik Levy, L Design

between something which is open and closed, between something solid and soft, and something which appears and disappears as it reflects it's environment."

It's hard to say exactly what Rocks is or are. Perhaps it is a bench, or a seat, or a piece of garden sculpture. Most simply, they are highly polished pieces of metal made to resemble the shape of a hunk of stone. But for Levy, they represent an almost ironic, or at least complex, relationship between humanity and the natural world. "When you have it at home, say as a sculpture or low coffee table or bench, you make what you want out of it," he says. "You bring a visual representation of notions that we know out of nature. When you bring this home, it reflects the home environment, it becomes part of the people and the interior design and the atmosphere. At the same time, it makes you feel something about nature, but it's a scientific and metaphoric nature." He continues, "Then, when it's outside, it brings the idea of man doing something, it brings this idea outside, among the rocks or the garden or at the swimming pool or on the roof."

To enhance this dichotomous vision, Levy focused his design efforts on the quality and size of the surfaces. "This feels like an object that has been sculpted, rather than a big rock that has broken off," he notes. "It's the proportion between the facets, the dimension of each facet, that fills in and creates the invisible rest of the object that will stay in the mind of someone." Levy explains that this notion of seeing what has been left out is critical to understanding the visceral impression created when you behold one of his Rocks. "If you look at a hand without a finger, you complete the hand. When you look at this, it has quite a bit of straight and horizontal surfaces and the eye wants to complete the cube. You'll see what was taken off more than what was left behind, because it's closer to the action. What you see is not the cube, but what's left. You see the contact surface of what was taken off. It's not that you see the cube, but you want to complete it in your mind. We look for the continuation of the surfaces. It's like typography—the words are actually read by seeing the space that's left around them."

What Levy wants people to see is not just the space from which the object may have been created, but also the environment from which the whole notion of the piece was derived. "If I make something that makes someone feel—for example, you can feel nature even if you're not seeing it, you feel the sense of rock before you've touched it—I send you to an emotional experience. This is one of the big successes of these pieces."

To create this complete sensory experience, Levy did some very basic and hands-on work. "I begin with, I went to the office on

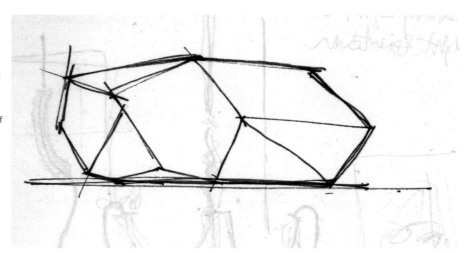

⟩ A sketch shows the facets and sculptural quality of the natural object that interested the designer, which he sought to re-create in a more ironic and challenging material. *Credit: Arik Levy, L Design*

⟨ This sketch shows the designer exploring the relationship of the shapes, sizes, and angles of the facets to one another, as well as the tension that is created between two objects placed together. *Credit: Arik Levy, L Design*

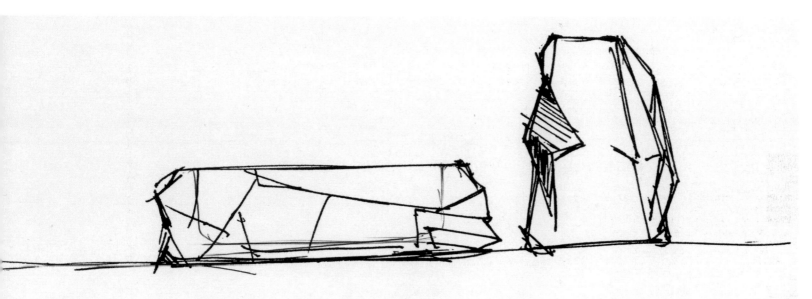

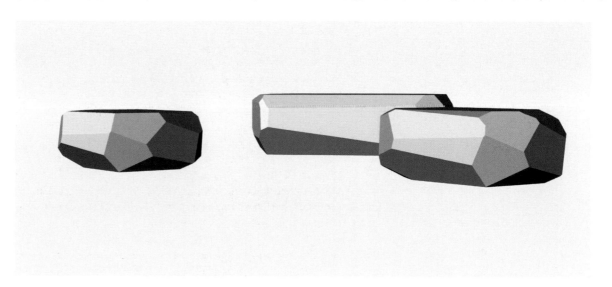

⟨ Another three-dimensional rendering of a group of Rocks allows the viewer to see the purity of each facet, without the visual confusion of the polished metal reflecting its surroundings. *Credit: Arik Levy, L Design*

Sunday, went to the workshop, took a few pieces of foam, ground them, and looked at it and ground it again, and looked at it again, and then said, 'That's it.' " Once he had this physical object, he and his staff created a three-dimensional file on the 3D modeler, and scaled it up to real size. Then, they created a kind of map of the image that could be laid flat and then folded back up into the desired shape. These files were sent to a workshop that specializes in custom bars and railings, what Levy refers to as "impossible stainless steel work." They laser cut 3mm ($\frac{1}{8}$") thick stainless steel sheets, following the map. Levy explains that where the surfaces change orientation, about half are banded, or folded, and about half are welded. "Not all parts are on a connecting axis," he notes. "When you have parts where there are three or five axes, you have to cut and paste, as it were." After the metal has been folded and welded, it is ground and polished to a mirror finish. "It reflects its environment," Levy says, "and makes things look soft or hard or empty or full."

Each Rock is handmade and totally empty inside. At the workshop, "They didn't even ask what is it," Levy recalls. "This was so odd, they didn't even ask. I said it has to be like this, and they just said, okay, okay, okay. Then they started making it and, just fell in love with it. It has an emotional relationship to them. It was very beautiful that people that are cutting and welding metal suddenly become emotional about an object that is not part of their own culture."

The Rocks come in three different sizes, and weigh about 30, 18, and 12 kilos (13 $\frac{1}{2}$, 8, and 5 $\frac{1}{2}$ lb.) each. Levy sees them working together, but is not prescriptive as to how. "They could be grouped, or used as just one or two. How you position them one next to the other, that is done intuitively because you create tension between the sizes. There's no single orientation, there is no one right orientation; there are many different ones. Because it is such an all around object, you can use it in many different ways. I don't suggest any particular thing." Levy clearly enjoys the confusion and intrigue created by coming upon a highly polished rock that appears to have fallen from a passing space ship. "I like the looks people give it," he says. "Some people just say, 'Wow I want it.' Some people come up, and we have a really nice discussion. It's like a jumping off point; it's not what it is, but what it makes people do or think or talk about."

The Rocks, no matter which shape or size you're looking at, defy easy categorization and can hardly be called furniture. It's a new kind of object that not only reflects, but seems to take on its surroundings. "It's connected into my more sculptural work," Levy says. "It's a really a good example for myself of where design and art meets today, which is a fine blurry border, where an object can have a function without being a bench, and can have an artistic function without being called a sculpture."

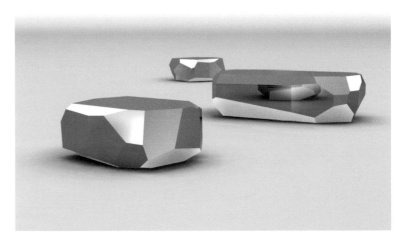

⊗ Top: Set outside, the Rock reflects its environment, making a statement for the designer about human influence on nature, and also proving to be a fascinating conversation starter. *Credit: Arik Levy, L Design*

⊗ Three-dimensional computer renderings of a group of Rocks show the possibilities imagined by the designer—not only are the pieces sculptural on their own, but they create new tableaus depending upon how they are grouped together.
Credit: Arik Levy, L Design

⊘ Opposite: Arik Levy gets a taste of his creation: "It refers to the 'feel before you see' idea," he says, "so when you put it in the mouth, you can feel the form."
Credit: Arik Levy, L Design

Swiss Benches, or *Los Bancos Suizos*, Alfredo Häberli

After getting a **call** from the Spanish company Bd Ediciones de Diseño, Alfredo Häberli kicked off his **creative process** the way a **short story** writer might, by first imagining his characters.

⊘ The complete line of *Los Bancos Suizos*, or Swiss Benches, by Alfredo Häberli is a versatile, mix-and-match, add-and-subtract, group of outdoor seating that allows people to gather for conversation and camaraderie, or even work while sitting down or standing up. *Credit: Bd Ediciones de Diseño*

⊘ Opposite: A series of sketches show the various characters Häberli imagined using his benches for everything from reading Neruda, to playing soccer or standing on your head. *Credit: Alfredo Häberli*

⊘ In this configuration, the Swiss Benches also function as an improvised soccer goal.
Credit: Bd Ediciones de Diseño

"Lucky for them, in Spain they have more sun than we do," Häberli says, describing how he got started designing his outdoor benches. "You can imagine the people spend more time outdoors, in the streets, in the piazzas, than we do. I just imagined people who were in a park. I thought of a couple, or a person who is alone, or a poet, or a guy who works at a bank, or a philosopher. So, I invent for myself this type of professional to create the shape of these benches to give them a stronger character than you would have in a typical bench." Häberli considered how a poet might sit in the park and ponder a poem on a warm afternoon, or how a couple might want to meet for an intimate lunch together, or a banker who sits in his office all day might need a respite from his desk. From this sympathy for how people could better use and enjoy public spaces, he created a uniquely practical, versatile, and beautiful outdoor furniture system.

Häberli points out that his process is not typical of most furniture designers. "My way of working is not a formalistic one," he says. "I don't have such a strong handwriting. There is always a little bit of humor, always very light, but in general, my pieces they are not minimalistic. My projects always have a thought behind. Just to come up with shape? That is not the way I'm working. It is not the shape which is the most interesting to me, but it's the thought behind the project."

For example, Häberli carefully thought through the needs of a busy professional who might wander into a park on his lunch break. "I was thinking of a banker who sits all the day, so I make the height of the bench a high bar so, when he wants to make a break, he can stand and read the newspaper or have a sandwich or a drink." Then, Häberli discovered something else interesting about this particular design. "When I was showing that, looking at the drawing, I saw it could also be a goal for kids who are playing soccer. And this is the way I love to do product, with some inspiration. It is not a normal bench, but it makes small steps in design history. It is a new typology which did not exist until today."

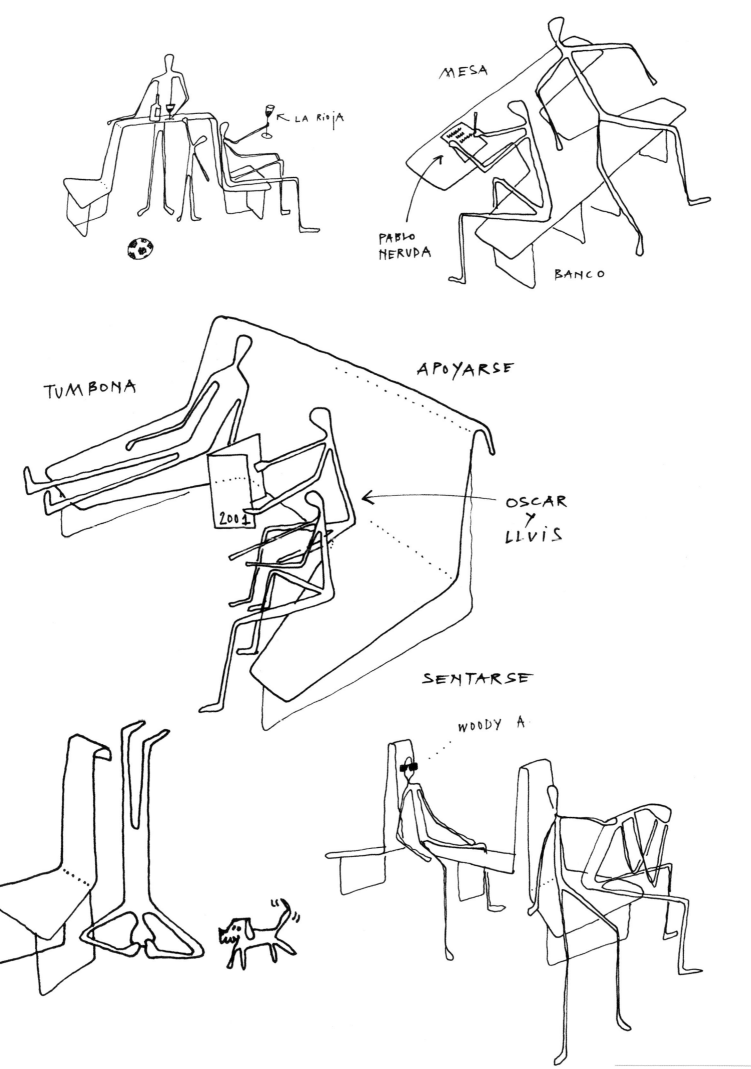

K LA RIOJA

MESA

PABLO NERUDA

BANCO

TUMBONA

APOYARSE

2001

OSCAR Y LLUIS

SENTARSE

WOODY A

The humor that Häberli values is also evident in the product's name. They considered calling the collection Time Out, but then realized that when you translate Swiss Benches into Spanish, a natural pun arises: the word for bench and bank is one and the same. "Even the name is trying to add value to the piece," Häberli jokes.

When it came to fabricating the benches, Häberli wanted the furniture to reflect its setting. A framework of galvanized metal tubes was covered with laser-cut sheet metal that had been stamped with a delicate pattern of small holes. "It's too small so you can't go in with a finger. You can't hurt yourself," he notes. The pattern itself" ". . . was inspired by flowers and nature and we transfer this pattern step-by-step to just holes at the end. But the first image was like flowers," he says. In addition to the galvanized version, the benches are also available ". . . painted in bronze, which is a color I love very much. It's inspired by the Mediterranean architecture," Häberli continues. "We're fed up a little bit with chrome. The bronze, it's warm, like wood, but still has the quality of metal to be outside all the year." For added flexibility, the pieces are screwed together, not only for ease of transport, but also so they can be assembled in different combinations of seats, benches, tables, or counters. This modularity means that the furniture can be configured as the site demands, from clusters that allow small gatherings to eat or play chess together, to a single, endless bench set along a pathway, to symmetric groupings that allow pairs or individuals a place to rest, to myriad of other possibilities. Including, of course, goalposts.

⊘ Bottom: A technical drawing shows not only detail about dimensions, but also the joints that allow the benches to be put together to create a cluster or string as long or compact as desired. *Credit: Bd Ediciones de Diseño*

⊘ In the Bd workshop, a paper print out of the nature-inspired patterns of holes is laid over a mock up to show the beauty and delicacy obtained by the cut outs. *Credit: Bd Ediciones de Diseño*

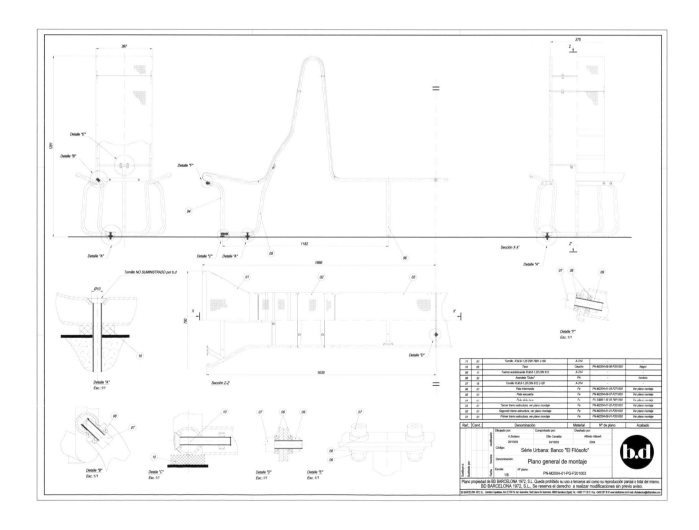

The biggest manufacturing challenge was to ensure the benches would be comfortable in spite of their material hardness. To get the correct ergonomics, Häberli looked back at the human bodies that were his initial inspirations. "If you look to the shape of the benches, in the lower back, you have a double S, and you will not believe it, but when you sit in that bench, it's a lot more comfortable than a lot of sofas," he reports. "We took a lot of care on that. You have a big support on your lower back. And the angle of the sitting, it goes a little bit down to the back, so your legs and knees are higher than your bottom," he explains.

Looking at Los Bancos Suizos now, Häberli reflects on the importance of patience and trusting your instincts. "It showed me that we have to believe in our feeling that comes from the stomach and just follow that route," he says. "And I learned that good ideas don't have a time." He points out that the same climate that brings people to the park to use his benches, also lends itself to a slower pace in product development. "It took us three years to develop this. Spain has beautiful weather so they don't work as much because they are always outside! I grew up in Argentina, so I should know this," he laughs. "But this idea is still valid three years later because it's a new typology of small inventions and completely new shapes created by these people I imagined I was designing for. Sometimes, you see things that are more quickly done, and after a year, well, it's not so interesting anymore."

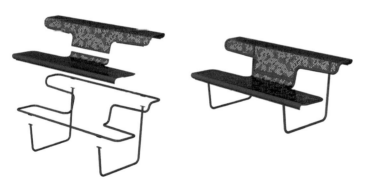

Häberli, in his characteristically humanistic way, is already well on his way to imagining additional users for the next round of Swiss benches/banks. "We are already working on new ones, including one for the homeless. I just hate it when, you know, they put bars in between the benches so the homeless people cannot lie down. I am making the opposite. I want to make a living room so the homeless can meet their friends and sit together all the afternoon. That's the next step," he says. "Another private bank."

Aspen Sofa, Jean-Marie Massaud When describing his design inspirations, Jean Marie Massaud returns **again and again** to **metaphors** from **nature** and literature.

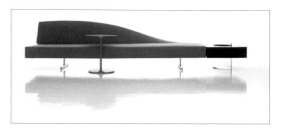

The Aspen Sofa is actually a collection of three pieces; a right and left version that can be used separately or combined into one large sofa, or a smaller, stand-alone version pictured here. *Credit: Nicola Zocchi*

"When you look at nature and how life is growing, it's not square," he says. "It's an ecosystem which is very rich in terms of life. It is the same thing as composing a sentence. This collection is speaking about furniture as a reef, a living thing, a solution that lets you use space in a different manner." And within this context, his Aspen sofa, developed for Cassina, is ". . . an articulation, a punctuation that gives it strength and strangeness in space."

The Aspen is actually three different pieces. There is a right and left version, each of which is an elegant study in asymmetry: one edge flows fluidly from two planes to a single surface, while the other edge appears chopped off in a bold, 90-degree stroke. These pieces can be used individually or attached to their mirror image to create a single, large sofa. Alternatively, there is a smaller, one-piece sofa of the same shape, the rounded mountain of its back rising gently from the flat plain of its seat. While Massaud enjoys all the pieces, he favors the individual halves: "Symmetry is death," he says. "Asymmetric is life."

In keeping with this metaphor, Massaud found developing the Aspen sofa was a natural process. He reports that one of the pleasures of working with Cassina is the creative freedom they offered. "Once they ask you to design for them, they already agree with your universe and your ideas," he says. "Of course, we had to discuss details and technique, but they are already with you, and they let you go creatively." Massaud was aware that his client had a predominant aesthetic, and he wanted to offer them something that broke their particular mold. "In the world of Cassina, things are quite precise," he points out. "I wanted to speak about fluidity, lightness, something that is not expected." Apparently, Cassina agreed, as the direction of the entire collection was articulated in a single meeting. "In the very first drawings, everything was expressed and they agreed with the whole attitude, which is about much more than shape," Massaud says. "It's about a way to understand and live within space. In this attitude, the sofa was not the finality, but part of the whole setting. I wanted to speak openly in space, with light in the room, to feel energy everywhere, but also create intimacy and connection."

Just like regarding a natural landscape, the contours of the Aspen sofa change dramatically, depending upon the angle at which you look at it. Made of injected foam on a stainless steel frame, a deep, structural slit turns what you expect to be a single, padded entity into two separate planes, jutting away from one another. According to Massaud, other, much more organic shapes were considered, but were rejected when it became clear that they would be too difficult to develop. "We arrived at something that is comfortable, but with a shape that expresses a story and looks like a piece of something folded," he explains.

⊗ The right and left versions of the Aspen can be combined to form one larger symmetrical sofa. Here, it is paired with an Auckland chair. *Credit: Nicola Zocchi*

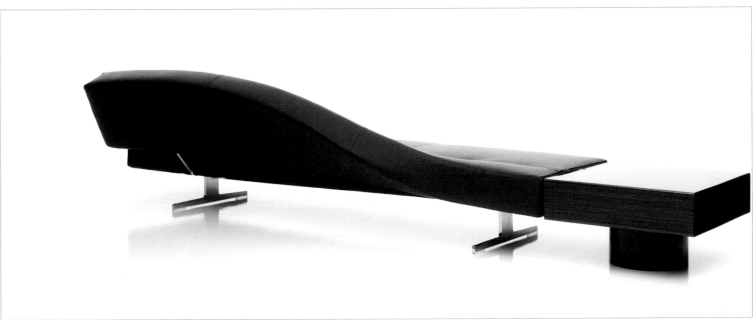

⊗ The most distinctive design element of the Aspen is not only the curve of the back, but also the surprising structural split that is especially dramatic when viewed from behind. *Credit: Nicola Zocchi*

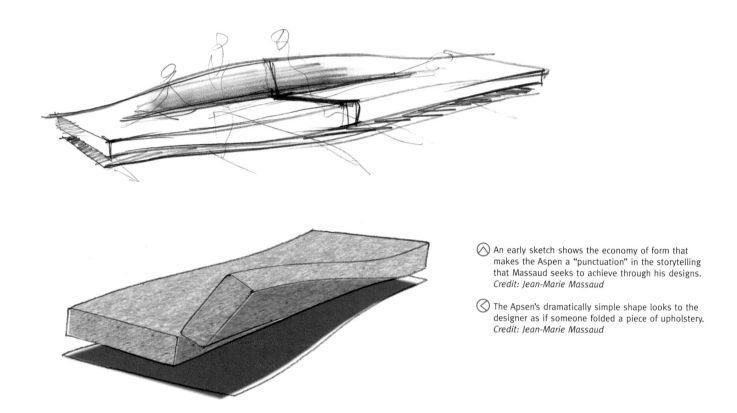

Massaud says he is surprised at how well the sofa has been received. "At first, it was just there to be a surprise, a kind of provocation. I thought people would smile and be entertained," he laughs. "But they don't see it as some kind of a monster. People actually want it."

Massaud envisions his sofa as an accent that is appropriate in a wide variety of contexts. "It's so different and pure that it goes with everything. I prefer to think of it in an eclectic universe," he says. "I like mixing avant garde and things from, say, my grandmother."

For Massaud, design functions as a metaphor for how we should live. "All life is based on eclectic references," he says. "If you propose a world where all is the same, then you are already dead. It is too artificial." To this end, Massaud suggests pairing the sophisticated silhouette of the Aspen with unusual fabrics, such as artificial fur or a bold color. Even florals. "I want to shake cultural references," he states.

The Aspen is the "continuation of a long story," for Massaud, who has been designing furniture for over fifteen years. When he graduated from college, he thought he wanted to do only product design. "But to have an influence in the market economy, you have to be an opinion leader, and in the design scene, this is done through furniture," he feels. Massaud works in partnership with an architect and has designed numerous products including crystal and fragrances.

When asked how all these efforts influence one another, he returns to his literary metaphor. "In architecture, you speak about the story, the statement, the universe, how people are living there. You can describe it like a fiction, a book, where all the elements of the lighting, windows, etcetera, are like words that speak side-by-side to tell a story. If you're telling the same thing all the time, it's boring. If it's part of a complex story, you begin to understand that you are in a special place."

Massaud feels strongly that design has to not just only function in the world, but also add real value to the story of our lives. "It's a question of meaning and contextual approach," he says. "It's not about form or shape. You have to ask: What is the human, cultural, or political context? What is the way of life of the people who will use this? What is important is the human part." Massaud continues, "Progress is not interesting just as technological movement, but only if it adds quality to the lives of people. Shape has to crystallize the meaning of the project. It has to express the exceptional time and place you will live in."

For Massaud, design is a process of making his personal vision consequential. "From the prism of my eyes, I am trying to express what is the content, what do you gain by living there or using this. It's a question of meaning more than style."

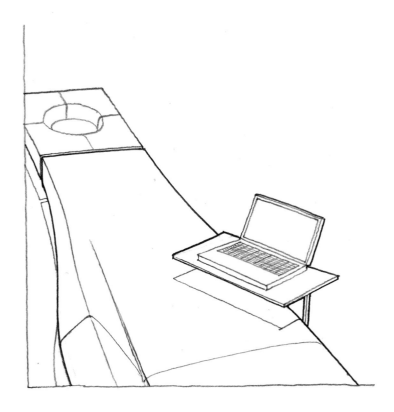

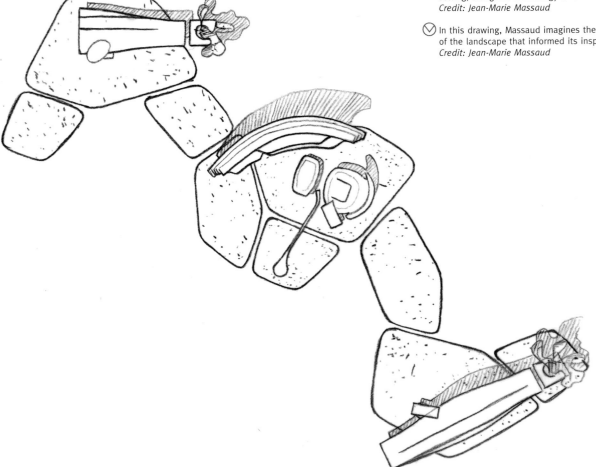

⬆ Left: Part of Massaud's goal in designing the Aspen was to create a form so pure that it would be comfortable in any setting and make a strong statement in eclectic collections.
Credit: Jean-Marie Massaud

⬆ The Aspen is equally at home in a domestic or commercial setting, alongside technology or the comforts of home.
Credit: Jean-Marie Massaud

⬇ In this drawing, Massaud imagines the Aspen sofa as part of the landscape that informed its inspiration and design.
Credit: Jean-Marie Massaud

Comet Sofa, Vladimir Kagan "I've always believed in furniture **liberated** from the walls of a **room**," says Vladimir Kagan. "Most of my **clients** were collectors of art, so they needed to liberate the walls for art **work**."

The Comet Sofa is a modular piece made of a central chair with a right and left end that can be added, removed, or reconfigured to create a wide range of seating options and orientations.
Credit: Michel Gibert, Roche-Bobois

With the Comet Sofa, Kagan continues his decades-long tradition of creating sensuous sofas that sit in the middle of a room and allow for a wide range of seating configurations. "These free-form designs have been the driving force of my designs," he says. "I like to make something that can be moved, rearranged, and allows you to sit in different directions." The Comet began when Roche Bobois came to Kagan looking for designs that reflected his quintessential design vernacular. "I went to visit them in their Washington, D.C. store," Kagan recalls. "I brought along a whole suitcase of designs, but all of a sudden, I was inspired and I started to sketch on the train. It just hit right," he says. "I do well sketching under abnormal circumstances. I work on airplanes, on the corner of a table in somebody's house—the inspiration hits that way." He says, "I'm a doodler. I was doodling. I always travel with a roll of tracing paper, so I start drawing at one end and keep going to the other."

The charge was to make a sofa that had the "Kagan" aesthetic written all over it, but to also make the piece modular so its configuration and colors can be customized by the end user. "We came up with this idea of a free-flowing sofa, with a central axis of a chair, and two free-form sofas at either end," says Kagan. "You can add or subtract color and make it very personal that way. You can customize the piece of furniture." He points out, "Manufacturers do not want to have a lot of frames and product on a shelf that makes up a collection. This collection has only three SKUs, and they love that. They don't need to carry a lot of different inventory. You have left and rights and you can drop off the back of the chair so it becomes a pouf. The whole thing is very flexible, yet with a very limited number of elements. The way the furniture pivots around the center round chair, you can open it up and make it a straight sofa or make it very tight and fit in a corner. You can have half in one direction and one in another. It can be ordered without a back, and then it would be a huge, open pouf that would give you seating in all directions."

Kagan adds, "The serpentine sofa comes from the late 1940s. Every manufacturer wants to license that product, so I have to think how can I give them something like that." For the Comet, Kagan says, "I worked with the serpentine concept and tried to bring it into the twenty-first century."

The Comet is made of layers of differing density foam over wooden frames. Roche-Bobois offers it with removable slipcovers in a wide range of fabric choices. "People enjoy it because you can play with it," says Kagan. "You could do it monochromatic or in quite contrasting colors. It becomes very personal, which is great, because color is very subjective and color is what identifies people."

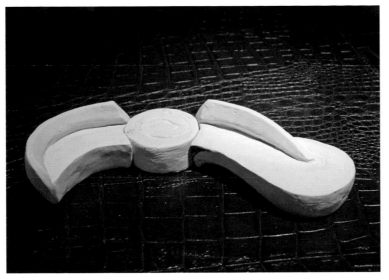

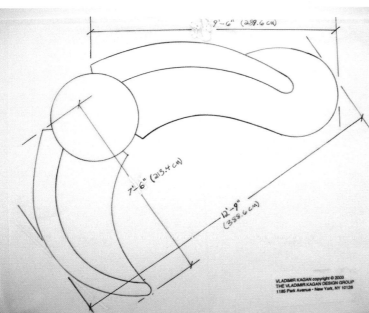

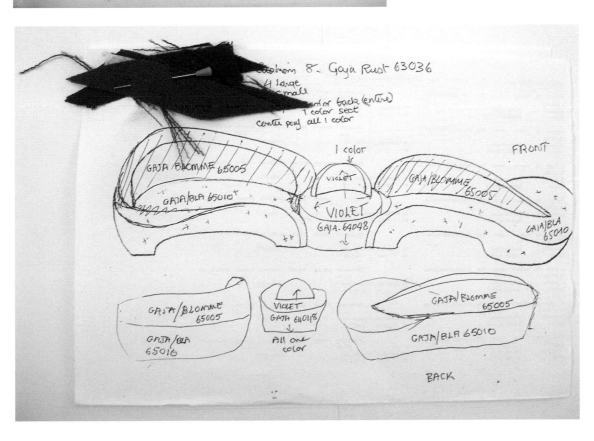

△ Above left: Clay models show the three component parts of a central chair with a sofa that extends off either end like the tail of a comet, hence the name. *Credit: Vladimir Kagan*

△ Kagan was prepared to show the manufacturer, Roche-Bobois, several design options, but on the train ride to the meeting, began sketching a new idea, which turned into the Comet. *Credit: Vladimir Kagan*

◁ When all three parts are used together, the Comet becomes a huge piece, almost 13' (4 m) feet in length. The pieces can be ordered without backs, so people can sit facing any direction. *Credit: Vladimir Kagan*

▽ The Comet is available in a wide range of fabric choices and is made with removable slipcovers over each piece, which allows customers to personalize the sofa. *Credit: Vladimir Kagan*

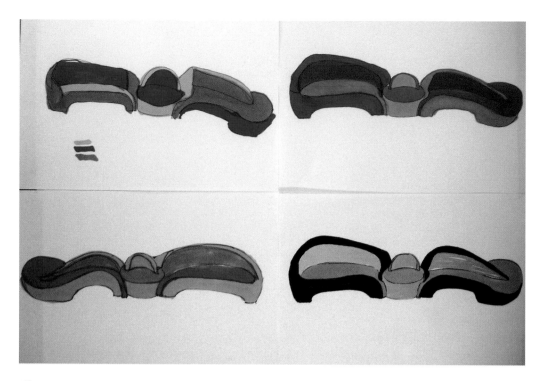

⊘ Color studies play up the trademark Kagan interest in free-flowing and organic shapes that help get the sofa off the wall and into the center of the room. *Credit: Vladimir Kagan*

⊗ Opposite top: The generous proportions, inviting shape, and multi-dimensionality of the Comet become fully realized in this full-scale prototype. *Credit: Vladimir Kagan*

⊗ Opposite bottom: The Comet can be ordered in monochromatic tones, but choosing different colors for each section and component part plays up the sensual lines as well as the piece's modularity. *Credit: Michel Gibert*

Kagan's interest in furniture design began early in his life and has continued for several decades. "My father was a cabinetmaker, and he needed me to help him in the shop," Kagan notes. "I studied architecture; I would prefer to be an architect, but necessity and reality drew me to furniture and that's what stuck. My father was a modernist, a very skilled craftsman," he says. "He made very boxy stuff. The organic stuff came to me later." And it came directly from nature itself. "When I was a teenager, my father said, 'Learn to draw,'" Kagan recalls. "I wanted to be an artist, and having artistic skills has been helpful. It's been a very important skill. I would draw from nature and doing so much drawing of nature, I sort of evolved a multilevel feeding of ideas. We would spend our summers in the Catskills, and we would sit on the rocks with the stream flowing through. It was such a wonderful way to sit, and I brought that concept in to the home—I call it interior landscaping."

Kagan's first pieces of furniture came out in the late 1940s, and many were not only icons in their own time, but are being rediscovered by a whole new generation who are giving them a fresh veneer of hipness. After so many years designing so many sofas, Kagan has no problem going back to the drawing board—or roll of tracing paper—and finding yet another way to express his personal design sensibility. "The very limitation is the challenge," he says. "I compare it to music. There are only so many notes in the scale. But using only those eight notes, think of all the magnificent music that has been written." He continues, "I am restricted by the anatomy of the human being, which dictates how a piece of furniture has to be made. Working with that very limitation is very challenging and frustrating. Architects can be much more sculptural and much more prima donnas, but they can design a building that doesn't work. But in a piece of furniture, the restrictions are so limiting that you have to behave yourself."

Unlike some designers who are always trying to reinvent themselves, Kagan also finds ongoing inspiration in his previous works. "I have the pleasure of revisiting myself because I've been doing this for so long. I was so far ahead of myself that there are things I've neglected. I go through archives with my clients, and what's in there stimulates my thinking. I don't like to recycle, I love making new, but you cannot get away from the idea that what goes around, comes around. I don't reject the past. I embrace the past."

Crescent Moon Sofa, Andrée Putman "It is my way to work," says Andrée Putman. "To be very **dreamy** and to tell myself lots of **stories**." Then she **adds**, "That's why I get along so well with **children**."

The Crescent Moon sofa was inspired as a companion piece to a rug that showed stars in the night sky.
Credit: Ralph Pucci International

Dreaming, stargazing, and contemplating the results of another project were the genesis of her Crescent Sofa. "I did a very big round rug," she explains. "The colors were, I think, at least five or six different dark blues. There was a lot of joy and happiness for all these blues to be mixed, because you hardly saw where they changed, but they had influence on each other, and I loved that. In these blues, I designed little stars of beige and gold and they were very small. In the end, this piece was called Milky Way." She continues, "This sky made me think of the Moon, and I wanted to do something with the Moon. I thought it would be incredibly nice to sit on the milky way of the floor and have the Moon for your body to sit on. You wouldn't find one person who didn't recognize the Moon when it starts to open, and it's that skinny Moon that does not last that long."

However, instead of creating a delicate crescent that hangs in the distance overhead, Putman brought her moon squarely down to earth. "I decided to make it so that it can be extravagantly big," she says. And extravagantly shaped. "What is interesting about the shape is that it really steals the show for people," Putman notes. "I like that expression very much—they steal the show by their shape, these pieces. The curve is very comfortable for the back," she adds. "The curve was the base of my idea. It has a croissant curve. Only the French could do that." For all the drama of its size and shape, the Crescent Moon Sofa achieves a feeling of lightness by a cluster of elegant feet that lift it delicately off the floor. "With feet, you have a rectangle or a square, and what I like is to put the feet on the corners of two squares facing each other obliquely," she explains. "I like that enormously."

The sofa itself is framed in a slender reveal of wood, and Putman kept the upholstery equally clean. "There is only one cushion for the whole seat, which is very unusual," she points out. "I like the idea that there are not too many cushions. I have a phobia for so many cushions," she says. "People like too many cushions to cover up the poverty of their taste. It's like they're hiding something."

Putman's design process involves bringing other people into her dreaming and storytelling world to create a seamless web of collaboration with the twenty people in her studio. "I work very classically," she says, and then quickly adds, "I don't draw very well. I speak a lot with the people who work here. I describe my vision, and they draw it out. There is no hierarchy. There are no disputes. It's very serene and wonderful. We believe very much in having fun—we need fun!" She and her team find and share inspirations gathered from a variety of sources. "We may bring in images that we saw that made us laugh or made us emotionally happy with a mix of color or a very strange and amusing idea," she says. "Of course, we are not going to use it as we find it, but maybe it is introduced in an interesting way, like a humorous detail."

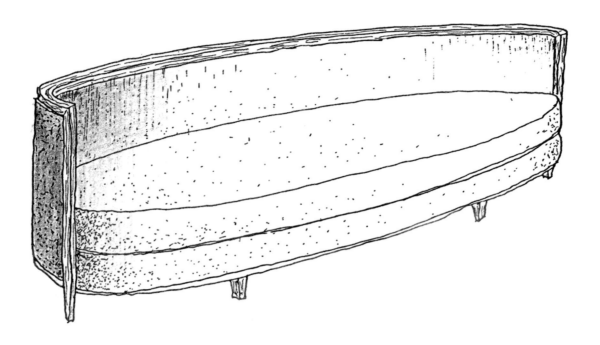

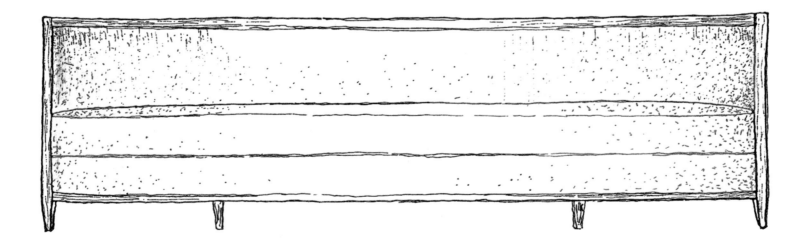

The Crescent Moon is a bit of a departure for Putman, who normally prefers that her sofas do not call attention to themselves; she describes the shape of the Crescent Moon as "eccentric" and "daring."
Credit: Andrée Putman

This mix of traditionalism and playfulness is something new for Putman's work in sofa design. "I only produce very classic and elegant couches where all the effort was to make them wonderfully comfortable and wonderfully proportioned, but not something with a lot of invention in the sense of shape," she says. "This one is really eccentric because of its shape. It is daring to have done that. In couches, I like them to disappear in the landscape of a living room, but this one doesn't disappear. As with many simple things, it appears more and more."

Ralph Pucci, gallery owner and producer of the Crescent Moon Sofa, agrees. "This is a classic. It's an iconic piece that is as fresh today as it will be in fifty years. It's a piece that will not tire, and I wanted the best manufacturing for it." For Pucci, the best way is the "old-fashioned way. It's all done in a small shop of just six men who do not rush. It's all hand done, with coils, a solid oak or mahogany frame, wrapped in cocoa mat, with foam cushions. It's built layer by layer, like a cake. This sofa will last a lifetime."

In addition to Putman's first inspiration of an oversized, 10′ (3 m)-long sofa, the Crescent is now available in 6′ and 8′ (1.8 and 2.4 m)-versions, as well as a club chair. It can be upholstered in leather or almost any fabric a customer wants, but Pucci points out that most often, luxurious fabrics are chosen. "We just did that sofa in a more showy way," he notes. "The frame was done in gold leaf. It looked very grand, not ornate at all."

For all its show-stealing qualities, ultimately it is the simplicity of the Crescent that makes it so appealing. "I believe in eclecticism," says Putman. "I believe you can have a pair of these couches, and just have a simple room with art on the wall and a few things on a table, and you'll have a very pleasant décor given by the shape of the curves on the sofa. It goes with all kinds of furniture. There is no limitation because of its simplicity." She adds, "The soft lines count and make it the backbone of a room. It's logical and easy, neither too sweet nor too austere. It something that brings, strangely, peace into the room because it's so comfortable for the body and also for the eyes." A result, no doubt, of the dreamy nature of its design inspiration.

⊗ The companion Crescent Moon club chair is manufactured in a similar fashion with layers of cocoa mat and foam cushioning over a coiled spring base. *Credit: Pucci*

⊗ Using a small shop and traditional methods, the Crescent Moon is made "the old-fashioned way" in oak or mahogany. *Credit: Ralph Pucci International*

⊘ ⊘ The Crescent Moon has grown into a complete line of sofas in 10', 8', and 6' (3, 2.4, 1.8 m)-versions, as well as a Club Chair. They can be upholstered in any fabric or leather.
Credit: Andrée Putman

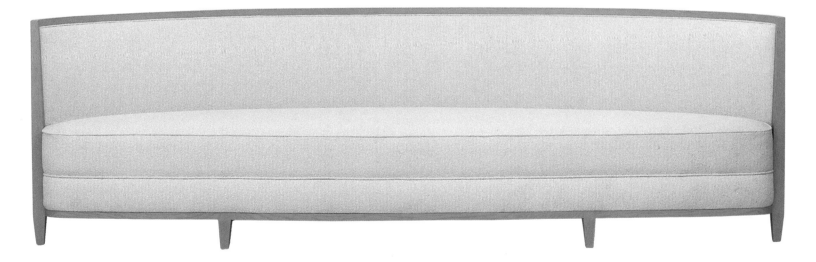

Fritz Sofa, Sarah Fels

"The idea was to **think** about how people might live in the **future**," recalls Sarah Fels of the beginning of the Fritz sofa project. "The initial brief was **so broad**, it was **almost** not a brief at all."

The Fritz Sofa expresses designer Sarah Fels' interest in faceted shapes as well as manufacturer Dune's expertise with upholstery to create a tightly tailored sofa with a timeless aesthetic. *Credit: Albert Vecerka*

While she often begins her designs with some kind of research, "this had more to do with thinking about poetic inspiration or images that stuck in my mind. I was thinking about a fairly diverse bunch of images, from the deco Chrysler building angularity, to the tech, cubist movement in architecture that produced all these crazy faceted objects and buildings, and also about punk spikiness. I was really interested in a faceted, angular language for furniture."

The ultimate shape of the sofa actually grew out of two other pieces of furniture. "The project really began as an armchair, and from that became an ottoman, and then a sofa," according to Fels. "That's not uncommon. When you start working on a project, you think about what else that idea can yield, and turning it into a family. In the context of the armchair, I was thinking about how this angular, formal language could conform to the body and the way people sit. I was thinking about the way a crooked arm and an elbow was shaped and how the chair could reflect that."

Fels was also keeping manufacturing in mind. While the producer, Dune, was not limited to any particular process, Fels knew that they were particularly skilled with upholstered pieces. "So, I was also thinking about projects that would be, in a way, advanced upholstery techniques, things that would show off what they can do really well."

To kick off her design process, Fels uses the old-fashioned tools of mechanical pencil and paper and begins to "sketch like crazy." She says the results usually range far and wide from where she started, but this is important to keep her mind open and her ideas fresh. She then sets the sketches aside for a period of time so that she can review them more objectively at a later date. Then it's time to sit at the computer. "I start making computer sketches, essentially, but they're actually renderings of wire frames of the object. And that is an amazing way for me to get to prototype the ideas quickly and find out why something that may have worked as a sketch is not working in 3D," Fels says. "I start thinking about the actual construction details a little bit and what they might be. But it's sort of a back-and-forth process, because thinking about the actual production drives the initial thoughts of what the idea can be; there's always this back and forth between where the form wants to go and what's possible production-wise. Ideally, the form reflects what the production process is. Those things should not be at cross purposes," she points out.

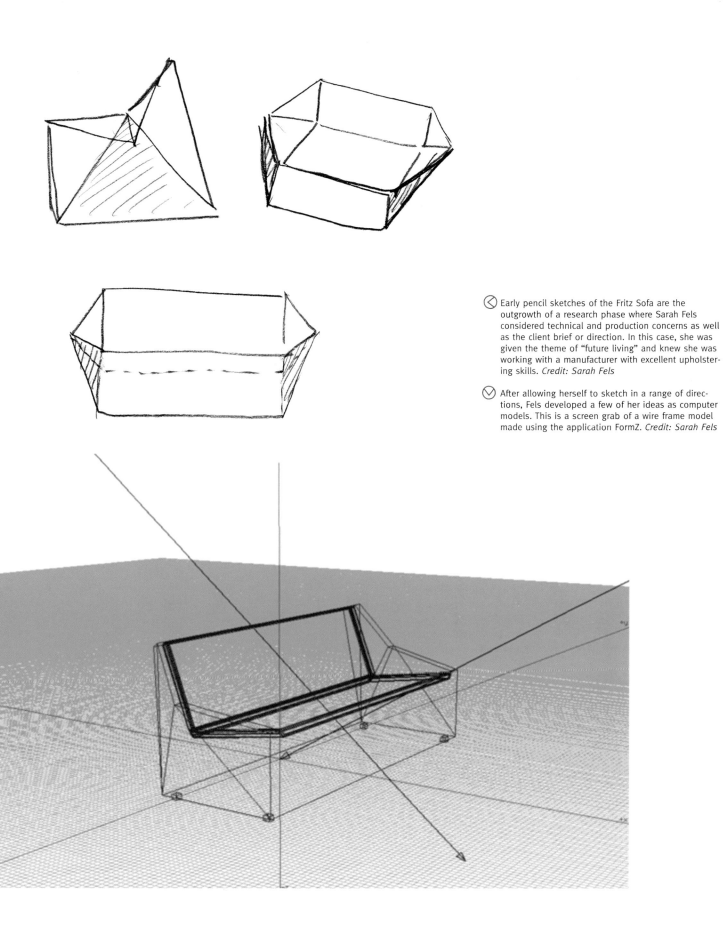

⊘ Early pencil sketches of the Fritz Sofa are the outgrowth of a research phase where Sarah Fels considered technical and production concerns as well as the client brief or direction. In this case, she was given the theme of "future living" and knew she was working with a manufacturer with excellent upholstering skills. *Credit: Sarah Fels*

⊘ After allowing herself to sketch in a range of directions, Fels developed a few of her ideas as computer models. This is a screen grab of a wire frame model made using the application FormZ. *Credit: Sarah Fels*

Once she has the form worked out, she presents these renderings to the client, showing the piece from various angles and elevations. She usually shows several ideas at once. In this case, after seeing all the options, Dune asked to return to her very first idea. "I had put it aside and the client came back and said remember that?" Fels recalls. "So we dusted it off. Sometimes it's not a linear process."

While Fels had set out to fully utilize all of Dune's upholstery capabilities, she didn't realize just how much of a challenge she was creating. "The formal idea really dealt with surfaces as opposed to the kind of puffy mass of an upholstered thing," she says. "In upholstery, it's very hard to get a crisp edge and a tight corner. But on the other hand, there's this traditional way of building a frame which is padded and sprung and covered in fabric, and that really does lend itself to these odd shapes. It took a lot of patience on the part of the people building it," she says. Unlike the more typical sofa, where dense cushions can hide a whole range of interior ills, with the Fritz, there was no room for error. "Every angle has to be correct for the whole thing to add up," Fels notes. "So the hard part was pushing the manufacturer to use all their frame building skills to arrive at what I had in mind. It was imposing a lot on the prototyper's patience and good will, but it all worked out in the end."

The solid mass of the sofa is relieved by the small feet peeking through at the bottom, which also addresses an important practical concern: "You always need some sort of foot," Fels says, "because floors are not even as a rule, and so if you just had the solid mass meeting the floor, it's almost guaranteed to be tippy. Feet save wear on the mass of the piece, and make it more stable on the floor." But equally important to Fels are the aesthetic considerations. "The feet also visually make for a somehow more pleasing transition from the object to the floor. Even for architects, there's always this question of how does the thing meet the ground, and it's a surprisingly difficult moment to finesse. But just by lifting this big, chunky thing off the ground a bit, you create this illusion that it's hovering, and it has this mysterious lightness. It's a more pleasing resolution."

Overall, the Fritz Sofa reflects both new and familiar design concerns for Fels. While the angularity is a different form than she usually creates, the focus on how the process helps create the form is a consistent theme in her work. "I'm always interested in my design work—not in a no-fun, didactic way—but in designing things that inform the user in some subtle way about how the object is made, or at least provoke an inquiry about how the object is made, and hopefully create some awareness that we live in a built environment. Because that, to me, is the sort of wonderful thing about

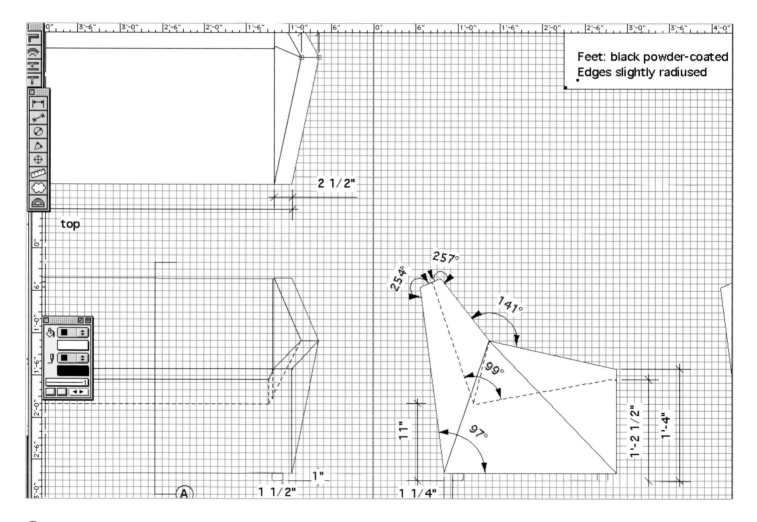

Using the program VectorWorks, the next phase in Fels's design process is to create a fully dimensioned mechanical drawing of the furniture piece. This screen grab shows a range of technical details such as angles and dimensions. *Credit: Sarah Fels*

⊘ In order to get a "clearer understanding of the form and construction issues," Fels does rendered computer models of her designs that show the real shape and dimension of the piece. *Credit: Sarah Fels*

⊘ In this computer model rendering showing front, back, and side views of the Fritz Sofa, Fels' interest in faceted shapes, tight corners, and clean upholstery is evident. *Credit: Sarah Fels*

design. It's this enormously powerful field in that everybody uses designed objects all the time, but it's kind of hidden in plain view. I'm interested in the potential of design to open up and reveal this amazing fact to people, and make them aware that things look the way they do for a series of reasons." Even if the impetus is not always intentional. "Sometimes, the reasons are not a brilliant idea; it might be an accident or someone's bad idea," Fels points out.

This awareness of design concerns and an emotional connection to furniture has been with Fels herself, apparently, since she was a child. "My grandmother had these armchairs in her apartment that I loved growing up," she says. "The group is named after my grandmother Fritzie, who my father called Fritz. So it's a tribute seating group."

⊖ The design of the Fritz Sofa grew out of designs for an armchair and ottoman. The entire collection is named after Fels' grandmother, whose armchairs hold a fond place among her early memories. *Credit: Albert Vecerka*

Iso Sofa System, Michael Sodeau

"The sofa **really** came about through the **design** of the leg profile," says Michael Sodeau of his Iso Sofa. "It's a weird, **awkward shape**," he says, "a **cantilevered** profile."

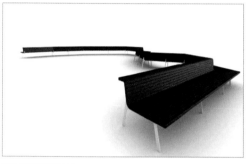

⃠ The Iso Sofa System by Michael Sodeau has been designed as a series of interlockable pieces that can be configured in a multitude of shapes to actually define the public spaces in which they're used.
Credit: David Simonds

⃠ Opposite top: A technical drawing of the leg profile gives accurate detail to the "weird, awkward shape" inspired by a road sign Sodeau passed regularly. The leg is cut from steel using a water jet, which leaves a clean finish. *Credit: Michael Sodeau*

⃠ Opposite bottom: A conceptual plan drawing shows the eleven pieces that make up the Iso Sofa System and outlines just a few of the many options it offers for defining space with seating.
Credit: Michael Sodeau

Asked by Modus to design a seating system for the contract market, Soudeau started working with a leg he'd originally envisioned for a chair. This strange silhouette was inspired by an equally odd source. "There's a route I take quite often coming to work," Soudeau explains. "And there's this road sign in Camden that shows the direction the roads go when they split. It was something I registered subconsciously and then turned into something three dimensional."

When he began reviewing the brief from Modus, Sodeau also found himself ". . . thinking on a grand scale, about seating hundreds of people." He then stepped back a bit farther, and started to consider how he could go beyond the simple functional demands of seating, and actually change the environment itself. "Instead of rows and banks of seating, as is traditional, I thought you could break up space in an interesting way and still seat the same number of people," Sodeau says. "It became more about changing the dynamics of an environment."

The sofa he has come up with can be configured into a multitude of shapes with different combinations of eleven components of varying lengths and angles. Each piece is bolted together at a leg joint. "The idea of the system is to break up space. Where more traditionally you'd have bench seats and chairs, say, for example, in an airport lounge, this allows you to redefine the space of a room," says Sodeau. "One advantage is that you can have the system actually snake back on itself. You can have social and antisocial seating, with pieces facing towards and away from each other."

Sodeau found that manufacturing became an integral part of the design process. "Initially, the leg was one piece," he says. "But there were some practical concerns with waste issues, so now we make it in two sections that allow us to have an extendable leg. The solution ended up being part compromise and part problem solving." Using 12 mm ($\frac{1}{2}$")-thick aluminum, the legs were cut with a water jet. The process is similar to laser cutting, but leaves a cleaner edge, which minimizes the need for finishing. The legs then receive an etching that gives them the look of light sand blasting. A coating is applied to protect the finish. Soudeau points out that this process is ". . . much more modern and allows you more flexibility in production because you're not required to do the massive production run all at once." The finish also allows all the components to look natural when put together, unlike, for example, brushed aluminum, where the patterns would need to match.

"The components are quite strange," he continues. "Usually, you'd have a heavy cast leg. But here, it's quite mechanical, the structure and the frame, but there's something quite light about it."

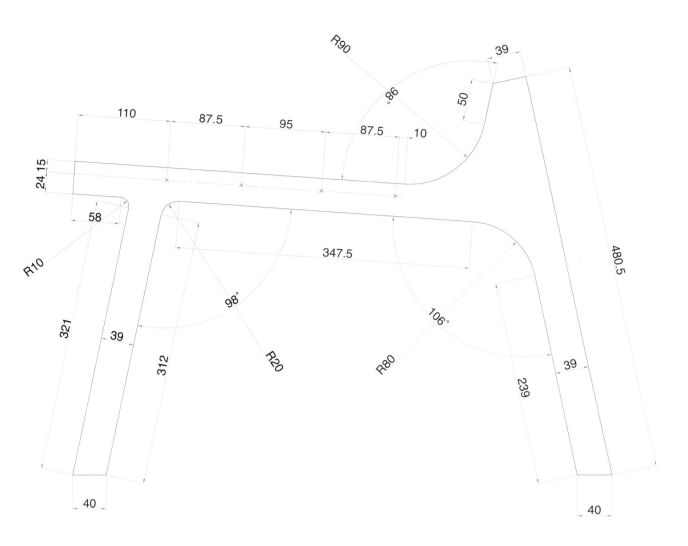

Michael Sodeau © 2003 – ISO seating system

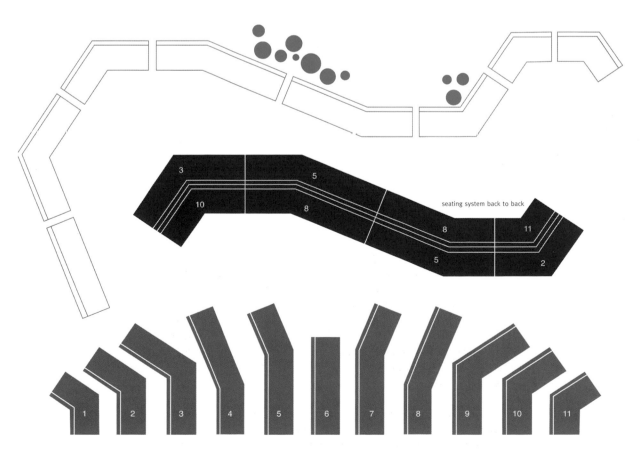

seating system back to back

The Iso Sofa is built on a fiberglass subframe that provides structure and strength in a very thin profile. The seat and back are made of layers of multidensity foam and quilted fabric. Finding the right balance between creating a slender silhouette and the practical concerns of comfort was Sodeau's biggest manufacturing challenge. "We've hit on an essentially satisfactory ground where the sofa is comfortable and the profile is as thin as possible, while retaining its comfort," he explains. "We also put cross members on the legs, which aren't visible underneath, to give it more support and structure." Developing the right upholstery technique required some trial and error. Much like "Goldilocks" in the fairy tale, Sodeau found one option was too hard, another too soft. His solution: combine them all in a layered sandwich of foam, Dacron, and the final, exterior fabric.

The return at the top edge of the sofa is an example of form doing double duty for both function and design. Coming just below typical waist height, the return is practical and elegant. "Because the system is fiberglass and made with a kind of extrusion rather than a mold, the return adds strength to the piece," says Sodeau. "And because it's public seating, it also provides an extra place to perch, or sit, or set something down."

Sodeau finds the entire process of moving a design from idea to reality part of the artistic challenge. "Most of the time, I have some subconscious ideas. But unless you sit down and rationalize your ideas, they won't turn into very much," he says. "The limitations of materials and manufacturing are inspirations. If anything, it would be more problematic if there were no constraints. Constraints are quite therapeutic. It's all in how you approach them, whether you see constraints as a closed door or an opportunity to try something different."

Sodeau also found some unexpected inspirations in designing for a commercial space. "The application is quite strange," he says. "Normally, when you design a piece of furniture or an object, you have a single person in mind who is going to walk in and buy it, who will consume the product. This is a different scenario in that it is something inflicted on people, in that it's public furniture. It's nothing you would choose. Someone is making a decision for everyone." Taking responsibility for the public space and public comfort became a part of his design process. "I wanted to pare it down to bare minimum and then add in what would be friendly elements," Soudeau says. "For example, the fold on the back to provide a perch, the quilting that adds a little more comfort. It makes it more engaging for the people using that public space."

The Iso System also embraces an unusual aspect of the unknown. While most furniture is bought as a complete and static object, this sofa becomes part of space planning itself. "It's almost an experiment, if you like. There's no easy way to try it out," Sodeau muses. "This piece will become part of the building and how it's used. It will direct foot traffic, for example." To be complete, the Iso System requires the active involvement of an interior designer or architect who will determine the sofa's ultimate shape. Sodeau is looking forward to some pleasant surprises. "There comes a point where you have to sort of cut the cord of a product and let other people use it, interpret it, engage it," he says. "Only then can you gauge whether it's a success or not."

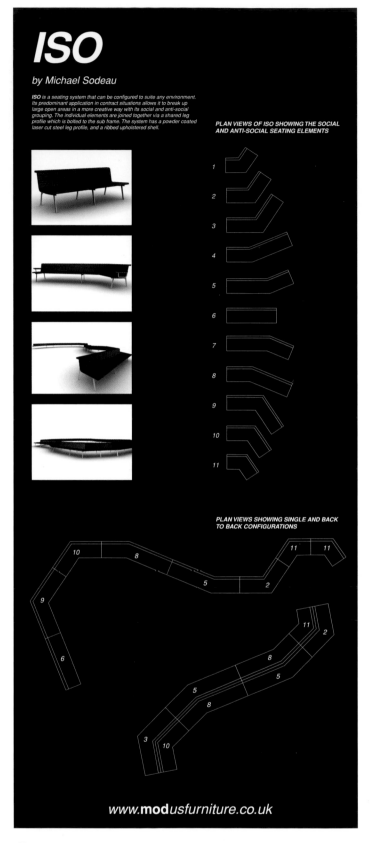

ISO
by Michael Sodeau

ISO is a seating system that can be configured to suite any environment. Its predominant application in contract situations allows it to break up large open areas in a more creative way with its social and anti-social grouping. The individual elements are joined together via a shared leg profile which is bolted to the sub frame. The system has a powder coated laser cut steel leg profile, and a ribbed upholstered shell.

PLAN VIEWS OF ISO SHOWING THE SOCIAL AND ANTI-SOCIAL SEATING ELEMENTS

PLAN VIEWS SHOWING SINGLE AND BACK TO BACK CONFIGURATIONS

www.modusfurniture.co.uk

⊗ A banner from the Milan Furniture Fair 2005, where the Iso was launched by Modus, shows the eleven different components to the system, as well as some snaking, circular, static, and back-to-back options among the multitudes of possible configurations.
Credit: Modus

⊗ A mold for the extrusion process will make the very thin fiberglass shell that is at the core of the entire Iso Sofa System. *Credit: Michael Sodeau*

⊗ Above right: The fiberglass shell is covered with a thin layer cake of various forms of padding and quilted upholstery to create a seat that is comfortable in spite of its very thin profile. The back return adds strength to the piece, and offers people a perch to rest a bag or themselves. *Credit: Michael Sodeau*

⊘ The steel frame is made so only the cantilevered shape of the leg will show in the final piece. The underlying crossbeams add support without being visible. *Credit: Michael Sodeau*

⊙ This computer rendering shows a few variations on the Iso Sofa configuration options, as well as the Sil Chairs that were the sofa's precursor. *Credit: Michael Sodeau*

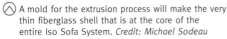

Trix Sofa, Piero Lissoni

"The idea was to **design** one moveable piece," says **Piero Lissoni** of his Trix convertible sofa. "If you like, it's a **really big pouf**. It's possible to sit, drink, make love—**why not?**—see the television."

The Trix uses a system of rubber bands and posts that allow three separate cushions to fold and unfold while staying close to one another. *Credit: Kartell*

Trix is a set of connected cushions that folds open or shut, allowing it to become a chair, sofa, or bed—there's even an integrated, removable, round tray. "Open one part, and then you transform it into a chair, move again and transform into an armchair, move again and transform into a bed," says Lissoni. "The movement is really simple because we designed a link system using one huge ring in rubber. You are totally free and it is up to you to decide every movement. If you like to use a lounge chair, you design a lounge chair; if you like to use a daybed, you design a daybed."

Its compact space and multiuse design make Trix especially appropriate in smaller living quarters. "Small spaces were in my mind," says Lissoni. "I'm also thinking for children, thinking for a simple bedroom. Imagine putting one in a bedroom for children and if you have a friend, there is one possibility to play, one possibility to sleep. Or if you have a small house and you invite some friends over, you can offer the possibility to sleep."

Several innovations make this versatility possible. The first is a contraption of rubber posts and bands that hold the cushions together, even as they allow them to be manipulated. "It's a special rubber," says Lissoni, "Like a huge O-ring, with rubber bands to keep pieces together. We are working with the resistance of the rubber around the resistance of the bottom to fix the cushions together. It's completely without mechanism. If you move the different cushions, the rubber is like a connection—it's my linking system." And it is this system that makes so many configurations possible. "It's not possible to divide, but it is possible to transform every moment," says Lissoni. "With this simple idea, I leave the decision to move the cushions up to you. Everyone now is a designer. Everyone is now ready to design our pieces and their life."

In addition, the Trix can be used indoors or out. Lissoni and the manufacturer, Kartell, designed and produced their own waterproof, polyester and nylon, elastic fabric that moves along with the cushions. "This fabric is like a huge net," Lissoni says. "The surface is designed because of the movement of the fabric; we have to design one fabric without the normal tension inside. It's in three dimensions. It's very thick and deep. It's like two nets connected—when you sit and move the fabric is completely elastic in all different directions. You don't see the movement, you don't see the effect," he notes. "Trix is possible to put outside next to the swimming pool, outside on the terrace. The fabric is the real trick of the product."

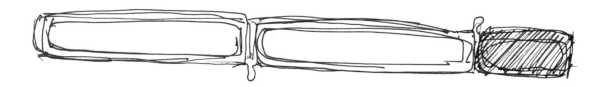

The Trix can be used as a chair, or a sofa, a lounger, or bed, and is especially useful in small, living spaces. *Credit: Piero Lissoni*

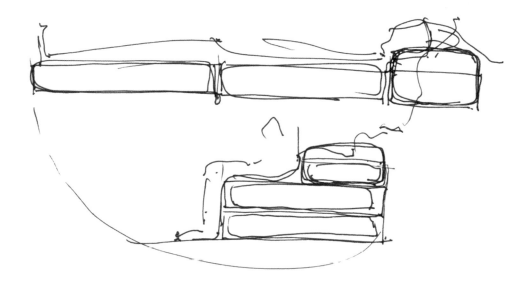

A computer rendering reveals the simplicity of the Trix mechanism—the friction of the rubber bands against the rubber posts hold each piece in place, even as it allows them to be reconfigured. *Credit: Lissoni Associati*

When folded all together, Trix can be used as an ottoman or small table, with a shallow plastic tray for holding snacks, a lamp, or other items. *Credit: Kartell*

Flip out one cushion, and Trix becomes a chair. A specially made, weatherproof fabric allows it to be used indoors or out. *Credit: Kartell*

Bottom: One more unfolding, and Trix turns into a lounger. Remove the plastic tray, and use it to carry drinks out to the terrace or poolside. *Credit: Kartell*

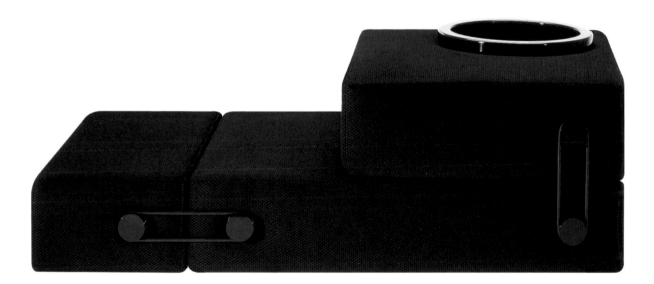

When completely unfolded, Trix becomes a bed with a mini, bedside table. Multiple densities of foam in the cushions ensure comfort. *Credit: Kartell*

The cushions themselves are made with layers of different densities of foam: "We were thinking about comfort, durability, elasticity, and so on," says Lissoni. One cushion has a cut out that holds the round tray. When Trix is completely folded into a cube, this tray allows it to work as a small table; when one cushion is unfolded, it becomes a side table. The tray can also be removed and set alongside the Trix when it is used as a lounger or a bed. Lissoni describes it as ". . . like the shadow of a tray. It is inside only 3 cm (1") deep, so you see only the foam. You use it like a tray or you pull it out and put it nearby to the bed, and it becomes a small night table for your watch, a small lamp, a book, for a water glass."

While the finished form of Trix is deceptively simple, it is just this quality that proved the most challenging to achieve. "It was very difficult to develop, difficult to simplify," says Lissoni. "If you don't use a lot of technology, you have to think very hard to make simplicity. When I start to talk about simplicity, it's like opening a nightmare. They look at you like in a horror movie—they think the nightmare has started again. But with Trix, we use a maximum of simplicity."

For Lissoni, there are critical differences between simplicity and the aesthetics associated with modernism in its minimal forms. "Why is it harder to talk about keeping things simple?" he asks.

"Think about some years ago, we were living in a special moment and everything, it was clean, minimal, and everyone liked to talk around simplicity. After some years, we are starting to think about some more freedom, and a lot of designers started to think about decoration like a new freedom and new point of view, a new voice, a new noise. I like the silence and the simplicity," he concludes. "We tried to make something clean, something simple, and we are thinking that real simplicity pays every day. It's an honest statement. If you want to use something like a super complicated piece, after a few months—or if you're lucky, after one or two years— but after that, it's boring, and you stop to use it. My target was like a minimal thinking that continues to live, and think, and talk, and use the minimal thinking again. And the simplicity is obviously simple, on the outside, but on the inside, you have to think with a lot of complexity. For a good simplicity, you have to think, and you have to solve a strong complexity."

Lissoni also expects some thinking from his customer. "I don't like to design bourgeoisie," he says. "Trix is sophisticated, but not bourgeoisie. It's not easy. You have to think. If you don't think, you don't buy."

Vero Sofa, Christian Biecher "I wanted to have a **very** well-drawn sofa and **armchair**," says Christian Biecher of the **initial** inspirations for his **Vero sofa**.

The Vero Sofa and matching chair reveal Beicher's interest in straight lines and substantive proportions in furniture. *Credit: Bernhardt Design*

"I wanted something modern and classic, that also went back to the history of modern design, the roots of geometry, the pure shapes of a square, triangle, and circle." He managed to achieve this tall design order by a somewhat surprising focus on simplicity. "I wanted something that was calm, almost banal, and yet precisely designed."

The Vero uses a series of straight lines and substantive proportions combined with two very judiciously used quarter-circles and some slender angles to create the desired aesthetic. "When you look at the front of the piece," says Biecher, "it's just blocks. But when you look at the side, you can see the curving angles at the top and bottom of the back. All of this is resting on legs set at a perfect 45 degree angle, so it's almost fragile." Biecher continues: "I like a sofa that is clearly detached from the floor. I like to have the space breathe around the piece. Then, to complete the whole thing, there is this use of color and texture that is showing the thickness and substance of the piece."

After considering it, then rejecting it, Biecher ultimately decided to include a long, low pillow bolster as a little element of comfort that gives some relief to the precision of his overall design. "My work is always a little bit stiff," he says. "I don't like soft things. I like straight things, something that holds itself." Of the pillow, he points out, "It's a little plus. It makes the sofa a little more sexy for those who might otherwise find it too strict."

Some of this adherence to the clarity of pure form perhaps stems from Biecher's background as an architect. "Probably there are certain shapes, color, and vocabulary that you can see in my work," he allows, "even though I try to forget that I am an architect when I go to design a spoon. Somewhere, I know that even if I think it's not the same type of work, these different skills are unified in a vision of the world, of what we can have. It's a way of looking at things, wanting to redesign the things that are around us, the chairs, the lamps, the buildings, the city."

Biecher begins his process of redesigning the world in his sketchbook. For the Vero, he remembers the design began with a chair. "I didn't even like the chair, I didn't like the proportion, but two pages later, it was immediately turned into a sofa. It still had the idea of the chair because the geometry didn't change." He then moved to the computer to work on proportion and other details. He tried both metal and upholstered armrests, but found the metal ones "scary" and so opted for the greater substance and comfort of upholstery.

Initial prototypes were made in plywood and white fabric. Primarily, they were used to find the right size for the armrests. "It was ultimately a sense of balance," Biecher says. "The piece had to look comfortable and inviting." Looking back, he reports that develop-

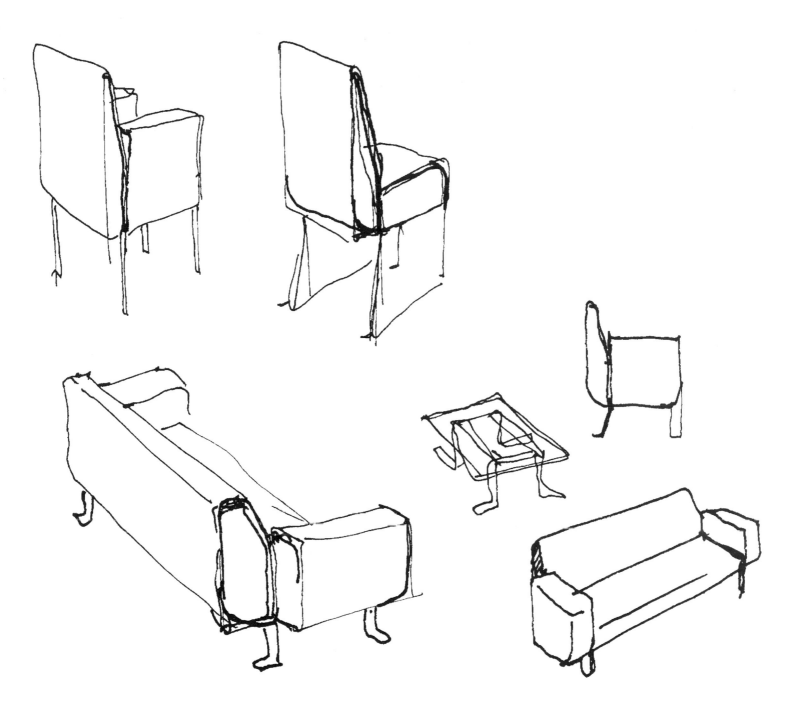

Top: The design of the Vero Sofa evolved from these early sketches of a chair; as is often the case, the chair was abandoned, even as, two pages further into the sketchbook, the Vero emerged.
Credit: Christian Biecher

Bottom: Preliminary sketches show how the entire grouping sets well-upholstered comfort floating above finely tuned legs. *Credit: Christian Biecher*

ment went quite smoothly. "Structurally, it's always calculated," he says. "The seat part, the bottom part of the sofa, it is quite thick, so it's easy to have it rigid. It's like a little bridge. The thicker it is, the more structure it has. Then the legs have to be strong enough in terms of the thickness of the steel. But it's very simple, technologically speaking."

This contrast between the delicacy of the legs and the substance of the overall piece is particularly pleasing to Biecher. Not only does he ". . . like the idea of a heavy piece floating on fragile supports," but he also wanted to veer away from the coldness of some modern design. "Most of the contemporary pieces that are sleek are also very anorexic. I want my work to be friendly, but designed. My work has flesh, and I like that. I want my pieces to be sensual, not anorexic. Anorexic is a negation of the senses."

Biecher ultimately decided to create a companion table for the sofa. "At first, I designed something that was beautiful in sketches, but very ugly in 3D," he says. Then, looking back at some earlier drawings, he found a shape that pleased him. "I'm very happy with this table. It has the silhouette of a martini glass, with straight legs and a triangle that holds a circle. It allowed me to express, with the minimum of materials, something that I love, something that I want in my own house. I love it because it is far from any design gesture; it is just essential and sculptural."

The Vero and its accompanying chair and table can take up comfortable residence in a variety of settings. "In the office," Biecher muses, "I see it in a lounge or waiting room. I could see it in a bar, or a restaurant, or a store. At home, this is also the type of seat I like to have because it is comfortable and a place where you can have conversation with your friends." He notes that although the Vero is usually shown by the manufacturer, Bernhardt Design, in strong contrasting colors, it is a piece that can take on a wide range of personalities. "In black leather, it is very corporate. If you upholster it in flowers or color, it looks very domestic," he says. "It was presented at a furniture fair in tweed and suede and it looked very James Bond. I love it even in flowered chintz."

Ultimately, Biecher sees himself as having created something that is adaptable to a wide variety of locales, atmospheres and users. "I don't want to design pieces that give lessons or dictate an attitude," he states. "I don't want pieces that tell you how to dress or to be. I want to design open and user-friendly pieces." He reflects: "It's ultimately not up to me to define my work, but I know the things I'm attached to."

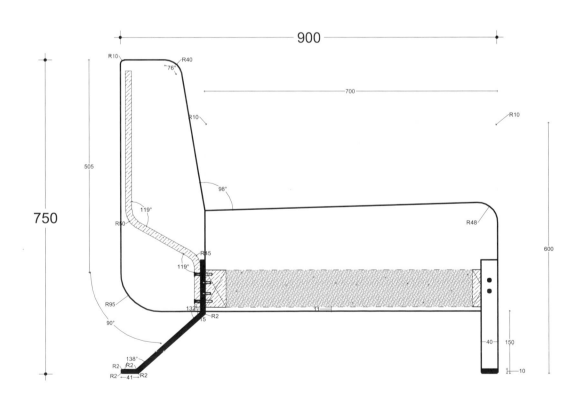

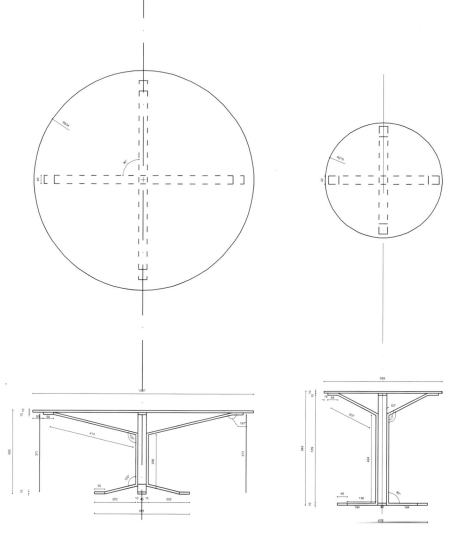

◁ Opposite top: Two prototypes reveal how the thickness of the arms creates a dramatic difference in overall balance and proportion. The designer notes that he prefers a designed sensual piece that has substance over the more contemporary "anorexic" designs. "Anorexic is a negation of the senses." *Credit: Bernhardt Design*

◁ Opposite bottom: Computer renderings show the clarity of geometric form that was Biecher's predominant design interest. *Credit: Christian Biecher*

▷ Shaped like a piece of fine, glass tableware, an accompanying table offers delicate balance to the generous form of the Vero Sofa. *Credit: Bernhardt Design*

▽ The strict lines of the Vero are enhanced by the drama of contrasting colors, even as they are softened by the long, low bolster pillow. *Credit: Bernhardt Design*

Marshmellow, Lars Dahmann "At first, we wanted to make handbags. We got inspired by finding some at **flea markets** in Asia," says **Lars Dahmann** of Lebello Design. "And I've always **liked** the minimalist aesthetic of **Asia**."

The Marshmellow Ottoman is made of colorful strands of woven plastic to be a playful, easy-to-pick-up-and-take-home piece of furniture. *Credit: Lebello USA*

What he ended up with instead of handbags were crayon-colored, woven plastic ottomans, manufactured in Asia. Playfully dubbed Marshmellows, this product was less the result of a desire to make furniture, than the desire to make, well, something. "We'd tried designing products for export into the American market," Dahmann says, "But we decided to make our own products. We wanted to have something that was instantly modern, but also classical. In terms of branding and naming, we wanted to have something that was very colorful and reflected the pop movement of the late '60s and '70s."

Dahmann found that furniture became a means for him to express his educational background and professional interest in both design and branding. "If you're just an industrial designer making CAD drawings—although this works for many companies—you miss the whole package, the branding, the positioning, the price point, the product naming, the graphics," Dahmann points out. "Having experience in all those areas, we create a product that has a brand within it. It allows us to control many aspects of our brand." In addition to the actual product, Lebello is also designing labels, tags, and packaging. "We're thinking of adding special carry bags for them," he says. "Packaging becomes very critical for the product."

In fact, carrying the product was a pivotal design concern. "My whole philosophy was to create a product that was easy to sell, easy to ship, easy to take home, to carry in your hands," Dahmann notes. "I didn't want people to have to order it, and then have a big box. I wanted it to be something that people could see in a window and put under their arm and take home."

An ottoman became the perfect vehicle to unite all these disparate goals. "Ottomans are really popular," Dahmann discovered. "People like little seats to put something on, but we didn't want to make a boring, square ottoman. There are not a lot of choices out there. We wanted to give the consumer the option to choose a lot of colors. In interior design, people are trying to create ambience in their home, and we wanted to have a large selection of colors that would be fun and playful."

Dahmann also wanted to manufacture the products in Indonesia. "Weaving is a traditional skill there, and I wanted to utilize the resources and skills they have. But it was difficult to find people who could weave in plastic, which is different than rattan. It requires more skill in terms of how you knot the plastic and it takes more strength because you have to pull harder on the plastic. It's challenging," Dahmann says, "but it's a new trend that's coming. People are turning more and more to plastic because it has a longer life expectancy and it can be used indoors or outdoors. It's smoother. But because it's a raw material that depends on the price of oil, it's more expensive."

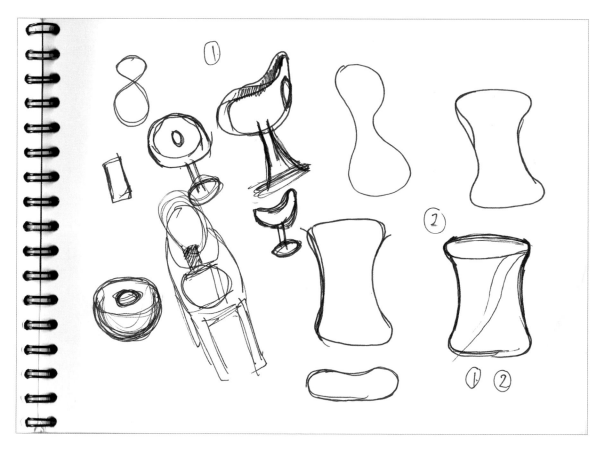

⬙ Top: Lebello was started to design, manufacture, market, and control the brand on a line of playful furniture that reflected the pop art sensibility.
Credit: Lars Dahmann

⬙ Further into Lars Dahmann's sketchbook, the form and sensibility of what would become the Marshmellow Ottoman begins to take shape.
Credit: Lars Dahmann

Using plastic was critical to giving the Marshmellow its signature attributes of bright colors, Pop sensibility, and indoor/outdoor versatility. So once they found a factory, Lebello spent a lot of time training the staff in quality and consistency. "It's quite a lot of headaches," Dahmann explains. "There's a lot of training involved in helping them come up with better solutions. You need to be involved in every step, especially when you go into producing the product. The more control you have over it, the more you can control the quality and consistency of the end product and you have a better relationship with the factory."

As part of his quality-control efforts, Dahmann specifies all the colors for the polycarbonate plastic strands using the Pantone Matching System, and insists on pigments from Germany and Japan, which he finds more durable and fade-resistant than the off-the-shelf varieties generally available. "Some very bright colors like orange or red, they will naturally fade no matter what," he says. "Naturally the darker colors will have a lot longer life span. Black is the safest color against UV light. But the most critical thing is to not use cheap plastic," Dahmann notes.

The Marshmellow comes in two sizes and two versions. "One is made with a bentwood frame and a solid core of rattan," Dahmann explains. "The other one has an anodized steel frame, which is the all-weather outdoor model. The rattan is slightly cheaper, but in terms of durability, the steel frame will last longer.

The rattan frame is for mostly indoor use." The steel framework is welded, while the rattan version is held together with stainless steel screws. He points out that in either incarnation, these pieces are time consuming to manufacture: "It takes a full day to make one."

After working with different prototypes, trying to determine the most comfortable height, Lebello settled on two sizes. "The smaller one is much shorter," Dahmann says. "It could be used for kids, or just to have your knees higher." The Marshmellow is topped off with a cushion that is covered in a cotton case that can be unzipped and washed. "The cushion is offset in an accent color," Dahmann points out, "to add more playfulness to the product."

When Lebello began to introduce the Marshmellow and other products, Dahmann found their inherent whimsy elicited inconsistent responses. "When we started," he recalls, "It was interesting to see what countries would be interested in our products. It was those that were more open—the Italians, the Spaniards, the Dutch—who were much more open to our products. The more conservative countries were not really into our products. We had a lot of American customers. Culture," he notes, "has an impact."

At the end of the day, for Dahmann, it's all about the color. "When I see them together," he says, "It's the color that really excites people. It's like fashion; we have a lot of colors so we can mix and match and create a really nice ambience."

A technical drawing gives the exact measurements of the two versions of the Marshmellow; the smaller version is child-sized. *Credit: Lebello USA*

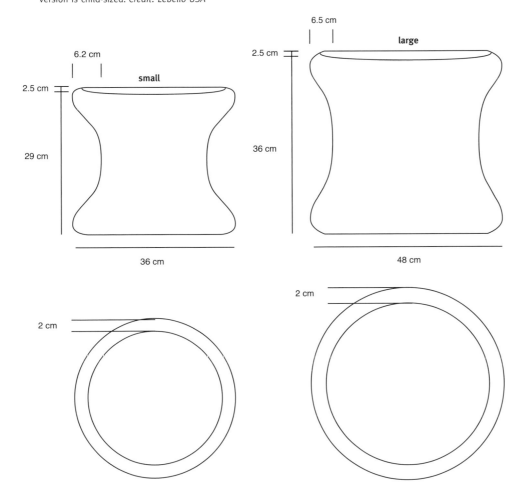

◇ Top left: The 2 mm and 3 mm ($\frac{1}{10}$ ") polycarbonate plastic strands used to weave the Marshmellow are custom-colored using the Pantone Matching System and dyes from Germany and Japan.
Credit: Lebello USA

◇ Top middle: The Marshmellow is woven using traditional Indonesian craftsmanship. *Credit: Lebello USA*

◇ Top right: The Marshmellow in rattan is woven on a bentwood frame and solid core of rattan. It is intended for indoor use. *Credit: Lebello USA*

◇ Bottom: The Marshmellow in mix-and-match, collectible colors is made of plastic strands woven over a steel base and is intended for indoor or outdoor use. *Credit: Lebello USA*

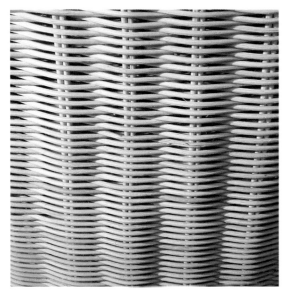

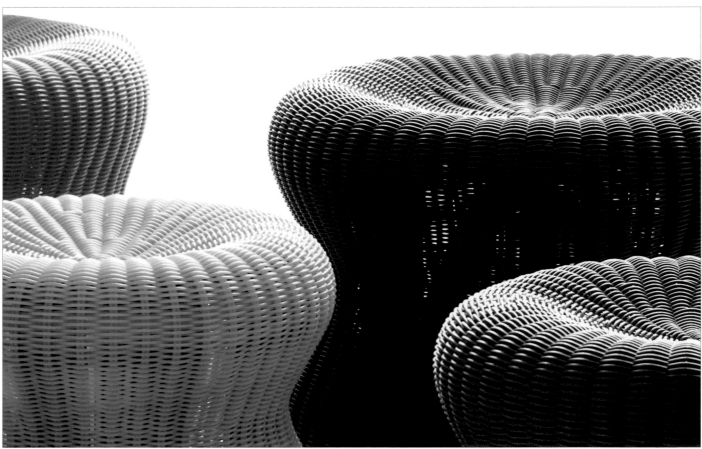

Sputnik Desk, Dario Antonini "The inspiration for the Sputnik came from my own **frustrations** with work desks and work **desk systems**," says Dario Antonini of **Orange 22**.

The Sputnik Desk is an oversized, glass-topped workstation inspired by spaceships as well as pragmatic concerns of modern office life.
Credit: Dario Antonioni/Orange 22

"I'd been designing work desk stations and modular systems for companies, and that got me to start thinking about the future of work and what a desk and work would mean or stand for in the future," he says. "Being so involved with computers and technology as I am, I couldn't separate my work from the digital realm, where we have all these peripheral devices that make our work life easier. The attempt was to create a simplified workstation that was ample enough to give you the workspace you need, but make it clean and unobtrusive."

Because Antonini has long been inspired by airplanes and space travel, it was inevitable that the desk would also have a bit of the Jetsons aesthetic as well. "I like to approach design from a narrative point of view," Antonini says. When he began designing his dream desk, he asked himself, "If you were sitting at the controls of a space ship or your master universe desk, what would that thing look like? What would it be like?" Sputnik became the answer to this question. "It would be an object that surrounded me and would facilitate bringing things to me, and my monitors would be around me and it wouldn't look heavy or obtrusive," he says. "It was about making work fun, creating something that makes you think, wow, I want to get behind that desk." And there was just one more thing the desk had to do. "It's also about making a desk that becomes a sculptural piece," Antonini adds. "It has a built-in wow factor."

While some of the Sputnik's inspiration may have come from outer space, it also fulfills a whole host of down-to-earth needs. In addition to being an oversized computer workstation, it has built in wire management, an accessory arm, and a pullout keyboard-and-more tray that is itself as large as some desks. The shape looks futuristic, but it's all about ergonomics. "If you diagram how the arms move during the course of a workday," says Antonini, "you get a beautiful drawing of the limits of the arm reach as it covers the work area. And when they launch rocket ships, they go at a specific angle to get through the atmosphere. We wanted to give the piece this kind of trajectory idea, where the curves are long and sweeping."

The work surface is also moveable. "The entire desktop surface rotates 15 percent in each direction on Teflon pads," notes Antonini. "This allows you to slightly rotate your desk to have perfect viewing of your monitor or multiple monitors. It gives you that additional comfort." The rotation is made possible by a supportive central column. "It's like a bicycle steering column," says Antonini. Because the glass weighs almost 200 pounds (91 kg), it requires substantive legs, which come off the central column out to the edges of the top, out of the way of chair and human legs. In keeping with his theme, Antonini designed this structure to "look like a lunar lander type of legs." He continues, "When you look at

⌄ At the factory, cardboard templates are used to "test where the different structural parts were coming off the main frame and to see where things were going to be in contact with each other," according to Dario Antonini of Orange 22. Credit: Dario Antonini/Orange 22

⌄ Antonini works out some design tweaks right on the factory floor. Antonini produces all his own products: "I'm not going to wait for these things to get made." Credit: Dario Antonini/Orange 22

⌄ Antonini found the greatest design/manufacturing challenges to be finding the right balance between support and unobtrusive elegance for both the leg structure and the keyboard/accessories tray. Credit: Dario Antonini/Orange 22

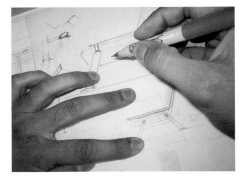

the mechanics of these exploration vehicles, they have fins or solar panels or some mechanical moving quality to them. This gives the desk that mechanical quality."

The open metal envelope hanging off the back of the desk was made to catch the tangle of cables that are an inevitable byproduct of the modern office. "Because we imagined two to three monitors on this thing, we needed to address the wire-management issue," says Antonini. "It was a must. I came up with the idea of making a contemporary-looking basket that holds all the wires so you don't have to feed them, you can just pile them in. It covers them visually, but it's an easy exercise."

In addition to a small accessory island, there is also an oversized keyboard/accessory tray. "Because the desk is so big," Antonini explains, "if you have something far away from you, you can't reach it. So this accessory arm puts things out of the way, but lets you bring them in close to you to keep your worksurface more clear. The keyboard tray has full extension glides, so when it's all the way out, it adds another quarter work surface to the desk." This feature also proved to be the most challenging from a manufacturing perspective. "The most complicated part of that desk was determining the configuration of the arms that were to hold the keyboard tray," Antonini notes. "We had drawn a series of solutions, and it took three or four iterations to get it clean and minimal."

Antonini and his company, Orange 22, handle their own production. "I'm not going to wait for these things to get made," he says. "I'm going to make them myself." In keeping with this attitude, Antonini balks a bit at being called a designer. "That label sometimes doesn't sit with me so well," he says. "I consider myself a maker of things." The hands-on habit came to him early in life. "Ever since I was a kid, if my parents bought me a toy, I took it apart," he says. "I wanted to see how it was made and what I could add to it. In that kind of tinkering, I learned to use my

⊗ A central post that functions like a bicycle steering column allows the desk's glass worksurface to pivot up to 15 percent in either direction, improving viewing angles and ergonomics. *Credit: Dario Antonini/Orange 22*

⊘ Sputnik's feet feature aluminum levelers covered with a white nylon pad to improve the aesthetics of the mechanism. *Credit: Dario Antonini/Orange 22*

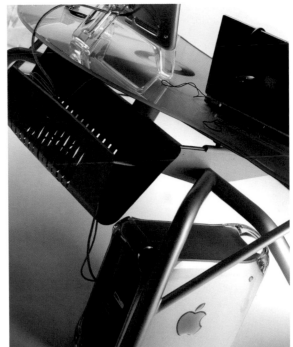

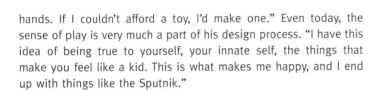

⊘ With a keyboard tray as large as a standard desk, the Sputnik becomes an oversized work station with plenty of room for multiple monitors and a modern, mixed-media work style.

⊘ Top: A metal basket hangs off the back of the Sputnik, ready to catch the inevitable pile of cables and cords of the wired work-force. *Credit: Dario Antonini/Orange 22*

⊘ The underside of the glass worksurfaces are lightly sandblasted for an opaque finish. *Credit: Dario Antonini/Orange 22*

hands. If I couldn't afford a toy, I'd make one." Even today, the sense of play is very much a part of his design process. "I have this idea of being true to yourself, your innate self, the things that make you feel like a kid. This is what makes me happy, and I end up with things like the Sputnik."

By managing his own manufacturing, Antonini feels that he can take more risks. "Part of the honesty of being a maker of things is a commitment to exploring and trying things that might not work," he says. "What happens in the design world a lot, or when we're working for clients, is that you have to get it right the first time around, and that fights against this innate sense of play. Part of why I started making our own products is so we can be free of the demands of high volume of sales, because selling this product is not the only way I make a living. The objects that come out of this approach and this mentality tend to be things that make people stop and say, 'What is this?' It's how you get people to dream a little."

Lo-Borg Cabinet, Nick Dine "I'm not a Trekkie," says Nick Dine, speaking about his Lo-Borg **cabinetry**. "It's just the **modern version** of a low sideboard." After a pause, he adds, "But I do know what the **Borg** are."

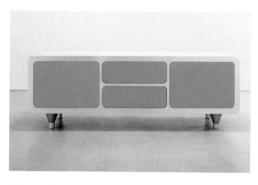

It turns out that the inspiration for the Lo-Borg and other pieces in this casegoods line came from a primal rather than futuristic fantasy life-form. According to Dine, "My very first inspirations were Fred Flinstone furniture, pieces that were carved out of one piece with no doors, just openings. Everything was reductive, not fabricated; it was like I took a gigantic rock and carved holes into it. I was unleashing my inner caveman."

Not too long after his Flinstone efforts, Dine designed a series of plastic laminate frames for Wilson Art picture frames. "We used laminate colors to create these simple, soft radius shapes. That language, which was a kind of zeitgeist of the times, sat well with me, and I decided I wanted to do a real project." This led him to design the Cy-borg, which translated the muted geometric shapes that Dine found so interesting to the doors of a cabinet made of wood and aluminum. "It had the aesthetic that was permeating design at the time," says Dine, "but I also felt that I wanted to keep developing it, and try and push the aesthetic beyond the initial hit that it had. I was taking a visual language that was out in the mainstream design culture and trying to make it my own. Of course," he quips, "it's not just me; it's every other jerk in the world, too. It's great when you're designing something and see fifty other people doing it. Then you know it's a great idea."

In addition to his work as a commercial and residential interior designer, Dine is also the design director for Dune, a company that manufactures limited edition, "innovative interior products." According to Dine, "Dune got this new technology paint, a special lacquer that enabled me to do these really graphic pieces, so we decided to do a line. I like these new versions with the paint instead of the wood and aluminum because they're about the graphic quality of the shapes," he notes.

To keep this graphic quality as clean as possible, the Lo-borg has no hardware on the doors and drawers, just touch latches. "I didn't really want it to read anything other than the graphic interaction of the colors," Dine points out. "I really like the tension of the color around the door and openings. It's that sort of buzzing that happens with your eye; it's that thickness of the radius trim and frame that's equal throughout. That's the visual language that permeates the series." He continues, "It's like the cabinet is the negative, and when you open it, the inside is the color of the front of the drawers."

The legs, which carry the color of the frame down to the floor, are made of cast aluminum. "I wanted something to sort of transition from the mass of the piece downwards that felt solid," Dine notes. "I wanted it to be organic, integrated into the piece, to

The Hi-Borg, 30"(0.8 m) × 22"(0.6 m) × 60"
(1.5 m), was envisioned as a storage unit for the bedroom, but Dine feels the strength and simplicity
of its graphic statement will make crossover to the
contract, or commercial, furniture world inevitable.
Credit: Albert Vecerka

Designing these laminate art frames for Wilson Art
started Nick Dine thinking about the other possibilities
for radius curves, and led him to design the Lo-Borg.
Credit: Albert Vecerka

Bottom right: The original Cy-Borg cabinet in aluminum
and wood, 72"(1.8 m) × 23 $\frac{3}{4}$ "(0.6 m) × 36"(0.9 m),
was the genesis for the development of a complete
line of case goods. *Credit: Albert Vecerka*

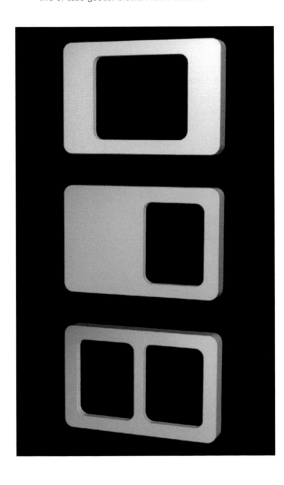

make a nice transition between the leg and the body. I have a tendency to sort of make things look rather industrial. This is a result of that. A lot of times, I want it to look like it wasn't designed, as if it was found in some kind of parts bin."

The Lo-Borg is made of birch plywood finished with a high-gloss polyurethane. According to Dine, "It's extremely difficult to get the finish just right. They burn a lot of time. It's a really time consuming piece to make. They're handmade, couture objects, but I wanted it to look like it was mass-manufactured." The Lo-Borg is available in innumerable colors and multiple drawer configurations. "Anything is possible," says Dine. "I love systems and I love the graphic relationship between the door and the body. It's infinite; I've just picked three archetypes to work with. I like evolving concepts and doing things that have a life outside the initial idea. It's like a friend that I keep visiting. This is another example of me finding and exploring a language."

For Dine, design ideas and vernacular are developed, not discovered. "I don't think ideas are owned by designers," he says. "They're kind of rented. If you have a moment of genius, for that one second that you have the idea, it's fabulous. But I look at stuff that's trying to be original, and I can always find a precedent. Designers as a whole have a sense of self that is grossly out of proportion to what they're actually doing. It's not uncommon for people to think they've made something new. But ideas are grown. They come from experimentation and growth."

As to how all this relates to the Lo-Borg, Dine is philosophical: "This piece is a particularly quiet and simple thing. You can find contemporary precedent for this piece, and I'm totally comfortable with that. It doesn't concern me because I'm much more concerned with aesthetic durability, and I think these things will be interesting to look at in ten years, even if they look dated. And they will," he adds. Dine trusts the promise of design evolution as well as technology to make old ideas new again. "Sometimes, something will be a couture piece for five years, and then they find a new technology or way to mass-produce it. Sometimes you revisit something in ten years, and you may find a way for it to carry you forward again."

For Dine, furniture provides a welcome creative reprieve from the bulk of his day-to-day work as a designer of commercial and residential interiors. "One of the things I like about furniture is that it's less pressurized in terms of what I have to achieve. I want it to be viable for the manufacturing, but at the same time I'm doing whatever I want, which is part of why I do it. I'm mostly in a service-based business. My interiors clients want my aesthetic, but there's always going to be lots of constraints and battles. It's like my clients are the screenplays I write for a living, and I view furniture like poetry I write for fun."

⊗ Dine finds the visual statement made by the tension between clean shapes and clear colors evident in the Cy-Borg cabinet intriguing. *Credit: Albert Vecerka*

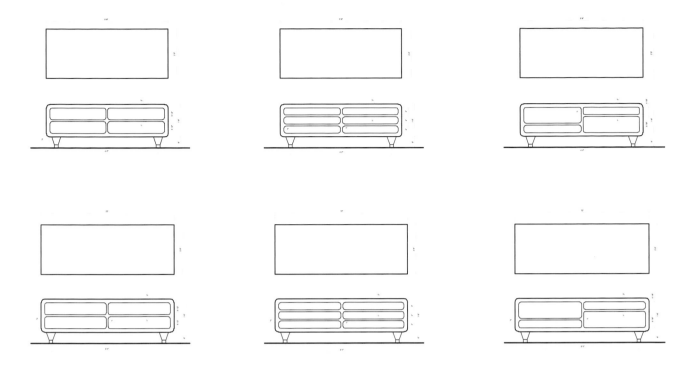

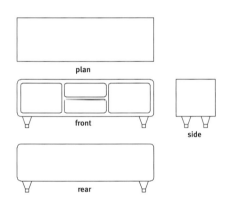

plan

front

side

rear

The Lo-Borg is available in a variety of drawer and door options, which make it viable as a stereo cabinet, dining room sideboard, or office credenza. *Credit: Nick Dine*

The interior of the Lo-Borg, $74"$ (1.9 m) $\times$ $23\frac{3}{4}"$ (0.6 m) $\times$ $26\frac{1}{4}"$ (0.7 m), is painted to match the drawers and doors in a labor-intensive process; touch latches keep the exterior surface clean and pure. *Credit: Albert Vecerka*

Boogie Woogie Shelving System, Stefano Giovannoni

"Magis asked me to design a **shelving system**," says Stefano **Giovannoni**. "I immediately recognized that a square unit was the best option for modularity. However, I also **realized** it would be quite **difficult to avoid** creating something banal."

⬡ The Boogie Woogie Shelving unit by Giovannoni Design is a modular system of identical plastic cubes that can be added to one another vertically and horizontally to create a bookshelf or room divider of any size. *Credit: Carlo Lavatori*

"I decided to give the face of the book unit fluidity, a sense of three dimensions, using the same three dimensional form that I created with the Fruitscape design for Alessi," he says. "I shifted the Fruitscape form from horizontal to vertical, and projected a square grid onto this curved landscape, creating the book unit modules," he continues. "It's funny that this product came from another product. This was the starting point, and it's something that is very special. I never succeeded to do such kind of transposition before, but I think it fits very well to this product."

The fruitscape is a "bowl," which is actually a flat piece of polished stainless steel with mounds dispersed over its surface for nesting individual pieces of fruit. "Each module is a small mountain like a wave," says Giovannoni. "For the Boogie Woogie, we used the same surface, and I cut off the top of the each mountain. It's like a projection of a grid where I create holes cutting off the higher level of the surface. Each module of the bookcase corresponds to a module of the fruit bowl." He continues, "I think this kind of transposition is very interesting in this project because if you saw the two together, you would not recognize that they came from the same place."

The Boogie Woogie unit was developed as a response to a very simple brief from furniture manufacturer Magis: "The bookcase has to be made out of one module that can increase in dimension horizontally and vertically," according to Giovannoni. "The risk was to create a product that would be very boring. It's not so easy because I like to create complexity from a very basic briefing. Using this surface, the result creates a product that is not flat, but has a full-dimensional way of creating interesting movement."

Each module is about 23" (0.6 m) square and made from injection molded ABS plastic in white, black, or red. The sides, bottom, and back of each piece are flat, while the front surface has a marked wave, picked up from the undulations on the Fruitscape. Modules are connected together vertically and horizontally to make a shelving unit of any size. In addition, they can be connected back-to-back to create a freestanding shelving unit or room divider where both the front and back undulate. The backs of individual modules can be left off, so the cubes are open. "The main piece includes the module with the front surface and eight sides—four outside and four inside the hole," explains Giovannoni. "This is one module, molded in one piece. The other module is the back panel. We have connectors that are made with

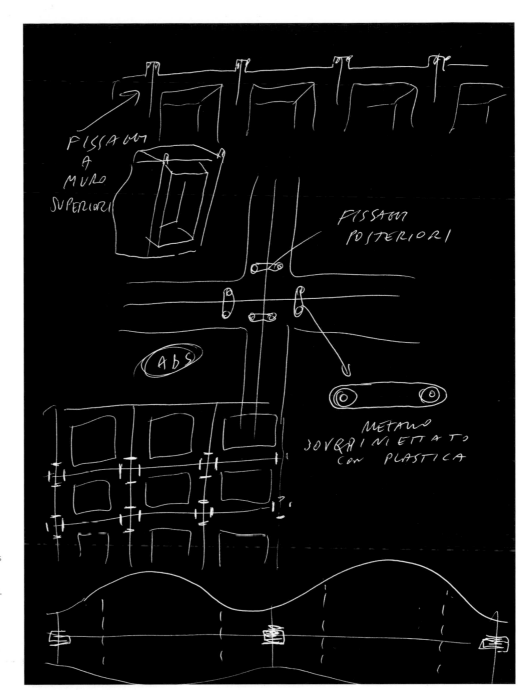

⊙ While Giovannoni does almost all his design phases directly on the computer, this early hand sketch shows his concept for metal fasteners embedded in each plastic cube that would allow the units to connect to one another, while maintaining a smooth presentation.
Credit: Giovannoni Design

⊙ The undulating face of the Boogie Woogie was inspired by a metal fruit holder Giovannoni designed, the Fruitscape (below). By taking the horizontal piece, making it vertical, and skimming the top off the mounds, the Boogie Woogie was born.
Credit: Giovannoni Design

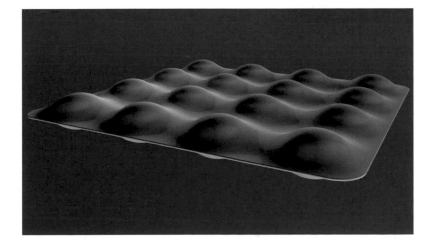

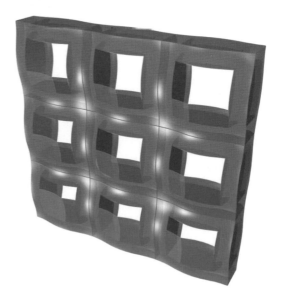

metal bars, coinjected between metal inside and plastic outside, so we can have the same surface of the main piece. There is also a particular designated piece for the top of the bookcase so you can fix the bookcase to the wall."

For Giovannoni, working in plastic is inseparable from the design process itself. "I like to work in plastic because plastic is the most flexible material," he says. "It's a material that you can develop according with your ideas. It's the most professional material for a designer because it's connected with huge investment and it's connected with an industrial way to conceive the product," he notes, referring to the tooling costs involved in making a mold for large scale plastic production.

Giovannoni feels very strongly that it is his responsibility as a designer to create products that will sell in high enough quantities to return the manufacturer's initial investment. "If you design in wood, you have no investment, but when you speak of plastic, it's a big investment, so it's a big risk for the company, and in the case of plastic, they need professional design. I like to work in plastic because it's a democratic material, it's the material for everybody, it's connected with huge numbers, and has many possibilities related to colors and shapes, and it's a very modern material. I'm interested in the industrial process, in big investment, and big sales."

For Giovannoni, an essential aspect of working in plastics is embracing technology. "The designer who works in plastic uses different tools," he says. "It's very important to have three dimensional perception of the product. We started with the most sophis-

ticated 3D software, and today we have the best knowledge in 3D modeling." Almost ten years ago, Giovannoni made a huge investment himself in Alias software, which he says is often used in car design. While the initial cost was "really a sacrifice, after that I increased my production, so it had very well paid for itself."

Now, every step of the design process happens directly on the computer. "I used to start with very small sketches with just the concept, but I never design by hand rendering anymore," Giovannoni reports. "After the first concept, we start directly on the computer, on 3D, and we develop a more and more precise idea of the product, continuously comparing one result to the next one. So it's a continuous modifying, and comparing, modifying, and comparing, optimizing the process to reach the best result. We develop prototypes by computer, from computer files, by machine, while the traditional way in furniture is totally different."

For all his interest in industry and technology, Giovannoni has given his product a decidedly humanistic name. "Boogie Woogie came out during the project because, if you look at it from the front, it looks very dramatic, but if you move towards the product, you can perceive that it moves a lot in horizontal and vertical direction," he explains. "This movement, it's like a dance that the product does. It reminds us clearly of the dance."

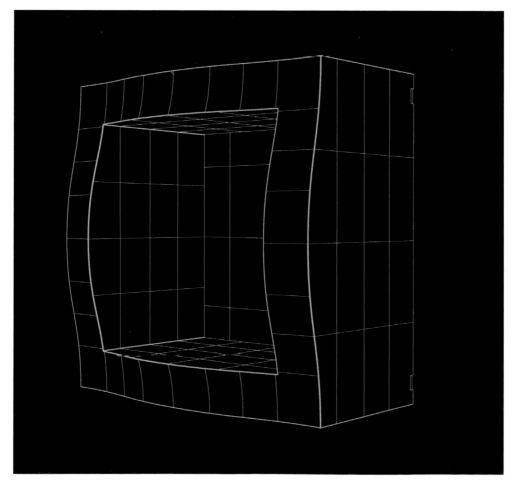

◁ Giovannoni felt that cubes were the best option for the modularity requested in the design brief, but was concerned they'd be too boring, so he gave the front face of each module a pronounced wave.
Credit: Giovannoni Design

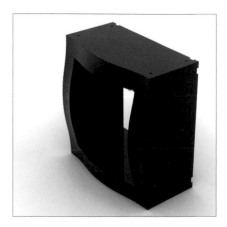

▽ Boogie Woogie units are made from individual cubes stacked and connected horizontally and vertically. Back panels can be added to close the units, or they can be left open. In addition, modules can be connected back-to-back to create a double-sided, freestanding room divider that has a wave pattern on both sides.
Credit: Carlo Lavatori

◇ For aesthetic purposes, the decision was made to move the injection point from the front of the individual unit to the base of an internal wall. An injection mold flow analysis considers temperature and filling of the mold and resulted in the design of independent cooling circuits that used water to keep the mold at a uniform cooling temperature. *Credit: Carlo Lavatori*

◇ Bottom: The Boogie Woogie uses high-technology and the "demo-cratic" material of plastics to create a shelving unit with a surface that dances more and more the closer you look. *Credit: Carlo Lavatori*

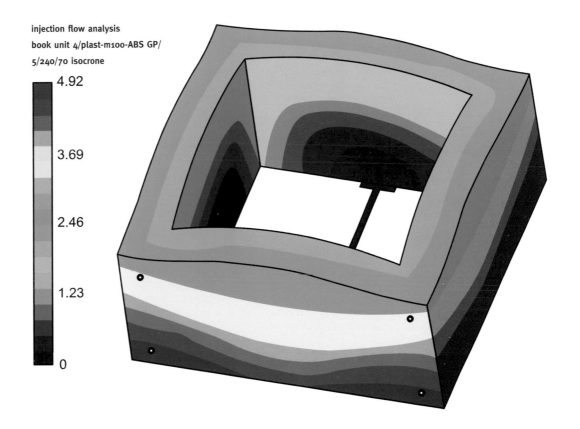

injection flow analysis
book unit 4/plast-m100-ABS GP/
5/240/70 isocrone

4.92

3.69

2.46

1.23

0

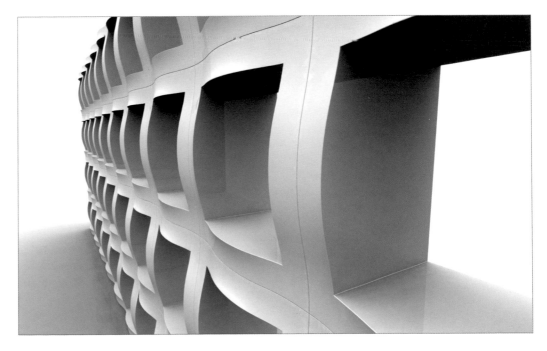

Exploding Log Shelving Unit, Chris Lehrecke

"There's these **two pulls** in the way I **design**," says Chris Lehrecke. "One is more the influence of my background in design and studying **furniture**, and the other is the **daily routine** of **building** things everyday that I've been doing for twenty years."

The Exploded Shelving Unit by Chris Lehrecke—shown here at the Pucci Gallery in New York City—is made from a single log sliced like sandwich bread.
Credit: Dan Howell

In each of these approaches, there are both formal and informal influences. While Lehrecke didn't attend architecture school, he does have a professional background in both architecture and design and grew up in the house of an architect. And he has been a long-time collector of furniture. Most important, he doesn't mind getting his hands dirty. "I started making things and looking at how machines work and how machines affect the way things are made and the way materials affect the way things are made," he says. Referring to his Exploding Log Shelving unit, he concludes, "This piece is a perfect example of me leaning towards the materials-and-the-machine" design sensibility."

The Exploding Log Shelf, like Lehrecke himself, is a product of its environment. After working in the highly urban setting of Brooklyn, New York, for twelve years, he moved his studio eight years ago to the countryside. "I bought an old church, and when the ten-acre field behind the church became available, I started warehousing logs," he explains. "I was doing everything from scratch, getting the logs, milling them, drying them, and going out to work with the sawyers. We'd take a log and put it up on this portable band saw, and start slicing it up the long way." As the pieces fell away from the log, the idea of creating a shelving unit by finding a simple way to simultaneously separate and connect the layers took shape in his mind. "Each time the log comes off, you have to lift it up, move it, and turn it over. You do this all day and you start to realize that the way the planks are coming off the tree are such a beautiful thing to see. It's so obvious, so simple and, like a lot of design, you wonder why has no one has done this before."

However, as once living things, logs do not respond to design challenges the same way many other materials do. "More often than not, you slice into a tree and it just doesn't work," Lehrecke points out. "You mill it up, and a lot of things can go wrong. There may be nails or ant colonies inside. There's a lot of tension in a log when it's growing, depending upon the conditions under which it's growing. When they dry, all the tension comes out and it can ruin the logs. You might put a log away in the drying shed and congratulate yourself for having this beautiful piece, and then it checks, which is like a big crack that goes down the center of a log." But for Lehrecke, this is all a welcome part of the process. When a log doesn't work for one project, he tries to find another use for it. "Maybe you have to cut it up and use it for legs. We try to roll with the punches and use every part of the tree for something. This is the fun part," he says, "where you just say, maybe I'll do a line of chairs this fall or use all the scraps for lamp bases."

⬙ Top left: One of the sources of Lehrecke's inspiration was this 200-year-old white oak in a field near his studio in New York State. *Credit: Dan Howell*

⬙ Top right: Lehrecke (in foreground) assists a sawyer with rolling a log of white oak onto a portable mill that can be driven to a site on the back of a pickup truck. *Credit: Dan Howell*

⬙ Bottom left: The mill cuts 2"(5 cm)-thick layers off the log, exposing the character and quality of the interior wood—and also sometimes uncovering some unwelcome surprises like ant colonies or old nails. *Credit: Dan Howell*

⬙ Bottom right: As pieces are pulled off the mill, they are loaded carefully in the order in which they were cut, and Lehrecke begins assessing them for furniture. *Credit: Dan Howell*

For the Exploding Log Shelves, Lehrecke gets logs through tree removal services. One of his favorite trees to use is catalpa. "It's one of most beautiful woods and almost never seen in furniture," he says. "The grain is very beautiful, very Asian. But there's not enough of it to create a market and it's very soft. Most companies want to work with harder, more durable wood. I love making furniture from wood that has no lumberyard or commercial value. There are these logs that are beautiful, but are not straight enough, or there's just not enough of it around. They have more character even if they'd don't have enough commercial value."

Lehrecke's prime concern with the Exploding Log Shelves is to preserve as much of the natural character of the tree as possible, while still creating a viable shelving unit. "The design dilemma," he notes, "was how do you do this with as little interruption as possible. This slight I beam I came up with was the most minimal means of supporting the shelves structurally, without interrupting it visually."

The supports are made of flat steel stock, about 4" (10 cm) wide $\times$ $\frac{1}{4}$ " (0.6 cm) thick, which are welded to another piece of flat steel that is invisibly morticedmortised into the wood. "When you look at it from the front, you almost don't see anything," Lehrecke notes. "That was the idea here. At certain angles, you don't pick up the metal at all, you just see the shelves suspended apart from one another."

The shelves are given the most minimal finishing treatments. The steel supports are oxidized with chemicals to make them black. As for the wood, according to Lehrecke, "We have a very simple way of dealing with wood. We find beautiful wood, we sand it to very fine grit, and then put two or three coats of wiping varnish on it, so it has a very minimal finish, but one that's protecting the piece. We want it to look like wood. We don't want to make it look like its been sprayed with a high-tech finish."

As fond as Lehrecke is of his raw materials, he remains pragmatic in his approach. "There are a lot of folks that talk to trees," he says, "but I'm not one of them. I just love the material. The more I've learned about it, the more interesting it becomes. I keep learning about which woods are good for what and what to watch out for in terms of working with them, and how they dry. It's never boring, and I keep learning things."

Lehrecke also finds that his eclectic background helps him find new ways to interact with this oldest of materials. "There seem to be two distinct communities of wood," he says. "One is the craft community, the people who went to woodworking and furniture-making school, and I didn't do that. Then there's the architecture and design-oriented community, and most of them have gone to architecture school and have not done much practical building. I fall somewhere between the two because I have a background in both, but I'm not overly influenced by either." However, to his neighbors in the countryside of New York State, "I'm the strange guy with the wood stumps. When they see some article in the *New York Times*, and see what someone paid for one of my pieces, they just laugh when I come into the country store."

⊘ Top. After their years in the shed, wood pieces are bought into Lehrecke's studio for another six months of drying. This piece is from a catalpa tree, a wood that Lehrecke is particularly fond of. *Credit: Dan Howell*

⊘ Each milled log is stored for two to three years of air drying. Seeing the logs in this form was Lehrecke's inspiration for the Exploded Log Shelving Unit. *Credit: Dan Howell*

The slender steel supports between each log slice provide structural strength without compromising the simplicity of the exploding log concept. *Credit: Dan Howell*

Layout Bookcase, Michele De Lucchi

"We want the client, the end user, to **rethink** the traditional layout of the **room**, and to introduce a **cupboard** that makes the **interior** not so rigid and **geometrical**, but more free and unconventional,"

The Layout by Michele De Lucchi for Alias utilizes extruded pieces of corrugated aluminum to create a curvaceous, stand-alone shelving unit that opens on both sides and allows a customer to redefine the living space. *Credit: Luca Tamburlini*

says Michele De Lucchi. "This is part of a layout process where you design the room in a totally unexpected way."

Unlike traditional shelving units that are invariably shoved up against a wall, Layout shelves are to be pulled out, into the room, where they become sculptural pieces that help define space. "The first idea was not to do a cupboard using a corner or wall of the room space, but to do a cupboard independent of the walls," says De Lucchi. "And I thought, instead of adding a wall, it would be better to add a curtain on the wall. A curtain is not a flat surface, but it is softer, and its surface is plastic. The project came out of combining the idea of a curtain with the technological possibilities of extruding aluminum. Because aluminum can be extruded in many different ways, this was a very possible and convenient technology."

The beauty of a Layout unit belies its practicality as a closed-door shelving unit. The system comes in several different sizes and heights, with doors on both sides, or with a flat back that can—in spite of its inspiration—be pushed up against a wall or into a corner. The interior shelves are made of wood painted aluminum, black, or ivory. The undulating aluminum doors have a matte finish and vertical corrugation that reflects light and creates movement by casting subtle and interesting shadows. Two structural uprights support the interior shelves and anchor the doors, which have no handles, but are opened with just the most gentle pressure on a small ridge that runs the full length of the door edge. The hinges are not only invisible to the exterior, but they also hold the doors open. This feature makes the shelves more easily accessible, and can also transform the unit into a kind of metal curtain, as originally imagined. De Lucchi notes, "Every functional part is invisible. You don't see hinges or handles. Everything appears as a smooth surface all around. This has been my aim, to make something that does not appear as a conventional cupboard."

Because the Layout is so unconventional, it serves many purposes. According to De Lucchi, "It can also be used as a room divider. Also, because it is open all over, you can use both sides; you can use any side. It provides new possibilities for the use and layout of a traditional space. The cupboard is no longer something to hide somewhere, but an object to put in front, to put in evidence, to design the shape of the space. It is not only geometrical and rigid, but can be much more rounded with the cupboard."

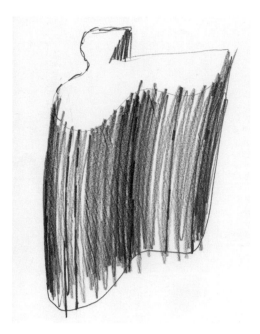
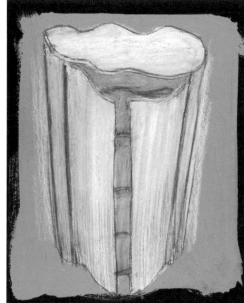

The material used also has an effect on how light is perceived and functions in a room. The extrusion process—which De Lucchi describes as being somewhat akin to watching spaghetti emerge from a machine—creates long, sinuous shapes of gently ridged, matte-finished aluminum. "It's very nice, , the reflections ist has of light," De Lucchi notes. "A normal cupboard is like a wall, so there is not the possibility of seeing the effect of the material. The Layout is really something that becomes different with the light. It reflects and creates a beautiful effect. Because it is not a flat surface, the many different lines, the composition with all the different lines and the curves makes the light bounce in different ways."

De Lucchi points out that Layout has become an entire system of furniture, rather than just a single unit. "It's a number of elements that can be composed in a number of variations. Right now we've developed the cupboard with all the internal equipment for the dining room and kitchen," he says, "And it is very comfortable to put dishes, glasses, pots other things that are round; this is easy to understand, because all the shape is very rounded." The cabinets are being offered in several different heights and shapes,

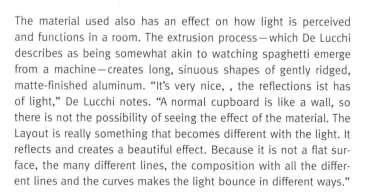

⊘ Early sketches reveal De Lucchi's interest in undulating forms that are reminiscent of curtains. *Credit: Michele De Lucchi*

⊘ Doors for a shelving unit take on the soft folds of fabric in this sketch that reveals the Layout's utilitarian and sculptural qualities. *Credit: Michele De Lucchi*

⊘ In the factory, prototypes are made of wood to finalize the shape of the curves. Production models are made from extruded aluminum, with painted wooden shelves. *Credit: Philippe Nigro*

including low, glass-topped versions. More options for other parts of the home are also under exploration. "We're also developing equipment for a cupboard in a bedroom," says De Lucchi. "We studied systems for storing clothes, shirts, socks, etcetera. The outside will be the same, but the inside will have boxes and drawers." In addition, De Lucchi anticipates commercial applications for the system. "Each year, we will introduce new combinations," he says. "Also something for the office. I anticipate it will have success in the office, because they are so conventional now. They need some new furniture, some new, fresh ideas."

De Lucchi is no stranger to creating "new, fresh ideas." Over his extensive career as an architect and designer, he has been a leading figure in radical and experimental movements like Cavart, Alchymia, and Memphis and has developed experimental products for a variety of manufacturers. He gives credit for some of this out-of-the-box thinking to his place of birth. "Generally speaking, we design in a more intuitive way," he says. "We do analysis and investigation afterwards. This is very peculiar to Italian design. It's our way; creation is a very free attitude. And then the investigation about what is the value of the project comes after. The investigation about the marketing, the best way to introduce in the market, and so on, is usually done in the second phase of the project."

But De Lucchi also values creative partnerships and the discipline imposed by commercial considerations. "It's very important, the relationship with the manufacturer," he says. "Because the best projects come out of the best relationships with the designer and the company, and usually the engineer in the company as well as the people in marketing and commercialization. Because design is not only a private act to express yourself, but more something that combines the aim of the designer together with the market life of the company."

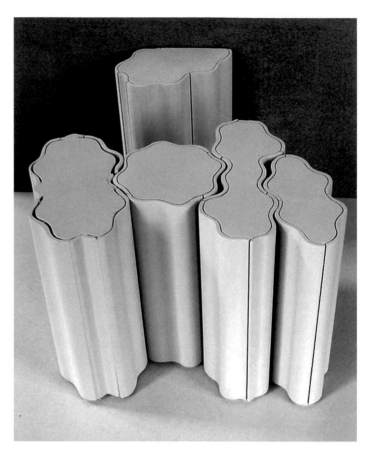

Above and top right: Small models show a variety of options for the Layout, including a flat-backed version that can be pushed against a wall and others that can be used as room dividers. *Credit: Michele De Lucchi*

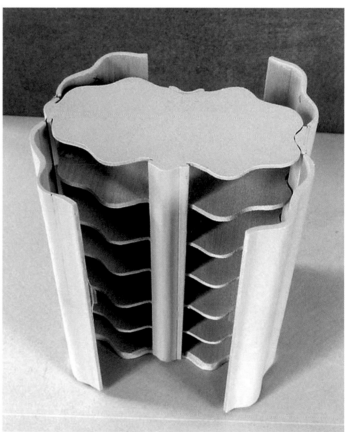

This model shows the undulating, double-opening doors that are the Layout's conceptual cornerstone. *Credit: Michele De Lucchi*

With its doors closed, the Layout offers an almost seamless face of flowing metal to the room; all functional details were designed to remain hidden.
Credit: Luca Tamburlini

Three—A Shelving Project Jakob+MacFarlane

Bookshelves are mostly the domain of **stark** ninety-degree **angles** given over to pure **function.**

Three—A Shelving Project is constructed from colored methacrylate, which is a very hard, flat, plastic that resists scratches and does not break.
Credit: Enrico Suà Ummarino

There could be no shelving unit that moves further from this paradigm than Three—A Shelving Project that Dominique Jakob and Brendan MacFarlane designed for Sawaya & Moroni. "The piece came from an urge to build a completely freestanding shelving unit in space," says MacFarlane. "The concept for the Three was to make a completely freestanding object that is both functional and spatial." In order to fulfill this tall order, Jakob+MacFarlane did no less than reconsider space itself. "We imagined the human body as creating the space, in a sense molding the object," MacFarlane explains. He sees the shelves as the expression of "a frozen moment in time."

MacFarlane explains that the process of design began by imagining a transparent matrix, a three-dimensional grid, if you will. He visualized a person walking around in this space. And then, he tried to picture the shape that this person "carved out of space" as they walked. "What they leave, moving with their body in a circle, is the shape of the bookcases," according to MacFarlane.

MacFarlane feels that this idea, as well as the ability to imagine and then create something in this way, comes directly from digital technology. "The kind of models we're doing are digital and transparent and allow us to see through things," MacFarlane points out. "We were interested in making real the kinds of things that you see in the digital world, looking at something almost how we'd read it as a digital model. There are ways of reading, layering, faceting, seeing something as a mesh, and this influences the vocabulary of the design object," he continues. "Meaning that the presence, or visual vocabulary of our piece is related to a simple grid that you would give any object predigitally, by giving it the coordinates *XYZ* in an organic or curvilinear or fluid form. This is then the expression of those kinds of coordinates."

The collision of design and technology is central to creation at Jakob+MacFarlane. "The digital world is a totally different process of creativity. It affects the way you think," MacFarlane says. "It brings you into a very—both good and bad—immediacy. You see the whole thing immediately, how it could be fabricated and made. Time is compressed, and you can see it all. That gives you, in a sense, more time to both appreciate the thing and, in a sense, be more proactive in the whole fabrication phase than a designer was before. It's so obvious that you want to fabricate it right away. Those kinds of barriers have been broken down. The designer becomes their own fabricator, and I think we'll only be seeing more and more of this."

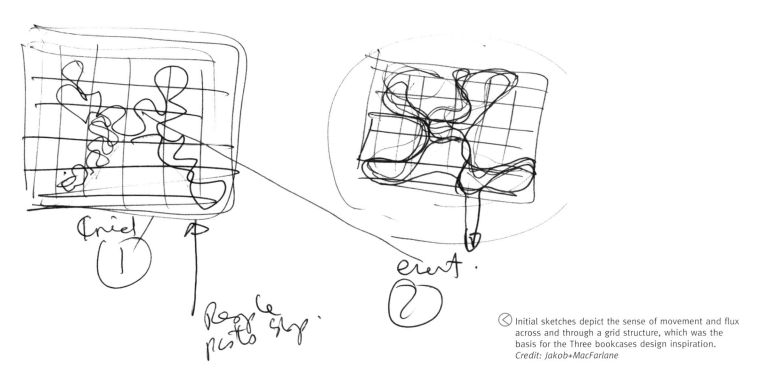

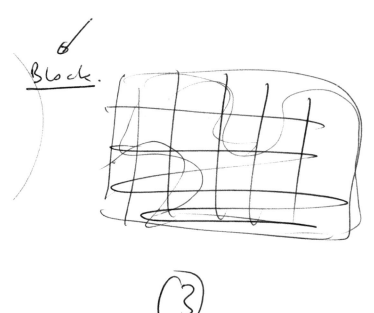

MacFarlane feels that the Three—A Shelving Project is ". . . furniture made from an event. There is this idea that our everyday spaces are filled with a complexity of force fields or spatial moments created by events. Digitally, we can now capture all of these movements and make the invisible visible. In some ways we are not trying to impose a design or a preconceived object but, rather, render something visible."

Of course, there are many, extremely down-to-earth concerns when trying to make the conceptual real. Jakob+MacFarlane worked with Sawaya & Moroni on an unusual fabrication technique. MacFarlane remembers how eggs were crated back in his native New Zealand thirty years ago, with flat pieces of cardboard that were cut to slip into one another to create three-dimensional support, similar to how wine bottles are kept separate in a cardboard box. He created digital drawings that reflect this simple, puzzlelike mechanism. These digital drawings, showing how the bookcases would be cut from plastic set in various horizontal and vertical planes, were sent directly to the maufacturer's cutting machinery. Once the individual pieces were made, they were assembled by hand and held together with invisibly applied screws and glue. MacFarlane points out that theoretically, the shelves could hold themselves upright simply by being slipped together, just as the cardboard divider does. But the glue and screws gives the final piece a critical measure of stability. "I think," MacFarlane muses, "that the childhood, almost toylike aspect of putting things together is part of the interest. It's also about revealing something that's already assembled."

Critical to the shelves' success was finding the appropriate fabrication material. "The challenge was to find the right plastic," says MacFarlane, "something that was flat enough and strong enough. Methacrylate is a very hard, flat, toughened plastic that resists scratching and doesn't break." Used as a shatterproof replacement for windows everywhere from hockey rinks to aquariums, methacrylate also has the advantage of retaining its translucency and making colors look particularly luminescent. MacFarlane points out that this translucency is critical to the overall design aesthetic. "We could have made it opaque, but transparency gives the object the ability to be seen all at once. In a sense, the object comes from a simple idea, but seeing it in transparency, we see something that appears much more complex than it is. This is something we're very interested in."

In a sense, Three—A Shelving Project is a reflection of the sculptor's adage, which claims that a sculptor simply releases the object from the stone. As MacFarlane notes, "When working directly with the material, the material gives you the answer. Ours is more conceptual in the sense that it's about the action of the body creating a resultant. You don't know what to expect to see, and then something emerges." He continues, "The strange thing about this piece is that it's context-less. We make a big point of saying that we're interested in context, but in this piece it's an event that created it. The piece is an outtake of someone moving. We've never stated a context and never had a preconceived idea about context. The idea is what it's all about."

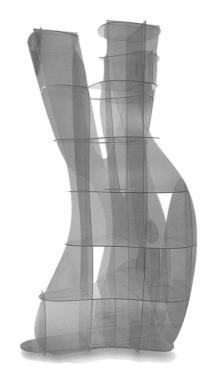

⊗ Inspiration for the three shelves came from a visualization of a person walking around in space. The designer tried to picture the shape that a person "carved out of space" as they walked.
Credit: Enrico Suà Ummarino

⊘ This computer rendering reveals the unfolding of each piece that goes into the Three bookcases. Note how the central image depicts the core piece, from which the parts have been exploded across three different directions. *Credit: Jakob+MacFarlane*

This rendering reveals what is left behind once the pieces that will become a bookshelf have been cut away. Depicting space in a three-dimensional form is a central design concept for the shelves. *Credit: Jakob+MacFarlane*

This rendering shows both what is left behind and what was made from the three dimensional grid of methacrylate. *Credit: Jakob+MacFarlane*

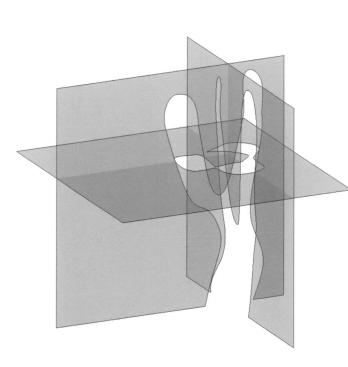

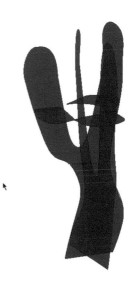

This rendering shows how the final bookcase will be cut from three pieces of methacrylate, set in three different axes. *Credit: Jakob+MacFarlane*

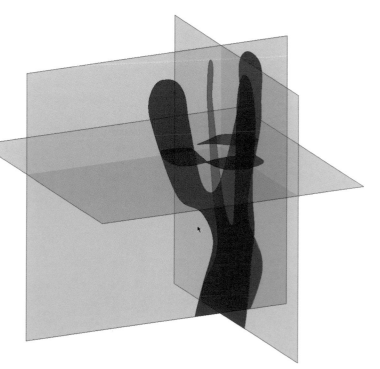

paper softwall, molo design

"We're always **playing** with materials on hand in the **studio**," says Stephanie Forsythe, **director** and designer at **molo design**, ltd. "As **designers**, we like to **focus** on one material and see all that it can do, rather than impose **ourselves** on the material."

The paper softwall uses honeycomb tissue like that found in party decorations to create a room divider that expands from a mere couple of inches into a flexible wall. *Credit: molo design*

In the case of the paper softwall, the initial inspiration was picked up at a dollar store. Working with expandable paper party decorations, Forsythe and her partner, Todd MacAllen, began looking into the expandable properties of tissue paper honeycomb, and the kinds of interesting 3D structures they could create. At the same time, ". . . we were also working on housing in Japan, at ways of making private space more flexible," says Stephanie. "In urban living, space is at a premium. We wanted to take these realities and find solutions that contribute to the quality of life and the free flow of air and light." With these concerns in mind, they began to imagine what would happen if they took one of those paper lanterns and made it much, much bigger.

The next step was to find a willing fabrication partner. They found a company in Pennsylvania that had been making paper party decorations for more than 100 years, and asked how big they thought they could take honeycombed tissue paper. "They were open-minded. It didn't faze them to go from paper wedding bells to walls," Forsythe reports. While the company only had to make small adjustments to existing machinery to accommodate molo's vision, they did find they needed to set aside a special room where they could warm the air to the proper temperature to cure the glue on this larger scale. Little by little, they worked up prototypes that increased in size from a column to a wall. Along the way, they discovered the material behaves differently as it grows. At first, with only fifty layers of paper, they found the honeycomb would spring closed. But by adding more layers, it would hold itself open, creating an expandable, flexible wall that absorbs sounds, captures and then diffuses light, and offers a uniquely soothing ambience through its delicate yet sturdy structure.

To add durability and handling ease, molo attached wool/felt end covers. To extend the wall, one holds onto the felt and pulls. "It sounds like rain, when you open it," Forsythe says. There are also Velcro® strips attached to the felt that allow one wall to be attached to another, for extra length or modularity. The felt can also be folded lengthwise so it sticks to itself, creating a column that gives additional support to each end. Finally, when the wall is collapsed on itself, it can simply be hung up in a closet, where the felt ends make it resemble nothing so much as a rolled blanket. "It's a bit like wrapping a book in a book cover," Forsythe points out. "We're giving the surfaces that get handled a lot a soft, yet sturdy, material. And felt has an affinity for the paper," she points out. "Felting and papermaking have a natural relationship."

The tissue paper honeycomb is stronger than it appears, with each sheet gaining strength from every other. Yet, it retains its delicacy and allows light to penetrate. *Credit: molo design*

By pulling the two ends of the paper soft-wall apart, a self-supporting wall is re-leased, accompanied by a sound not unlike a gentle rainfall, according to the designer. *Credit: molo design*

In part, the beauty of the paper softwall comes from its stunning simplicity. Which is, in turn, the direct result of molo's design sensibility. Trained as an architect, Forsythe says, "The headache always comes down to where materials are joined, and no one wants to take responsibility for the joint. There are so many possibilities when you simplify things. There's this idea of focus, of paying attention to one material and seeing what it can do." Plus, there are practical concerns that make it easier to modify what already exists. "Our general philosophy is to look for existing tools and infrastructure. After all, we can't afford to make our own machines," she says, "so we look for materials that are out there and for new ways they can be used."

The base material of the softwall is 400 layers of off-the-shelf tissue paper treated with flame retardant. The resulting product is surprisingly durable; Forsythe reports that the family dog, as well as a couple of young, rambunctious nephews have not been able to damage the paper softwall they use in the studio. "If you bump into it or the dog runs into it, the wall has so much flex, it just bounces away," she says. "And the honeycomb structure means each individual sheet borrows from the others for strength. But we look at it like we're living with a Japanese Shoji screen, which gets patched over time, only adding to its character. The same can happen with the softwall." Still, it is paper and water will destroy it, so molo design has introduced a softwall made from a non-woven polymer textile. In addition, they are looking at working with artists to create unique, limited editions of paper softwalls.

Molo design is also exploring other building and product possibilities for paper honeycomb. They are making smaller versions with an interior tunnel that could hold a lightbulb, creating a cool-to-the-touch, space efficient, ambient lamp. They're also looking at embedding LEDs into the honeycomb to create a collapsible lamp. But the most exciting possibilities involve increasing the product scale even more. Working with Common Ground, a New York City nonprofit looking to use innovative design solutions to address the homeless problem, molo design is creating full rooms of collapsible, single occupancy housing made from honeycomb textile. They are currently working on a test program that puts these rooms into a raw space in New York's Bowery neighborhood. While there are many concerns with everything from fire codes to wear and tear from constantly shifting tenants, Forsythe feels these are surmountable challenges that can allow the softwall to become an important addition to the catalog of building-system possibilities.

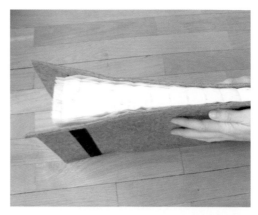

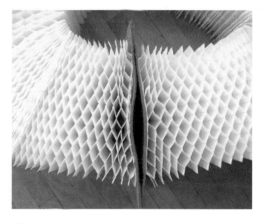

⬡ Top: The paper softwall is made with hundreds of layers of fire-retardant tissue paper, folded and collapsed in between two soft bookends of felt. *Credit: molo design*

⬡ Middle: The felt ends of the paper softwall feature Velcro® strips that can be adhered together to provide extra support to the ends. *Credit: molo design*

⬡ Bottom: Two softwalls can be connected together with Velcro® strips for extended length. *Credit: molo design*

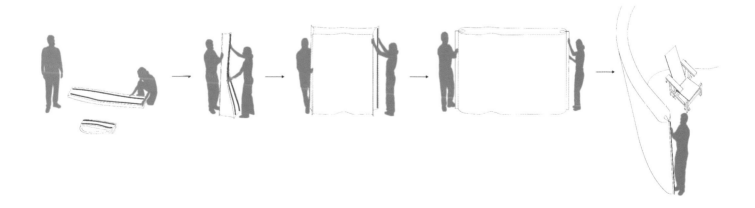

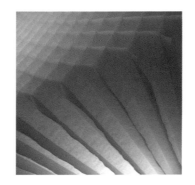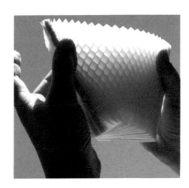

⊘ molo design is continuing to look at the possibilities for designing with both honeycomb paper and textile. They are considering objects from lighting to temporary shelters for the homeless. *Credit: molo design*

⊖ Opposite bottom: The paper softwall is commercially available at two standard heights of 6′ (1.8 m) tall and 4′ (1.2 m) tall. Both are 1′ (30 cm) thick and expand from $1\frac{1}{2}$ " (4 cm) when closed, to up to 20′ (6.1 m) long. *Credit: molo design*

Molo design has made the paper softwall commercially available at two standard heights of 6′ (1.8 m) tall and 4′ (1.2 m) tall. Both are 1′ (30 cm) thick and expand from $1\frac{1}{2}$ " (4 cm) when closed, up to 20′ (6.1 m) long. Molo created a buzz when they used early prototypes of the paper softwall for their own booth at the ICFF (International Contemporary Furniture Fair) in May 2004; the 2005 show marked their official product launch. But even before its commercial introduction, the paper softwall was awarded a jury pick from *Architectural Record* magazine as one of the best products of 2004, and New York's Museum of Modern Art recently added a paper softwall to their permanent collection.

In the meantime, Forsythe and MacAllen have been carting softwalls to museum shops and potential retail outlets. "We can fit two paper softwalls into our suitcases," she says. "It's really funny when we bring them out and put them up in a store or on the sidewalk. People giggle as it opens, and then keeps opening and opening to 20′ (6.1 m) or more. They can't believe this much wall can come from just $1\frac{1}{2}$ " (4 cm) of thickness."

Davos Bed, Theo Williams "I'd never done a **bed** before,"

says Theo Williams, explaining the **inspiration** for his Davos bed. "But I'd been **snowboarding** a lot, and I'd done **skateboard** ramps as a kid.

The Davos Bed's defining feature is its curved headboard, inspired by skateboarding ramps Theo Williams built as a kid—the angle is perfect for boarding as well as sitting up and reading in bed.
Credit: Puntozero

We used to split up orange boxes and bang them back together. So, I just remembered what I did as a kid. It was just a natural curve. Nothing else really."

This focus on the simplicity of a solution is not idle modesty, but a central part of Williams' design philosophy. "I hate having all this excess stuff," he says. "In the end, it's all rubbish. Really, it's just mind-boggling how much stuff you see and most of it's not worth it. I like something to last; I like things that are not too fancy. You need something that kicks off a little bit of an emotion, but is not over decorated, not calling attention to itself. There are lots of things that grab your eye, but twenty-four hours later . . ." Williams continues, "If it's really simple, you fall in love with it, and every time you look at it, you see something a bit different about it," he concludes.

For all its unadorned elegance, there is nothing austere about the Davos Bed. "The curve invites you to go lie on it and sit up on it," Williams notes. "It's got just that right angle so you need only one or two cushions to sit up. You can have a completely empty room, and it can be quite lovely. I find when you have all these accompanying pieces in a room, it's all a bit arrogant and loud." Another critical design element is the way the mattress snugs into the notch created by the curving backboard deviating from the base. "When you have a straight line and a curve," Williams notes, "there is a natural place where they have to meet and it's really quite obvious." As would be expected, achieving the "obvious" and "simple" resolution was the result of lots of hard work. According to Williams, "We had to try to get the curve just right. We made card models, made some solid ones, nailed bits together, faked it, glued it, to get the right thing. There are industry standards, but it was mostly trial and error. We even tried some that were much shorter, but it lost its aesthetic." He pauses and then, laughing, adds, "I'd get really dirty in the factory, just trying it over and over."

Ultimately, the production is as uncomplicated as the gesture of the bed would suggest. It is made from four pieces—a backboard, two sides, and an end—held together with a chrome-plated, steel T, that runs the length of the top piece, which is then mounted on a base. Working from the original concept, Williams has designed a sofa, chaise lounge, and two tables in addition to the bed, to make a complete Davos line, available in several options of materials and finish. The wood bed is made with a solid leg that runs the full length of the front and back. "I wanted the bed to have a heavy appearance from the front view," Williams notes, "using a solid base/leg support. I did not want to see what was under the bed. But from the side, the furniture appears very light and the curve of the wood can be easily read."

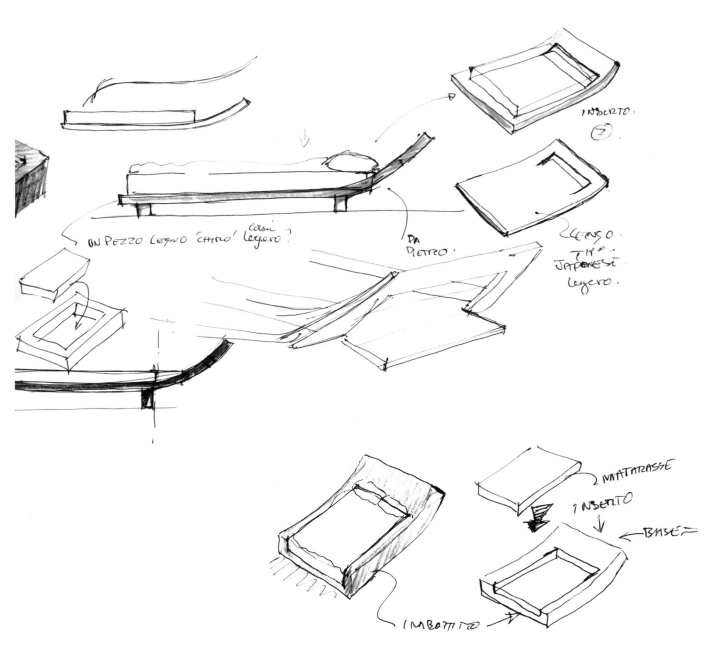

⌃ Top: An early sketch shows all the key elements to the Davos: the sloped headboard, the simple line of the leg, and the opening into which the mattress slides. *Credit: Theo Williams*

⌃ Another early sketch describes the mattress being held by the bed. In final versions, the supporting sidewalls are removed and the mattress is snugged into the simple notch created by the curved headboard meeting the supporting back piece. *Credit: Theo Williams*

⌃ Middle: Williams took a photo of a prototype on the factory floor and then drew his corrections to the rough edges and headboard proportion directly onto the picture in order to accurately visualize the results. *Credit: Theo Williams*

⌃ Bottom: An early prototype uses supports and clamps to get the angle of the headboard just right and to create a surprisingly simply means of keeping the mattress in place. *Credit: Theo Williams*

There's also a padded leather version with four, slender feet at each corner. "In the leather, we used chrome," Williams explains. "It's a much darker, richer material. And the chrome actually reflects the floor, so you see this perfect curve."

Ever frugal, Williams says that the bulk of the piece is made as inexpensively as possible. "We used the cheapest wood possible underneath," he says, "to keep the cost down. We used very economical materials. I'm quite conscious about saving money and materials. I don't want to waste materials and money. But," he adds, "the veneer is just perfect. It has a perfect finish."

As for the final product, Williams reports, "It's purely the way I wanted it. I've always wanted a bed like this for my room. When I'm working without a brief, I make things that I would want to live with. I try not to look at too many magazines, and not do too much research. I just want to think about what I would like. It's very instinctive. I do the first thing that comes to mind."

There is one other version of the Davos—the original, actually— that ironically defies the spare economy that is at the core of Williams' design and manufacturing principles. "In keeping with its snow-inspired beginnings, this bed was pure white," Williams says. "It was extremely expensive. It had twenty coats of lacquer. Davos is one of the best places to go skiing in Switzerland, and when you see the white one and the name, it all clicks." The other versions evolved when they began to consider how and where the bed would actually be used. "The white one had more interest for hotels," Williams notes. "The leather is more for the home really. It seemed quite natural to go from something quite expensive to something much more economical, and then create something in the middle, which is the leather. Which," he notes, "also became the most popular."

While Williams says the white wood version is the most pure because it harkens back to the skate ramps that were the bed's genesis, and concedes that it is "a bit odd to look at the other ones," when asked which bed he sleeps on himself, he chuckles, clears his throat, and admits "Well, the padded leather one. It's very rich. The room just has the bed in it."

The wood version of the Davos gives a nod to skateboard-ramp roots, while creating a thoroughly modern and elegant statement that makes it a stand-alone piece. *Credit: Puntozero*

A pure white Davos Chaise was inspired by snowboarding in Switzerland. It took twenty coats of
lacquer to create the pure white finish.
Credit: Puntozero

Lublin Daybed, Jacek Ostoya

"When I was a kid, every other **summer**, we'd visit family in Poland," **recalls** Jacek Ostoya. "I remember at my **aunt's house** in the town of Lublin, on the **eastern** side of Poland, there was a **daybed** in their living room."

The Lublin Daybed is named after the town in Poland where, during summertime family reunions in his childhood, Jacek Ostoya took naps on the daybed in his aunt's living room while the adults chatted in the living room. *Credit: Bruce Khan*

"If I wanted to take a nap, I'd be laid down there, while they sat at the table talking. Rooms did double duty because people didn't have much space. This daybed was multifunctional, working as a couch or converting to a bed. It stuck with me. I liked the idea of furniture doing double duty," he says.

An architect, Ostoya began to design a line of furniture after his brother-in-law, Peter Brayshaw, opened up a millwork shop. "He worked at the Guggenheim Museum, doing installations and working in their wood shop to make platforms or funky installations for artists that would facilitate exhibiting the art," explains Ostoya. "He learned woodworking and millworking, and then I come from an architecture background, but I'm all thumbs when it comes to shopwork." They began working together, with Ostoya designing the pieces, sharing his ideas with Brayshaw, who then figures out how to make the ideas real. "I'll do the sketches and get together with Peter, and he'll look at it from a construction standpoint and we'll discuss connections and such," Ostoya says. "It's definitely a collaboration. It's a symbiotic relationship."

When Ostoya began designing, he wanted his furniture to express a similar, familial sensibility. "When we started the furniture, I saw that in modern furniture there's a lot of plywood and that swoopy, plasticy stuff," he notes. "And I love that, but I wanted something different. I wanted to build things that I wanted in my own house." And to build things inspired by the piece he napped on at his aunt's house during those long-ago summers in Poland. "I wanted this furniture to do a little more than the obvious use," he says. "We've tried to incorporate this idea of furniture doing double-duty."

Because of Brayshaw's background and skills, making furniture in solid wood was an obvious choice. Ostoya says, "I have no interest in Shaker or mission furniture, but did want to use that lasting joinery that will survive and can be handed down." And have a modern look and feel. "We asked ourselves how we can do solid wood but pare it down to the architectonic shape. Some people might say simple means dumb, but to me it means clean."

The Lublin Daybed is not only a place to sit, or nap, or look at the view out the window—remove the cushions and they become seats, while the bed transforms itself into a coffee table. Made from solid walnut and walnut plywood, with brushed stainless steel supports and wool cushions, this multipurpose piece expresses an understated candor. "I like honest materials," says Ostoya.

△ Top: As part of the effort to make multfunctional pieces of furniture, the Lublin has a cubby built right in to hold books or an extra blanket. Or, simply put the cushions on the floor where they become seats, and the daybed is transformed into a coffee table.
Credit: Bruce Khan

△ Left: Jacek Ostoya is trained as an architect; his brother-in-law, Peter Brayshaw, is trained as a wood-worker. Together, they have developed the Mebel line of furniture, which is made in this workshop.
Credit: Peter Brayshaw

△ Right: Mebel's design mandate is to make furniture with a modern aesthetic using solid wood and tradi-tional methods that ensure the pieces will last.
Credit: Peter Brayshaw

As part of this honesty, Ostoya and Brayshaw also decided the piece should explain its own construction. "When we made the decision to not use veneers, we wanted to expose the end grain and how this piece is constructed, so we did solid pieces all around the perimeter. This allowed us to use mortise and tenon joinery for the edges and facilitated cutting out the cubbyhole." This cubbyhole is both an aesthetic and functional choice. "I like the idea of carving out of it," Ostoya says. "It's an organic form with a cutout from a machine. You can see the hand of man, the machine versus the organic piece of wood." And then he adds, "Also if you're lying there, you can put your book underneath, which keeps things clean like us architects like it."

This cubby presented one of the only significant manufacturing challenges. Ostoya points out that routers used to cut something like this always leave a bit of a radius in the corners of the shape. "I wanted the corner to be right angles, so we had to hand-cut those. I drove Peter a little bit crazy with this," he confesses.

The asymmetrical shape of the legs was derived from another piece in the collection. "I developed three pieces at the same time because I wanted a collection that all hung together," he says. "The shape of the legs came from the double bench. The legs and the cushion form one volume that is intersecting the wood. I wanted to imply a larger volume, and the metal, by delineating the edges, implies a volume."

The legs are adhered to the wood with a metal plate that is screwed into the bottom of the daybed. The wood is finished with a conversion varnish. "We wanted the most natural finish on the wood to let the wood speak for itself," says Ostoya. "Walnut has great coloration and the grain is very expressive. I know a lot of people use a hand-rubbed finish, but that can stain. We wanted to compromise between a real heavy finish and something that lets the natural beauty show through." Finally, the cushions are covered in wool, with an oval bolster held into place with a Velcro strap. "Segmenting the cushions gives the cushions a little rhythm as they go down the piece," he notes.

Making furniture as a family business has given Ostoya a new appreciation for the demands of manufacturing and woodworking. "If you're doing furniture as one-offs," he says, "it's easy to look at furniture like sculpture. But when you look at manufacturing, there's that whole question of how can you keep the integrity of a handmade, solid piece of wood." He's also considering more carefully how his designs affect the production process. "I'm trying to look at things from the eye of a builder," Ostoya says. "My brother-in-law will still crack jokes about 'You stupid architect,' and we do sort of design without knowing what the real world is like. I just know what I want it to look like, and we have the tendency to hand-off the design and say, 'Make it like I want it.' Now, as we move forward with new pieces, I'm finding myself thinking of the construction aspects to things. I have a greater respect for the building aspect of things. I have a greater appreciation for the design that is within the construction."

Top: The Lublin Daybed is made of the walnut planks shown here alongside the planer that gives them their first-pass smooth finish. *Credit: Peter Brayshaw*

The Lublin Daybed coffee table is constructed as a closed box in order to show wood grain and handcrafted construction techniques to full advantage. Here, two sides are being assembled. *Credit: Peter Brayshaw*

▷ The walnut daybed receives a light "conversion" varnish, which accentuates the wood grain but will not stain as hand-rubbed finishes sometimes do. *Credit: Peter Brayshaw*

▽ The Lublin's cushions and bolster are covered with a gray wool fabric that complements the steel leg structure. *Credit: Bruce Khan*

Landscape 05 Chaise, Jeffrey Bernett

"A chaise is a very **interesting** piece," according to Jeffrey Bernett. "In the furniture world, it's probably the piece that's **closest to sculpture**."

The Landscape 05 is a kind of line extension of an earlier chaise. After considering all the possible real-world uses of a chaise, Bernett added an arm to make a few more human poses possible. *Credit: B&B Italia*

"And doing a chaise is very daunting because you get compared to the very best right off the bat. Eames, le Corbousier, Mies van der Roe, Kierholm—all of them designed iconic chaises."

Bernett has designed two closely related chaise lounges for B&B Italia. "A number of years ago," he explains, "we did a chaise for B&B that was both highly publicized and commercially viable. The owner of B&B said that it had captured all the spirit and integrity of the company in one product, and it turned out to be the most successful marketing piece they'd done in twenty years." When B&B more recently came back to Bernett with the simple request that he "design another big hit," he presented six or seven different ideas, one of which was a chaise that was reminiscent of the one they'd already done. "We thought there was something to build on there," Bernett says. "We wanted to create something that captured a spirit of design and promoted balance, harmony, and a level of sophistication, and at the same time put forth a piece that was very representative of B&B." B&B agreed and asked him to pursue this second chaise design.

"A lot of chaises are thought of as a place for a fifteen-minute nap," Bernett notes, "Should you fall asleep, at some point your arms will fall and wake you up because there are no armrests," he explains, comparing the first chaise, which had no arms, to the second. "So we thought a lot about performance, about how people might use this piece, and how we could make it more functional. We thought all along about the problem of how to support the arm and the body and do it in a beautiful way. By adding the arm, it makes the piece a touch more dynamic, and visually it's a little more interesting. It allows a person to drape, lie in different positions across the piece, be a bit more lazy and comfortable in how you use it and fit into it."

Bernett thinks of the two chaises as "kind of like brothers," and points out that with the Landscape 05, "you're looking at an asymmetric shape that evokes an emotion." But he also emphasizes that function must come first: "You have to solve the problem in the correct way or it won't perform well, and B&B sells furniture that performs well; once we solved the performance issues, then we could go ahead and make it beautiful."

The shape itself posed some interesting production challenges. Because the profile of the chaise is so thin and yet covers such a long distance, ". . . we had to create enough structure and stability in the frame so that it would be torsionally stiff enough to not rock, but also have the seating performance and comfort that is so important to B&B," Bernett reports. "The seating performance requirement can be a tough challenge." This particular challenge was solved by developing a steel skeleton, over which polyurethane foam is injected and then upholstered.

⬡ Top: The basic asymmetrical single-armrest form of the Landscape 05 was quickly achieved, as shown in this computer rendering.
Credit: Jeffrey Bernett

⬡ A computer rendering of the back view of the Landscape shows the extremely slender profile, which created some manufacturing challenges, as it had to also be torsionally stiff enough to support a reclining body.
Credit: Jeffrey Bernett

At the B&B factory, a mold is prepared for the main section of the chaise. *Credit: B&B Italia*

The steel skeleton for the Landscape 05 is necessary to create a structural frame that is strong enough to support the length of the chaise. *Credit: B&B Italia*

Below left: The underlying steel frame provided the added benefit of a headrest that can easily be attached and detached with internal magnets. *Credit: B&B Italia*

The steel frame for the Landscape 05 Chaise is covered with a thin layer of polyurethane foam. The final product is available in a range of upholstery options, including leather and industrial felt. *Credit: B&B Italia*

Stability was also a critical concern when it came to the leg design. Two legs made of a single continuous loop run the entire length of the chaise, creating an elegant support that is also sufficiently rigid.

The underlying metal structure provided an additional, unexpected benefit to the headrest design and functionality. "You have to think about how someone's using the piece," Bernett emphasizes. "If you're taking a nap, your head is in a different place than if you're watching television or reading a newspaper. When you're working in a pure manner, these attachments can be quite cumbersome and loud in the overall scheme of the project. In this case, because there is an underlying structure of steel slats, we came up with the idea of using magnets that connect the headrest to the steel and allow it to be adjusted in endless ways, and also to be easily removed. There's no other physical attachment needed."

While the headrest is always offered in leather, and the chaise itself is available in a range of fabrics, Bernett also suggested a special fabric for the Landscape 05. "Going back to my interest in the contemporary art world, I've always thought industrial felt was interesting. It's made of all the offcuts and waste cuts from the carpet and sewing industry, so it's sort of a recycled product. We did all kinds of research into the material and sent it over to B&B because we thought it would be interesting for them to bring a new fabric to a new product." Bernett appreciates the particularly soft and tactile quality of the felt, and the way it accentuates the feeling of comfort the chaise evokes.

Bernett credits the success of this project to the collaboration between his office and B&B. "Working with B&B, I feel very fortunate, because in B&B you have a company that is truly an industrialized producer that really tries to push innovations, and all along tries to sell a high-quality product that functions very well and is beautiful. There's not that many companies that can hit that mark on all those levels. We've had the good fortune to make pieces that are commercially very viable, but are also aligned with B&B's core values, and have become icons for the company as they're trying to create their image of how the world sees them."

According to Bernett, there were few hiccups in the development of the Landscape 05. "We hit the target pretty easily," he says. "The right thing to do was pretty obvious. Sometimes, it's great when you prevail after a longwinded project, but it's also satisfying when you can achieve your vision right off the bat. It's kind of like stepping up to the plate and hitting a home run. Not that you don't hit a lot of foul balls, but everything sometimes comes together all at once. For this project, we saw the prototype, and we were done."

Even though Bernett may have made this particular home run look effortless, the Landscape 05 is the result of strategic design thinking, logically applied. "Simply put," Bernett says, "product design is three-dimensional problem solving where the result is a tangible object that takes into account function, price, value, and human needs and conditions. So in any given problem, whether it's a bathroom fixture or an airplane seat, you have to identify the tasks and challenges to overcome, and then go about the design process. Then, if you can design in a manner that ideally makes the space nicer to be in, and makes you want to spend more time at home, or makes a chair that is healthier to sit in, or performs better, all along you're improving the quality and value of life. Generally speaking, design is all about improving the quality of life."

The Landscape 05 went from prototype to final form with no changes, a rare home run in furniture design and manufacturing.
Credit: B&B Italia

contributors

Agence Patrick Jouin (116)
Patrick Jouin
Paris, France
33.1.55.288.920
agence@patrickjouin.com
www.patrickjouin.com

Alfredo Häberli Design and Development (132)
Alfredo Häberli
Zurich, Switzerland
41.1.380.32.30
studio@alfredo-haberli.com
www.alfredo-haberli.com

Alias (184)
www.aliasdesign.it

aMDL SrL (184)
Michele De Lucchi
Milan, Italy
39.02.43.00.81
www.amdl.it

Artifort (12)
www.artifort.com

Atelier Satyendra Pakhalé (44)
Satyendra Pakhalé
Amsterdam, The Netherlands
31.20.41.97.23.0
info@satyendra-pakhale.com
www.satyendra-pakhale.com

B&B Italia (204)
www.bebitalia.it

BD Ediciones de Diseño (132)
www.bdbarcelona.com

Bernhardt Design (160)
www.bernhardtdesign.com

Biecher & Associes (160)
Christian Biecher
Paris, France
33.1.49.29.69.39
info@biecher.com
www.biecher.com

Ronan Bouroullec, Erwan Bouroullec (36)
Saint-Denis, France
33.1.48.21.04.02
info@bouroullec.com
www.bouroullec.com

Blu Dot Manufacturing and Design (16)
John Christakos, Maurice Blanks, Charles Lazor
Minneapolis, MN, United States
612.782.1844
jchristakos@bludot.com
www.bludot.com

Cassina (136)
www.cassina.com

CCD (52)
Christopher C. Deam
99 Osgood Place
San Francisco, CA, United States
415.981.1829
www.cdeam.com

CDS/Consultants for Design Strategy (204)
Jeffrey Bernett
New York, NY, United States
212.334.9109
jbernett@cds-us.com
www.cds-us.com

Chris Lehrecke Furniture (180)
Chris Lehrecke
Bangall, NY, United States
845.868.1674
info@chrislehrecke.com
www.chrislehrecke.com

Claesson Koivisto Rune Arkitektkontor (72)
Mårten Claesson, Eero Koivisto, Ola Rune
Stockholm, Sweden
46.8.644.58.63
arkitektkontor@claesson-koivisto-rune.se
www.claesson-koivisto-rune.se

Dahlstrom Design AB (124)
Björn Dahlstrom
Stockholm, Sweden
46.867.34200
info@dahlstromdesign.com
www.dahlstromdesign.se

Dine Murphy Wood (172)
Nick Dine
New York, NY, United States
212.226.7171
nick@dinemurphywood.com
www.dinemurphywood.com

Tom Dixon (48)
London, United Kingdom
44.207.400.0500
info@tomdixon.net
www.tomdixon.net

Driade (60)
www.driade.com

Dune (148)
www.dune-ny.com

Edra (24)
www.edra.com

em [collaborative studio] (84)
Emmanuel Cobbet, Mark Yeber
Los Angeles, CA, United States
310.289.0181
info@emcollection.com
www.emcollection.com

Estudio Campana (24)
Fernando Campana, Humberto Campana
São Paulo, Brazil
55.11.38.25.34.08
campana@campanadesign.com.br
www.campanabrothers.com

Fels Design (148)
Sarah Fels
New York, NY, United States
212.529.4334
mail@felsdesign.com
www.felsdesign.com

Ana Franco (96)
Horminga Design
Studio City, CA, United States
818.943.4321
analufranco@hotmail.com

Friends of Industry (64)
Harri Koskinen
Helsinki, Finland
358.9.7268.90.90
info@friendsofindustry.com
www.harrikoskinen.com

Adrien Gardère (20)
Paris, France
33.1.40.26.10.37
a.gardere@free.fr

Giovannoni Design (176)
Stefana Giovannoni
Milan, Italy
39.02.48.70.34.95
studio@stefanogiovannoni.it
www.stefanogiovannoni.it

Jakob+MacFarlane (188)
Dominique Jakob, Brendan MacFarlane
Paris, France
33.1.44.79.05.72
jakmak@club-internet.fr
www.jacobmacfarlane.com

Jenkins Design and Development (100)
Jeffrey B. Jenkins
Alexandria, VA, United States
703.519.9445
jeff@jeffreyjenkins.com
www.jeffreyjenkins.com

Jonas Wannfors Designers DBSD (88)
Jonas Wannfors
Stockholm, Sweden
46.8.44.20.980
info@wannforsdesign.com
www.wannforsdesign.com

Kartell (156)
www.kartell.it

Konstantin Grcic Industrial Design (68)
Konstantin Grcic
Munich, Germany
49.89.55.07999.5
office@konstantin-grcic.com
www.konstantin-grcic.com

L Design (128)
Arik Levy
Paris, France
33.1.44.78.61.61
contact@ldesign.com
www.ldesign.fr

Lebello USA (164)
Lars Dahmann
Los Angeles, CA, United States
310.500.0393
sales@lebello.com
www.lebello.com

Lissoni Associati (156)
Piero Lissoni
Milan, Italy
39.02.65.71.942
info@lissoniassociati.it
www.lissonipeia.it

Lovegrove Studio (80)
Ross Lovegrove
London, United Kingdom
44.207.229.7104
studio@rosslovegrove.com
www.rosslovegrove.com

LYX Furniture and Light (88)
www.lyx.com

Magis (176)
www.magisdesign.com

Matali Crasset (28)
Paris, France
33.1.42.40.99.89
matalicrasset@wanadoo.fr
www.matalicrasset.com

Matt Sindall Design (76)
Matt Sindall
Paris, France
33.1.43.14.05.47
msindall@noos.fr
www.mattsindall.com

Mebel Furniture (200)
Jacek Ostoya
San Francisco, CA, United States
415.379.8689
info@mebelfurniture.com
www.mebelfurniture.com

Michael Sodeau Partnership (152)
Michael Sodeau
London, United Kingdom
44.207.83.35.02.0
info@michaelsodeau.com
www.michaelsodeau.com

Michael Wolfson Design (108)
London, United Kingdom
info@wolfsondesign.com
www.wolfsondesign.com

Modus (152)
www.modusfurniture.co.uk

molo design (192)
Stephanie Forsythe, Todd MacAllen
Vancouver, British Columbia, Canada
604.696.2501
info@molodesign.com
www.molodesign.com

Monica Förster Design Studio (40)
Monica Förster
Stockholm, Sweden
46.86.11.22.09
monica.forster@swipenet.se

Montina (64)
www.montina.it

Sawaya & Moroni (188)
www.sawayamoroni.com

Nola (124)
www.nola.se

Orange 22 Design Lab, LLC (168)
Dario Antonioni
Los Angeles, CA, United States
213.972.9922
info@orange22.com
www.orange22.com

Barber Osgerby (112)
Edward Barber, Jay Osgerby
London, United Kingdom
44.207.680.9222
mail@barberosgerby.com
www.barberosgerby.com

Palomba Serafini Associati (32)
Ludovica Palomba , Roberto Palomba
Vigasio, Itlay
39.04.57.36.41.81
press@palombaserafini.com
www.palombaserafini.com

Parallel Design (92)
Ali Tayar
New York, NY, United States
212.989.4959
mtayar@rcn.com
www.alitayar.com

PearsonLloyd (8)
Luke Pearson, Tom Lloyd
London, United Kingdom
44.207.377.0560
info@pearsonlloyd.co.uk
www.pearsonlloyd.co.uk

Perimeter Editions (20)
www.perimeter-editions.com

Poltrona Frau (40)
www.poltronafrau.it

Andrée Putman (144)
33.1.55.42.88.55
Paris, France
archi@andreeputman.com
www.andreeputman.com

Readymade Projects, Inc. (104)
Stephen Burks
stephenburks@readymadeprojects.com
www.readymadeprojects.com

Roche-Bobois (140)
www.roche-bobois.com

Ron Arad Associates (60)
Ron Arad
London, United Kingdom
44.207.284.4963
info@ronarad.com
www.ronarad.com

Ligne Roset (36)
www.ligne-roset-usa.com

FeliceRossi (28)
www.felicerossi.it

Sfera (72)
www.ricordi-sfera.com

Studio Massaud (136)
Jean-Marie Massaud
Paris, France
33.1.40.09.54.14
studio@massaud.com
www.massaud.com

Studio Patrick Norguet (12)
Patrick Norguet
Paris, France
33.1.48.07.29.95
patrick.norguet@wanadoo.fr
www.patricknorguet.com

Studio Urquiola (56)
Patricia Urquiola
Milan, Italy
39.02.29.29.52.27.01
patriciaurquiola@tiscali.it
www.patriciaurquiola.com

TZ Design (120)
Mark Goetz
New York, NY, United States
212.741.2334
info@TZdesign.com
www.TZdesign.com

Vladimir Kagan Design Group, Inc. (140)
Vladimir Kagan
New York, NY, United States
212.289.0031
info@vladimirkagan.com
www.vladimirkagan.com

Theo Williams (196)
Amsterdam, The Netherlands
31.06.52.57.01.01
info@theowilliams.com
www.theowilliams.com

Zanotta (32)
www.zanotta.it